# Get Going
# with Microsoft® Excel

S. S. Khalsa

SIGMA PRESS
Wilmslow, England

**Typeset and Designed** by Sigma Hi-Tech Services Ltd, Wilmslow, UK

**Cover Design** by  Design House, Marple Bridge, UK.


**Published by**
Sigma Press, 1 South Oak Lane, Wilmslow, Cheshire SK9 6AR, UK


**ISBN: 1-85058-264-5**

**British Library Cataloguing in Publication Data**
A CIP catalogue record for this book is available from the British Library

**Printed by:** Interprint Ltd, Malta

# Here's how to Get Going . . .

*Get Going with Microsoft Excel* consists of six parts:

1. A comprehensive illustrated guide to Excel
2. Exercises for practising Excel basics
3. Models using Excel in practice
4. Solutions to the exercises in part 2
5. Quick reference to commands, functions and macros
6. Index

*Get Going with Microsoft Excel* can be used both in the classroom as a textbook, and by individuals sitting at their own desk who want to get going with Excel.

The exercises in this book follow a thread of continuity, following a theme and building on it as each new Excel function is put to use.

This book is updated to include the newest functions in Microsoft Excel for MS-DOS, version 3.0. All features which are only available in Excel 3.0 are identified by the following marker:

**Excel 3.0**

The first pages of the book explain how to install and start Excel.

## Training suggestions:

Excel contains an on-line tutorial. Going through this tutorial is a good way to orient and familiarize yourself with the workings and environment of Excel. Note that neither the mouse nor the number pad on the righthand side of the keyboard can be used with the tutorial. However, outside of the tutorial, you are encouraged to use the mouse and the number pad as much as possible.

Part one of this book gives an explanation and example of the various facets of Excel. As you go over each topic in part one, note that examples are provided which illustrate the relevant commands/ formulas. If you are training others, it might be advisable to simplify the examples at times, for instance if you are using the blackboard.

The exercises are found in part two of the book. They are organized according to and in the same order as the topics covered in part one. After finishing each sequence in a chapter, you (or class participants) can then complete the appropriate exercises.

There are three sets of exercises which run through the various facets of Excel. One set is based on the model of an employee list, the next set on an accounts receivable list, and the third set on a tax return. You can use one, two or all of these sets, according to the amount of time you have.

In part four of this book, you will find solutions to the exercises given in part two.

Part three of *Get Going with Microsoft Excel* contains the following models:

a) financial analysis
b) invoice system
c) payroll system
d) price analysis

These models illustrate how Excel can be used in a more advanced way, with spreadsheets linked together with macros, and customized dialogue boxes for more friendly user interface. In a more advanced setting, you can go through the models in part three, and try to reconstruct the models again, perhaps with slightly altered format and variables. Note that these models are also available on disk.

To familiarize yourself with user-error handling in Excel, study chapter nine in the book, which explains how to diagnose and remedy the most common errors made by users in Excel.


## The author

For the past four years, Sardar Singh Khalsa has been involved in development, documentation and training in Microsoft Excel. He has travelled throughout Norway giving courses from 1 to 3 weeks in Excel, and he has also put together and coordinated Excel course material for Norsk Data, a leading Scandinavian computer developer, and for the Norwegian government. The author has already published several books on database, spreadsheet and operating systems.


Note: This book has been written entirely in Microsoft Excel, with the exception of a small number of screen photographs.

# CONTENTS

---

## *Part One – A Guide to Excel*

# Part Two – Exercises

# Part Three – Models

---

A disk is available containing the models from Part 3 of this book.
To obtain the disk, send £10 to cover production, post and packing (plus
VAT at the current rate if you are in the UK) to:
Sigma Press, 1 South Oak Lane, Wilmslow, Cheshire, SK9 6AR, UK.
Cheques payable to Sigma Press; Access and Visa accepted.
Offer valid for the UK and Europe only. Specify 5.25" or 3.5".

# Part 1  ‖  Excel basics

|  | D4 | =today-C4 | | |
|---|---|---|---|---|
|  | A | B | C | D |
| 1 |  |  |  | 19.Nov |
| 2 |  |  |  |  |
| 3 | acct.nr. | balance | due | overdue |
| 4 | 482379 | 485.34 | 23.Nov |  |
| 5 | 482380 | 7274.00 | 19.Nov |  |
| 6 | 482381 | 495.20 | 14.Nov | 5 days |
| 7 | 482382 | 896.56 | 9.Nov | 9 days |
| 8 | 482383 | 4952.30 | 5.Nov | 14 days |
| 9 | 482384 | 986.60 | 31.Oct | 19 days |
| 10 | 482385 | 8593.00 | 26.Oct | 23 days |
| 11 | 482386 | 56.40 | 22.Oct | 28 days |

# Get Started

Read the following pages to learn how you can get started with the Excel spreadsheet program.

## What is Excel?

Microsoft Excel is a spreadsheet program which also has substantial graphic capabilities and database functions. In addition, there is a large variety of macros and built-in functions which can be used in administrative, mathematical, statistical and financial applications.

B1         =PMT(Interest/Periods,Periods*Years,Loan)

|   | A | B | C | D | E |
|---|---|---|---|---|---|
| 1 | Annuity | -237 | Period | Interest | Principal |
| 2 | Loan | 9000 | 1 | -90 | -147 |
| 3 | Interest | 12% | 2 | -89 | -148 |
| 4 | Periods | 12 | 3 | -87 | -150 |
| 5 | Years | 4 | 4 | -86 | -151 |

Excel is a Windows-based product, and is well integrated with other Windows products, whether they be word processing, desktop publishing or database products.

Like other Windows products, Excel is equipped with pull-down menus where you can choose commands either by pressing a key or clicking with the mouse. With these menu commands, you can edit, format, sort and name your data. Results appear instantaneously on your screen.

|   | A | B | C | D |
|---|---|---|---|---|
| 1 | Emp.no. | Name | | Init. |
| 2 | 1524 | And | Anders | AA |
| 3 | 1853 | Bond | James | BJ |
| 4 | 4862 | Hansen | Hans | HH |
| 5 | 1524 | Hansen | Knut | HKN |
| 6 | 3548 | Poirot | Hercule | PHE |

| Data |
|------|
| Find |
| Extract |
| Delete |
| Sort |

You can also use menu commands to change the height and width of cells, change the colour of text or spreadsheet lines, and remove gridlines or let them remain, as you wish.

In addition, you can link several files together, so that when numbers are updated in one file, the other files are also updated automatically.

## Versions of Excel

Since the first version of Excel for MS-DOS appeared on the market, a number of subsequent, improved versions have come out. These are listed below with a short description. The additional features in versions 2.1 and 3 are described in further detail later on in this book.

Version 2.0    First version of Excel for MS-DOS and WINDOWS.

Version 2.1    A number of internal improvements, can define dialogue boxes graphically (further described in book).

Version 2.1c    Same as version 2.1, but runs with WINDOWS 3.

Version 3.0    Runs with WINDOWS 3, a number of additional functions and graphic features (further described in book).

## Install Excel

You need the following three Excel disketts:

1. Setup Disk (Diskett 1)
2. Documentation Disk (Diskett 2)
3. Library Disk (Diskett 3)

You then do the following:

1. Enter MS-DOS Executive.

2. Choose the system box in the upper left corner and choose:

   **Close**

   The following message appears:  "This will end your Windows session"

3. Press RET.
   "C:\>" or "C:\USER>" appears on the screen.  If not, type:

   **CD\**

   ... and press RET.

4. Insert the diskett called "Setup Disk".

5. Type:        **A:SETUP**              ... and press RET.

   Follow the instructions as they appear on the screen, and insert
   each of the other disketts when instructed.

6. When you have done this, take out the last diskett and restart your
   PC by pressing:

   | CTRL | | ALT | | DEL |

## Start Excel

To start the Excel program, you do the following:

1. Enter MS-DOS Executive.

2. Choose the directory:   **WINDOWS**

3. Choose:                          **EXCEL.EXE**

   Then choose:              **Worksheet**

   An empty worksheet will then appear on the screen.

( **Excel 3.0** )  To start Excel in version 3.0, click with the mouse at the Microsoft Excel icon.


## Start the online tutorial in Excel

There is a good online tutorial in Excel. To start it, you choose from the top menu:

   **Help - Tutorial**

# 1. How does a spreadsheet work?

**Cell addresses**

A computer spreadsheet is divided into cells, and each cell has an address. For example, the cell in the 3rd column in the 8th row has the address C8.

**Select cell**

To move to a cell and enter information, you click using the mouse, or move to it using the arrow keys on the keyboard. The cell you have chosen is called the active cell. In the example below, the active cell is C2. Note that the active cell is indicated at the top left of the spreadsheet.

C2

|   | A | B | C | D |
|---|---|---|---|---|
| 1 |   |   |   |   |
| 2 |   |   |   |   |
| 3 |   |   |   |   |

**Enter text**

In each cell, you can enter information in the form of text or numbers. In the example below, we have entered text in cell C2. Note that even though the text takes more space than the cell, it simply spills over to the next cell.

|   | A | B | C | D |
|---|---|---|---|---|
| 1 |   |   |   |   |
| 2 |   |   | The text continues ... |   |
| 3 |   |   |   |   |

**Enter numbers**

In the example below, we have entered numbers into cells A2, B2, A3 and B3.

|   | A | B | C | D |
|---|---|---|---|---|
| 1 |   |   |   |   |
| 2 | 3465,32 | 798,21 |   |   |
| 3 | 45 | 35% |   |   |

# 1a. Navigating

There is always just one active cell on the worksheet. You know which cell is active by the darker box around it. The active cell in the example is B2. The cell reference to the active cell can be found up to the left of the formula bar.

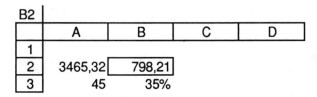

To move the cursor from one cell to another, either click with the mouse at the desired cell, or press the arrow keys.

To move the cursor to the beginning of the line, press: | Home |

To move the cursor to the end of the line, press: | End |

To move the cursor to the beginning of the worksheet, press:

| CTRL | | Home |

To move the cursor to the end of the worksheet, press:

| CTRL | | End |

To move the cursor down one screen picture (ca. 20 lines), press:

| PG DN |

To move the cursor up one screen picture (ca. 20 lines), press:

| PG UP |

To move the cursor over one screen picture (ca. 10 columns), press:

| CTRL | | PG DN |

To move the cursor back one screen picture (ca. 10 columns), press:

| CTRL | | PG UP |

## 1b. Selecting cells

When you are entering data or formulas, simply move the cursor to the desired cell and start typing.

If you want to format, name or do anything else with the cells, you need to select them first. You do this either by clicking and dragging with the mouse over the desired cells, or by pressing:

| Shift |    ... and one of the arrow keys.

Cells which are selected are shown in dark, except for the active cell which has a dark frame. In the example below, we have selected the cells A2:C3.

A2

| | A | B | C | D |
|---|---|---|---|---|
| 1 | | | | |
| 2 | 3465,32 | 798,21 | | |
| 3 | 45 | 35% | | |

**Select rows and columns**

To select an entire column, you click at the column heading (A,B,C ...). In the example below we have selected column B.

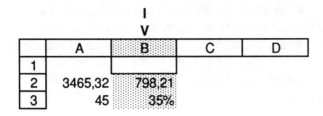

| | A | B | C | D |
|---|---|---|---|---|
| 1 | | | | |
| 2 | 3465,32 | 798,21 | | |
| 3 | 45 | 35% | | |

To select an entire row, you click at the row heading (1,2,3 ...). In the example below we have selected row 2.

| | A | B | C | D |
|---|---|---|---|---|
| 1 | | | | |
| --> 2 | 3465,32 | 798,21 | | |
| 3 | 45 | 35% | | |

To select the entire worksheet, click at the blank square in the upper left corner, as in the example below.

| | A | B | C | D |
|---|---|---|---|---|
| 1 | | | | |
| 2 | 3465,32 | 798,21 | | |
| 3 | 45 | 35% | | |

To select several areas at the same time, press:

| CTRL |   ... while you choose the different areas.

In the example below we have selected the areas A2:A3 and C2:D2.

| | A | B | C | D |
|---|---|---|---|---|
| 1 | | | | |
| 2 | 3465,32 | 798,21 | | |
| 3 | 45 | 35% | | |

## 1c. Write formulas

You can perform mathematical operations on any numbers on the spreadsheet, and place the results wherever you want. To do this, you choose the cell where you want your result, and write an equation. In EXCEL, this equation is called a formula. In the example below, we are writing an equation to add the contents of cells A2 and B2 together.  We start with:

=

Then we click with the mouse at the first cell we are operating with, or we can type the cell address (more chance for error):

**A2**

Then we type the operand:                    **+**

Then we click with the mouse at the next cell we are operating with (or  type it):

**B2**

To finish our formula, we press:            | **RET** |

The entire formula then looks like this:

**=A2+B2**

In the example below, we have typed this formula in cell D2. Note that as long as cell D2 is the active cell, the formula will be shown in the formula bar at the top.

| D2 | =A2+B2 | | |
|---|---|---|---|
| | A | B | C | D |
| 1 | | | | |
| 2 | 3465,32 | 798,21 | | 4263,53 |
| 3 | 45 | 35% | | |

**Operands and parentheses**

In addition to +, you can also use - (subtraction), / (division), and * (multiplication). Note that Excel executes multiplication and division before addition and subtraction. Thus, if you want addition or subtraction executed first, you need to enclose the operation in parentheses.

In the examples below, the formula in D2 adds the contents of A2 and B2 together and then multiplies by B3, while the formula in D3 multiplies B2 by B3 and then adds A2. As you can see, the result is quite different.

D2　　=(A2+B2)*B3

|   | A | B | C | D |
|---|---|---|---|---|
| 1 |   |   |   |   |
| 2 | 3465,32 | 798,21 |   | 1492,236 |
| 3 | 45 | 35% |   | 3744,694 |

D3　　=A2+B2*B3

|   | A | B | C | D |
|---|---|---|---|---|
| 1 |   |   |   |   |
| 2 | 3465,32 | 798,21 |   | 1492,236 |
| 3 | 45 | 35% |   | 3744,694 |

**Edit contents of cell**

If you go to a cell where data or a formula is entered, and begin to type, you will automatically delete anything that was there before. If you want to merely edit the contents of a cell, then click with the mouse up in the formula bar, or press the F2 key. In the example below, we have edited the formula in cell D3 so that it divides the result by A3.

D3　　=(A2+B2*B3)/A3

|   | A | B | C | D |
|---|---|---|---|---|
| 1 |   |   |   |   |
| 2 | 3465,32 | 798,21 |   | 1492,236 |
| 3 | 45 | 35% |   | 83,21541 |

## 1d. Choosing menu commands

You can use many commands, such as to open or save files, or to
copy, move or format data. Instead of typing out these commands,
you choose them from the top menu. Using the mouse, you click once
at your choice. Using the keyboard, you hold down the ALT key,
type the underlined letter of your menu selection, and then simply
type the key to choose a command from the pull-down menu.

In the example below, we are choosing the File - Save command
from the menu. With the mouse you would click once at File
and once at Save. With the keyboard, you would hold down the ALT
key and type F (for File), and then S (for Save).

| File |
|------|
| New |
| Open |
| Close |
| Link |
| Save |

## 1e. Taking care of files

**Save file
under new
name**

If you are saving your work for the first time (or saving your work under
another name) use the menu command:

**File - Save as**

A dialogue box appears on the screen. Type in your new file name.
What appeared first in the text box in black will be overwritten.
Press RET or click at OK in the box to confirm.
A valid file name must:

1) be no longer than 8 letters/digits
2) begin with a letter
3) not contain blanks, slashes ( / ) or periods ( . )

In the example below, we have called our file "custlist".

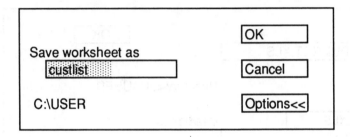

**File types**     The correct file type is added automatically, so you needn't
type it in. The file types in Excel are:

        XLS ......... normal worksheet
        XLW ........ workspace
        XLC ......... chart
        XLM ......... macro sheet

**Save file**      It is always wise to save your work at least once every 15 minutes.
**under same**     When you save a file without changing its name, choose the menu
**name**           command:
                            **File - Save**

**Open and**       If you have finished working on a file, you can close it without going
**close files**    out of EXCEL. Then choose:

                            **File - Close**

To close your file and close the EXCEL program, choose:     **File - Exit**

To open an already existing file, choose:     **File - Open**

A dialogue box will then appear on the screen. Choose the
file you want to open from the list box by clicking with the mouse
(or ALT F and then arrow keys). Confirm with RET (or OK).

In the example below we are opening the file called BUDGET.XLS.

```
Open
                                                    ┌──────────┐
                                                    │    OK    │
                                                    └──────────┘
File Name :   ┌─────────────────────┐
              │ BUDGET.XLS          │
              └─────────────────────┘
                                    Directory is C:\USER

      Files                   Directories
      ┌──────────────────┐    ┌──────────────┐
      │ ANALYSIS.XLS     │    │ [ .. ]       │
      │ BUDGET.XLS       │    │ [ -A- ]      │
      │ CALANDER.XLS     │    │ [ -C- ]      │
      │ CUSTLIST.XLS     │    │              │
      └──────────────────┘    └──────────────┘
```

**Open
empty sheet**

To open an empty sheet, choose:

**File - New**

A dialogue box will appear, where you can choose if you want to
open a worksheet (normal spreadsheet), a chart (for diagrams) or
a macro sheet (for macro instructions). Most often you will be
opening a worksheet.

## 1f. Windows

You can have more than one file open at the same time. The space on the screen given to each open file is called a window. The file you are currently working on is called the active window.

**Activate window**

To move from the window you are working on to another window, click with the mouse at that window, if it is visible on the screen. If it is not, choose:

**Window**

Your open files will be listed in the pull-down menu. Choose the one you want to work on. The window holding this file will then appear on the screen.

In the example below, we are working on FILE1.XLS, and are choosing FILE2.XLS.

| Window |
| --- |
| New Window |
| Arrange All |
| Hide |
| x  1. FILE1.XLS |
| 2. FILE2.XLS |
| 3. FILE3.XLS |

**Show all files**

To display all open files simultaneously on the screen, choose:

**Window - Arrange All**

Note that while all files are visible, only one window is active.

**Show same file twice**

To have the same file you are working on displayed on two windows, choose:

**Window - New Window**

This command can be useful if you want to work on one part of your spreadsheet, while at the same time looking at another part.

In the example below, we have opened a new window for FILE1.XLS. Note that EXCEL calls the two windows FILE1.XLS:1 and FILE1.XLS:2

B5

### FILE1.XLS:1

|   | A | B | C | D | E | F |
|---|---|---|---|---|---|---|
| 1 | Annuity | -500 | Interest | Principal | Balance | Period |
| 2 | Loan | 59581 | -447 | -53 | 59528 | 1 |
| 3 | Interest | 9% | -446 | -54 | 59474 | 2 |
| 4 | Periods | 12 | -446 | -54 | 59420 | 3 |
| 5 | Years | 25 | -446 | -54 | 59366 | 4 |
| 6 |  |  | -445 | -55 | 59311 | 5 |

### FILE1.XLS:2

|   | A | B | C | D | E | F |
|---|---|---|---|---|---|---|
| 296 |  |  | -22 | -478 | 2445 | 295 |
| 297 |  |  | -18 | -482 | 1963 | 296 |
| 298 |  |  | -15 | -485 | 1478 | 297 |
| 299 |  |  | -11 | -489 | 989 | 298 |
| 300 |  |  | -7 | -493 | 496 | 299 |
| 301 |  |  | -4 | -496 | 0 | 300 |

**Move and size windows**

You can adjust the size of windows on the screen by clicking with the mouse on the borders of the windows and dragging. To move windows (and dialogue boxes) simply click at the title box on the top centre of the window, and drag.

(move)          (size)

### FILE1.XLS:2

| B | C | D | E |
|---|---|---|---|
|  | -22 | -478 | 2445 |
|  | -18 | -482 | 1963 |
|  | -15 | -485 | 1478 |

**Create workspace**   You can create a workspace of files which are linked together.  This way, when you open the files, instead of having to open them all one at a time, you can merely open the workspace. All the files stored in that workspace will be opened automatically and placed in the same way on the screen as when you created the workspace. Also, the most recent, updated version of each file will always be opened.

To create a workspace, choose:

### File - Save Workspace

A dialogue box appears. Give your workspace a name, and press RET.

When you want to open the workspace next time, you will recognise it by its file-type, XLW. When you open the workspace, all the files which are a part of the workspace will be opened in their most recently updated state, and will be presented on the screen in the same way as when the workspace was last saved.

# 2. Editing the spreadsheet

There are a number of commands to edit data in the spreadsheet.
Most of these commands are located under EDIT in the main menu.

## 2a. Deleting and inserting data and cells

**Clear contents
of cells**
You can clear the contents of cells. Choose:     **Edit - Clear**
Then choose ...  **Formulas**

... or press the shortcut keys:

| **DEL** | and then: | **RET** |

In the example below, we are clearing the contents of cells A2 to D2.

|   | A | B | C | D |
|---|------|---------|--------|-----------|
| 1 | January | February | March | 1. quarter |
| 2 | 6565,00 | 782,40 | 456,20 | 7803,60 |
| 3 | 34,35 | 798,21 | 789,50 | 1622,06 |
| 4 | 48,20 | 154,00 | 243,70 | 445,90 |
| 5 | 872,00 | 53,00 | 879,20 | 1804,20 |

(before clearing)

|   | A | B | C | D |
|---|------|---------|--------|-----------|
| 1 | January | February | March | 1. quarter |
| 2 |  |  |  |  |
| 3 | 34,35 | 798,21 | 789,50 | 1622,06 |
| 4 | 48,20 | 154,00 | 243,70 | 445,90 |
| 5 | 872,00 | 53,00 | 879,20 | 1804,20 |

(after clearing)

**Delete cells and contents**

You can also delete cells entirely. To do this, choose:

**Edit - Delete**

By deleting cells, you create a hole which has to be filled, either by shifting the other cells left, or up. A dialogue box appears and gives you this choice. In the example below, we are deleting cells A2 to D2, and shifting the other cells up.

|   | A | B | C | D |
|---|---|---|---|---|
| 1 | January | February | March | 1. quarter |
| 2 | 6565,00 | 782,40 | 456,20 | 7803,60 |
| 3 | 34,35 | 798,21 | 789,50 | 1622,06 |
| 4 | 48,20 | 154,00 | 243,70 | 445,90 |
| 5 | 872,00 | 53,00 | 879,20 | 1804,20 |

(before deleting)

|   | A | B | C | D |
|---|---|---|---|---|
| 1 | January | February | March | 1. quarter |
| 2 | 34,35 | 798,21 | 789,50 | 1622,06 |
| 3 | 48,20 | 154,00 | 243,70 | 445,90 |
| 4 | 872,00 | 53,00 | 879,20 | 1804,20 |
| 5 |  |  |  |  |

(after deleting)

**Insert**

To insert cells into the sheet, select the cells over which or to the left of which you want to insert new cells, and choose:

**Edit - Insert**

By inserting cells, you force the other cells either to be pushed to the right, or down. A dialogue box appears and gives you this choice. In the example below, we are inserting cells above A2 to D2, and shifting the other cells down.

|   | A | B | C | D |
|---|---|---|---|---|
| 1 | January | February | March | 1. quarter |
| 2 | 6565,00 | 782,40 | 456,20 | 7803,60 |
| 3 | 34,35 | 798,21 | 789,50 | 1622,06 |
| 4 | 48,20 | 154,00 | 243,70 | 445,90 |
| 5 | 872,00 | 53,00 | 879,20 | 1804,20 |

(before inserting)

|   | A | B | C | D |
|---|---|---|---|---|
| 1 | January | February | March | 1. quarter |
| 2 |  |  |  |  |
| 3 | 6565,00 | 782,40 | 456,20 | 7803,60 |
| 4 | 34,35 | 798,21 | 789,50 | 1622,06 |
| 5 | 48,20 | 154,00 | 243,70 | 445,90 |
| 6 | 872,00 | 53,00 | 879,20 | 1804,20 |

(after inserting)

**Insert more than one row/column** To insert several columns or rows of cells, instead of selecting only one column/row over or to the left of which the new cells are to be inserted, you select the same number of rows/columns that you want inserted. In the example below, we are inserting two rows of cells above cells A2 to D2.

|   | A | B | C | D |
|---|---|---|---|---|
| 1 | January | February | March | 1. quarter |
| 2 | 6565,00 | 782,40 | 456,20 | 7803,60 |
| 3 | 34,35 | 798,21 | 789,50 | 1622,06 |
| 4 | 48,20 | 154,00 | 243,70 | 445,90 |
| 5 | 872,00 | 53,00 | 879,20 | 1804,20 |

(before inserting)

|   | A | B | C | D |
|---|---|---|---|---|
| 1 | January | February | March | 1. quarter |
| 2 |  |  |  |  |
| 3 |  |  |  |  |
| 4 | 6565,00 | 782,40 | 456,20 | 7803,60 |
| 5 | 34,35 | 798,21 | 789,50 | 1622,06 |
| 6 | 48,20 | 154,00 | 243,70 | 445,90 |
| 7 | 872,00 | 53,00 | 879,20 | 1804,20 |

(after inserting)

## 2b. Copy and move

**Copy
data**

You can copy data or formulas from one cell to another. Suppose you want to copy the contents of cell A2 and place them in cell A4. You first select cell A2. Then choose the menu command:

**Edit - Copy**

Next select cell A4 and press:　　　　　　| **RET** |

When you copy a cell which contains a formula with cell addresses, such as =A2+B2, the cell addresses will change when you copy to another cell. Suppose cell D2 has this formula, and you copy from cell D2 to cell D4. Since D4 is two cells down from D2, the cell addresses will change from A2 and B2 to A4 and B4, and thus the formula will become =A4+B4.

In the example below, we have copied from A1 to B1, from A2 to A4, and from D2 to D4. Note that text and numbers remain the same, while the cell addresses in the formula change.

D2　　　　　=A2+B2

|   | A | B | C | D |
|---|---|---|---|---|
| 1 | Text 1 | | | |
| 2 | 34,32 | 798,21 | | 832,53 |
| 3 | 45 | 35% | | |
| 4 | | 53 | | |

(before copying)

D4　　　　　=A4+B4

|   | A | B | C | D |
|---|---|---|---|---|
| 1 | Text 1 | Text 1 | | |
| 2 | 34,32 | 798,21 | | 832,53 |
| 3 | 45 | 35% | | |
| 4 | 34,32 | 53 | | 87,32 |

(after copying)

You can also copy a range of cells in the same way as you would a single cell. First select the range of cells you want to copy. Next, choose Edit - Copy in the menu. Then move the cursor to the top righthand cell in the area you want your range copied to, and press RET.

**Move data**

To move the contents of one or more cells, choose: **Edit - Cut**

Select where you want the cells copied and press: | **RET** |

In the example below, we have moved the data in cells A1:B3 to C1:D3.

|   | A | B | C | D |
|---|---|---|---|---|
| 1 | Text 1 | Text 1 |   |   |
| 2 | 34,32 | 798,21 |   |   |
| 3 | 45 | 35% |   |   |

(before moving)

C1

|   | A | B | C | D |
|---|---|---|---|---|
| 1 |   |   | Text 1 | Text 1 |
| 2 |   |   | 34,32 | 798,21 |
| 3 |   |   | 45 | 35% |

(after moving)

**Copy results of formulas**

You can copy the results of formulas, without copying the formulas themselves. This may be useful if you want to update data and at the same time preserve the results you had from before.

To copy results of formulas only, select the cells containing the formulas and choose: **Edit Copy**

Select where you want to copy the results (in some cases this might even be where the formulas are now) and choose:

**Edit - Paste Special**

In the dialog box, choose: **Values** and then: **OK**

Finish by pressing: | **ESC** |

In the example below, we have copied the formula in cell D2 to D4 with Edit - Paste Special. Compare the results with the example on page 21.

D4          832,53

|   | A | B | C | D |
|---|---|---|---|---|
| 1 | Text 1 | Text 1 |   |   |
| 2 | 34,32 | 798,21 |   | 832,53 |
| 3 | 45 | 35% |   |   |
| 4 | 34,32 | 53 |   | 832,53 |

(after paste special)

**Convert rows
<--> columns**

You can convert columns of data to rows, and visa versa. To do this, select the data you want to convert and choose: **Edit - Copy**

Select where you want to copy the results and choose:

**Edit - Paste Special**

In the dialog box, choose: **Transpose**

(before Transpose)

|   | A | B | C |
|---|---|---|---|
| 1 | January | February | March |
| 2 | 6565,00 | 782,40 | 456,20 |

(after Transpose)

|   | A | B |
|---|---|---|
| 1 | January | 6565,00 |
| 2 | February | 782,40 |
| 3 | March | 456,20 |

**Automatic
inserting
of cells**

You can cause spaces to be inserted automatically when pasting in information.

To do this, choose Edit - Copy to copy your cells. Then move the cursor to where you are pasting in your cells and choose:

**Edit - Insert Paste**

In the example below we are copying information about James Bond to row 4.

|   | A | B | C | D |
|---|---|---|---|---|
| 1 | ID | Last name | First name | Init. |
| 2 | 1853 | Bond | James | JB |
| 3 | 4862 | Hansen | Knut | KHA |
| 4 | 3548 | Poirot | Hercule | HEP |

(before copying with insert paste)

|   | A | B | C | D |
|---|---|---|---|---|
| 1 | ID | Last name | First name | Init. |
| 2 | 1853 | Bond | James | JB |
| 3 | 4862 | Hansen | Knut | KHA |
| 4 | 1853 | Bond | James | JB |
| 5 | 3548 | Poirot | Hercule | HEP |

(after insert paste)

**Move cells with automatic adjustment**

In the same way as when you copy, you can move cells with Insert Paste. In addition to cutting and pasting, spaces are inserted for the moved cells AND the empty spaces where the cells were moved from are deleted.

In the example below we are moving information about James Bond to row 6.

|   | A | B | C | D |
|---|---|---|---|---|
| 1 | ID | Last name | First name | Init. |
| 2 | 1524 | And | Anders | AA |
| 3 | 1853 | Bond | James | JB |
| 4 | 4862 | Hansen | Knut | KHA |
| 5 | 1524 | Jones | James | JJ |
| 6 | 3548 | Poirot | Hercule | HEP |
| 7 | 5244 | Corleone | Vito | VIC |

(before moving with insert paste)

|   | A | B | C | D |
|---|---|---|---|---|
| 1 | ID | Last name | First name | Init. |
| 2 | 1524 | And | Anders | AA |
| 3 | 4862 | Hansen | Knut | KHA |
| 4 | 1524 | Jones | James | JJ |
| 5 | 1853 | Bond | James | JB |
| 6 | 3548 | Poirot | Hercule | HEP |
| 7 | 5244 | Corleone | Vito | VIC |

(after insert paste)

**Copy to more than one cell**

You can copy the contents of a cell to many cells at the same time. For example, you could copy the contents of D2 down to D3, D4 and D5 all at once. First, starting from the first cell, in this case D2, you select the range, in this case D2 to D5. Then choose from the menu:

### Edit - Fill down

Similarly, you can copy the contents of, for example, A2 to B2, C2 and D2. Then the command is:

### Edit - Fill right

You can also copy upwards and to the left. To do this, select the cells, and then press the SHIFT key while you choose:

### Edit - Fill up        ... or ...
### Edit - Fill left

In the example below, we are copying the formula in cell D2 to D3, D4 and D5. Note that the cell addresses in the copied formulas have changed. In working with columns and rows of figures, the Edit - Fill commands can thus be considerable time-savers.

D2        =A2+B2+C2

|   | A | B | C | D |
|---|---|---|---|---|
| 1 | January | February | March | 1. quarter |
| 2 | 6565,00 | 782,40 | 456,20 | 7803,60 |
| 3 | 34,35 | 798,21 | 789,50 | |
| 4 | 48,20 | 154,00 | 243,70 | |
| 5 | 872,00 | 53,00 | 879,20 | |

(before copying)

D5        =A5+B5+C5

|   | A | B | C | D |
|---|---|---|---|---|
| 1 | January | February | March | 1. quarter |
| 2 | 6565,00 | 782,40 | 456,20 | 7803,60 |
| 3 | 34,35 | 798,21 | 789,50 | 1622,06 |
| 4 | 48,20 | 154,00 | 243,70 | 445,90 |
| 5 | 872,00 | 53,00 | 879,20 | 1804,20 |

(after copying)

**Absolute and relative referencing**

In some cases you may not want cell addresses inside formulas to adjust when being copied or moved. To do this, insert $. This can be done manually in the formula, or by selecting the cell address you wish to lock, and pressing:

> F4

Thus A2, for example, would become $A$2.
We would call A2 a relative reference, and $A$2 an absolute reference.

In the example below, we are locking the cell A2 in the formula in D2, so that when we copy the formula, A2 remains the same. Note that C2, the other cell reference, changes.

D2          =C2*(1+$A$2)

| | A | B | C | D |
|---|---|---|---|---|
| 1 | Bonus | February | Salary | 1. quarter |
| 2 | 10% | Anders | 3420 | 3762 |
| 3 | | Bond | 2980 | |
| 4 | | Christie | 2540 | |
| 5 | | Davis | 3640 | |

(before copying)

D2          =C3*(1+$A$2)

| | A | B | C | D |
|---|---|---|---|---|
| 1 | Bonus | February | Salary | 1. quarter |
| 2 | 10% | Anders | 3420 | 5215500 |
| 3 | | Bond | 2980 | 4544500 |
| 4 | | Christie | 2540 | |
| 5 | | Davis | 3640 | |

(after copying)

**Name cells**

Another way to lock cells is to name them. For example, you could name cell A2 'Bonus'. Once you have named the cell, you insert the name into all formulas on your spreadsheet which contain the named cell, so that the cell address is replaced by the cell name. For example the formula in D2 above would be '=C3*(1+Bonus)'. Naming cells makes the formulas easier to read and maintain.

To name a cell, select the cell you are naming (for example A2 above) and choose:

**Formula Define Name**

A dialogue box will appear. If the cell you selected has a label over or beside it, EXCEL will suggest this label as a name. The address of the selected cell will be suggested as the address. You can change either the name or cell address by editing in the appropriate box. Confirm by pressing:

| RET |

Using the example above, we have selected ce'l A2. Since the text "Bonus" was in the cell over A2, EXCEL has suggested this as a name.

| | | OK |
| --- | --- | --- |
| **Name:** | Bonus | |
| **Refers to:** | $A$2 | |

Once you have named a cell, you can use that name in all formulas on the spreadsheet which use that cell (such as A2 in the example above). To replace all existing references to A2 in all formulas on the spreadsheet, choose:

**Formula - Apply Names**

A dialogue box appears. Check that the cell names you want inserted are selected, and then press RET. In our example, wherever the cell address A2 appears in formulas on the spreadsheet, A2 will be changed to 'Bonus'.

The procedure then for naming cells in your spreadsheet is:

1) Write your formulas.
2) Name all cells which will be used repeatedly in formulas
   (Formula Define Name).
3) Insert names in formulas (Formula Apply Names).
4) Copy formulas as needed.

In the example below, we are giving cell A2 the name "Interest",
inserting it into all formulas, and then copying the formulas. Note
that when the formula in C2 is copied, "Interest" continues referring
to the same cell (A2).

C2          =A2*G2

|   | A | B | C | D |
|---|---|---|---|---|
| 1 | Interest | | Interest | Savings |
| 2 | 10% | 1989 | | 5000,00 |
| 3 | | 1990 | 500,00 | 5500,00 |
| 4 | | 1991 | | 5500,00 |
| 5 | | 1992 | | 5500,00 |

(before naming)

C2          =Interest*D2

|   | A | B | C | D |
|---|---|---|---|---|
| 1 | Interest | | Interest | Savings |
| 2 | 10% | 1989 | | 5000,00 |
| 3 | | 1990 | 500,00 | 5500,00 |
| 4 | | 1991 | | 5500,00 |
| 5 | | 1992 | | 5500,00 |

(after naming)

C5          =Interest*D4

|   | A | B | C | D |
|---|---|---|---|---|
| 1 | Interest | | Interest | Savings |
| 2 | 10% | 1989 | | 5000,00 |
| 3 | | 1990 | 500,00 | 5500,00 |
| 4 | | 1991 | 550,00 | 6050,00 |
| 5 | | 1992 | 605,00 | 6655,00 |

(after copying)

**Sort
data**

You can sort data in any column or row. For example, you have
an employee list which includes ID number, employee name
and initials. You could sort by any one of these three - that is,
by ID number, by name or by initials. To do this, you select
the data you want sorted (without headers). Then choose:

**Data - Sort**

A dialogue box then appears. For first key, you choose the first
cell in the column/row you are using to sort by. In the example below,
the list is to be sorted by last name. So here, you choose the first
cell in the last name column, in this case B2. Then you indicate if you
want your data sorted in ascending (default) or descending order.

You can also choose a second and third sort key. In the example
below, we have chosen first name (C2) as the second sort key.

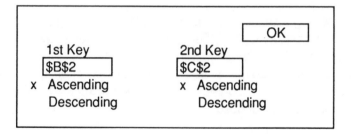

29

The pictures below show our list before and after sorting.

|   | A | B | C | D |
|---|---|---|---|---|
| 1 | ID no. | L. name | F. name | Initials |
| 2 | 4862 | Hansen | Knut | HKN |
| 3 | 1524 | Hansen | Hans | HH |
| 4 | 3548 | Poirot | Hercule | PHE |
| 5 | 1853 | Bond | James | BJ |
| 6 | 1524 | And | Anders | AA |

(before sorting)

|   | A | B | C | D |
|---|---|---|---|---|
| 1 | ID no. | L. name | F. name | Initials |
| 2 | 1524 | And | Anders | AA |
| 3 | 1853 | Bond | James | BJ |
| 4 | 4862 | Hansen | Hans | HH |
| 5 | 1524 | Hansen | Knut | HKN |
| 6 | 3548 | Poirot | Hercule | PHE |

(after sorting)

**Number series**

Instead of writing a series of numbers manually, you can generate them automatically, as long as they increase at an even proportion, for example, a series of numbers from 5000 to 6500, increasing each time by 250. To do this, write your first number. Then start from this cell and select the rest of the cells where you want the number series to appear. Then choose:

**Data - Series**

A dialogue box will then appear, where you choose step value and stop value. If you want the number to increase by 250 each time, then for step value you would type 250. If you wanted the numbers to go no further than 6500, then stop value would be 6500.

| Step value : | 250 | Stop value : | 6500 |
|---|---|---|---|

The pictures below show before and after Data - Series is chosen.

| | A | B | C | D |
|---|---|---|---|---|
| 1 | 5000 | | | |
| 2 | | | | |
| 3 | | | | |
| 4 | | | | |
| 5 | | | | |
| 6 | | | | |
| 7 | | | | |

(before)

| | A | B | C | D |
|---|---|---|---|---|
| 1 | 5000 | | | |
| 2 | 5250 | | | |
| 3 | 5500 | | | |
| 4 | 5750 | | | |
| 5 | 6000 | | | |
| 6 | 6250 | | | |
| 7 | 6500 | | | |

(after)

## 2d. Linking spreadsheets

**Link single cell**

You can link different spreadsheets, so that when figures are updated on one sheet, the other sheets will automatically be updated. A simple way to do this is to link single cells with cells on another sheet. To do this, go to the cell you want linked to the other sheet and type:

**=**

Then choose:   **Window**

Select the file that you want to link to.
Select the cell you want to link to and press:      | **RET** |

Hereafter, if the cell on the linked-to sheet is changed, then the linked cell on the first sheet will change accordingly.

In the example below, we have linked cell B15 on the active file to cell B1 on FILE2.XLS. Note that just as when you write a formula and select a cell address on the same sheet, EXCEL includes it automatically in the formula. The same occurs when you select a cell on another sheet. Only in the latter case, the file name is included, followed by "!".

| B15 | =FILE2.XLS!$B$1 | | |
| --- | --- | --- | --- |
| | A | B | C | D |
| 13 | Expenses | | | |
| 14 | Rates | 150 | | |
| 15 | Loan | 500 | | |
| 16 | Electric. | 125 | | |
| 17 | Phone | 345 | | |

FILE2.XLS

| | A | B | C | D | E | F |
| --- | --- | --- | --- | --- | --- | --- |
| 1 | Annuity | 500 | Interest | Principal | Balance | Per. |
| 2 | Loan | 59581 | -447 | -53 | 59528 | 1 |
| 3 | Interest | 9% | -446 | -54 | 59474 | 2 |
| 4 | Periods | 12 | -446 | -54 | 59420 | 3 |
| 5 | Years | 25 | -446 | -54 | 59366 | 4 |
| 6 | | | -445 | -55 | 59311 | 5 |

**Link a group of cells**

You can also link a group of cells to cells on another sheet, through a single action. To do this, move to the other sheet, select the cells you want to link to, and choose:

**Edit - Copy**

Then move back to the first sheet, select the top left hand cell in the area you want linked to the other cells, and choose:

**Edit - Paste Link**

32

**Arrays**

Edit - Paste Link creates an array of cells linked to the cells on the other sheet. This array is different from a normal group of cells with individual formulas. These array cells cannot be moved, edited or deleted individually (although they can be individually formatted or copied).

The array range can be moved, cleared or deleted by selecting the whole range, and then choosing the appropriate menu command.

**Edit an array**

To edit the array cells, select any cell in the array and edit the formula in the normal way. When you have finished, press:

```
| CTRL |

| SHIFT |          | RET |
```

The result is that all cells in the array are edited in the same way.

In the example below, we have linked the cells I3:I35 in the first sheet to the cells E3:E35 in FILE2.XLS. The { } signs in the formula in I3 indicate that this formula is part of an array.

I3     {=FILE2.XLS!$E$3:$E$35}

| | G | H | I | J | K |
|---|---|---|---|---|---|
| 1 | | | | | |
| 2 | 1.quarter | 2.quarter | 3.quarter | 4.quarter | |
| 3 | 7161,25 | 8425,00 | 7803,60 | | |
| 4 | 1372,35 | 1614,53 | 1622,06 | | |
| 5 | 715,57 | 841,85 | 445,90 | | |
| 6 | 986,00 | 1160,00 | 1804,20 | | |

FILE2.XLS

| | A | B | C | D | E | F |
|---|---|---|---|---|---|---|
| 1 | | July | August | Sept | 3. quarter | |
| 2 | | | | | | |
| 3 | Region 1 | 6565,00 | 782,40 | 456,20 | 7803,60 | |
| 4 | Region 2 | 34,35 | 798,21 | 789,50 | 1622,06 | |
| 5 | Region 3 | 48,20 | 154,00 | 243,70 | 445,90 | |
| 6 | Region 4 | 872,00 | 53,00 | 879,20 | 1804,20 | |

**Dynamic linking of spreadsheets (DDE)**

Suppose you open a spreadsheet which is linked to another spreadsheet. You are asked if you want to include the most recent updates. If you answer 'yes', your data will be updated without you having to open the linked spreadsheets.

In the formula, cell references to unopened spreadsheets are shown with full path description.

B2   =C:\SALES\TROMS.XLS!$H$34

|   | A | B | C | D |
|---|---|---|---|---|
| 1 | 1991 Sales in Northern Norway (in mil.) | | | |
| 2 | Troms | 4568 | | |
| 3 | Nordland | 6452 | | |

You can also open all the linked spreadsheets with a command. Choose:

**File - Links**

A dialogue box appears. Press SHIFT while you click in the listbox at the files you want to open.

**DDE with other applications**

You can also write a formula directly into Excel which refers to an unopened spreadsheet. You must then give the path. In the example above, you would type in cell B2:

=C:\SALES\TROMS.XLS!$H$34

You can also directly write a formula which refers to another application, for example Q+E. Then you write the application's name, followed by a pipe ( | ) and then path, file name and reference as above.

In the example below we are referring to information on a Q+E query file.

=QE|ANSATTE.QEF!ALLE

**Undo mistake**

If you have made an error, and want to undo it, the command is:

**Edit - Undo**

In the example below, we sorted by last name, but neglected to mark the last column. If there were hundreds of names, this could result in a minor catastrophe. To undo this mistake, we now use the Edit - Undo command.

|   | A | B | C | D |
|---|---|---|---|---|
| 1 | ID no. | L. name | F. name | Initials |
| 2 | 1524 | And | Anders | HKN |
| 3 | 1853 | Bond | James | JJ |
| 4 | 4862 | Hansen | Knut | PHE |
| 5 | 1524 | Jones | James | BJ |
| 6 | 3548 | Poirot | Hercule | AA |

(mistaken sorting)

|   | A | B | C | D |
|---|---|---|---|---|
| 1 | ID no. | L. name | F. name | Initials |
| 2 | 4862 | Hansen | Knut | HKN |
| 3 | 1524 | Jones | James | JJ |
| 4 | 3548 | Poirot | Hercule | PHE |
| 5 | 1853 | Bond | James | BJ |
| 6 | 1524 | And | Anders | AA |

(after edit-undo)

**Help**          If you need help on a specific menu command, press:

> [ SHIFT ]

> [ F1 ]

A large question mark will appear. Click on it with the mouse and drag it to the menu command on which you want information.

You can also look up information in an online index. To do this, press:

> [ F1 ]

# 3. Formatting your spreadsheet

You can format your spreadsheet in a number of ways to make it more clear and readable. You format by selecting the cells you want to format, and then by choosing a format command from the menu. Then, no matter what data is entered into those cells, that data will follow the format you defined for that cell. You can format:

- number type
- print font and size
- lines over, under or on the sides of the cell
- row height and column width

## 3a. Number format

Numbers can be formatted in the following ways:

- with a specified number of decimals shown
- with commas or periods to indicate thousands and millions
- with text, for example, "US$"
- as a date
- as a percentage
- in a certain colour (red, yellow, blue or green)
- with spaces in between
- positive numbers with one format, negative numbers with another, for example negative numbers in red

To format numbers, select the cells you want to format, and choose:

**Format - Number**

A dialogue box will then appear on the screen. Choose the number format you want from the list box and press RET (or OK).

Below are some number formats, and what the result would be
for the numbers 3452,758, -5,87, 0,674 and 32987.

| General | 3452,758 | -5,87 | 0,674 | 32987 |
|---|---|---|---|---|
| 0 | 3453 | -6 | 1 | |
| 0,00 | 3452,76 | -5,87 | 0,67 | |
| #.##0,00 | 3.452,76 | -5,87 | | |
| 0,00;[red]-0,00 | 3452,76 | -5,87 | 0,67 | |
| 0;0 | 3453 | 6 | 1 | |
| 0,0% | | -587,0% | 67,4% | |
| d.mmm.åå | | | | 24.Apr.90 |

Note: if you want nothing to be shown if a value is 0, use '#', and
if you want '0' shown if a value is 0, use '0'.
For example: 52 with the format  #.##0,00  will be shown as: 52.00
52 with the format  0.000,00  will be shown as:  0,052.00

**Negative/
positive**

A number format can specify one format for negative numbers and
another format for positive numbers. You then use semicolon (;) as
divider, so that the format to the left of the semi-colon is for positive
numbers, and the format to the right is for negative numbers. See
the format "0,00;[red]-0,00" in the example above.

**Date**

In the above example, the date appears quite differently in general
format as it does in date format. For Excel, the 24th of April, 1990 is
the 32987th day after Jan. 1, 1900. Because of this, you can calculate,
for example, the difference in days between today's date and
June 25th, 1989.

Note that number format has nothing to do with the mathematical value of the number. In the example below, the formula in cell C2 adds the contents of cells A2 and B2. In the second figure, cells A2 and B2 have been formatted to show no decimals. Still, the formula in C2 uses the actual mathematical values of A2 and B2 (4.5 and 3.5), so that the result is the same. The actual value of a formatted cell is shown in the formula bar, as shown in the example below (cell B2).

Note that a decimal point is designated in Excel by a period (.)

| C2 | | =A2+B2 | | |
|---|---|---|---|---|
| | A | B | C | D |
| 1 | | | | |
| 2 | 4,5 | 3,5 | 8 | |

(before formatting)

| B2 | | 3,5 | | |
|---|---|---|---|---|
| | A | B | C | D |
| 1 | | | | |
| 2 | 5 | 4 | 8 | |

(after formatting)

**Customized format**

You can also create your own number format, instead of choosing one from the box. Then you merely type your format in the input box below. Note that to add text, such as "US$", you enclose it in quotation marks. In the example below, we have written our own format to show the number in red with no decimals and followed by "days overdue" if positive, and nothing shown if negative.

```
Format Number                              OK

  General
  0
  0,00
  #.##0
  #.##0,00
  #.##0 Kr;-#.##0 Kr

  Format :   [Red]0" days overdue";""
```

In the example below, we have formulas to calculate overdue payments for a list of accounts. The number formats we have used are:

| | |
|---|---|
| Cells A4:A11 | **0** |
| Cells B4:B11 | **0,00** |
| Cells C4:C11, D1 | **ddmmm** |
| Cells D4:D11 | **[Red]0" days";""** |

| D4 | | =today-C4 | | |
|---|---|---|---|---|
| | A | B | C | D |
| 1 | | | | 19.Nov |
| 2 | | | | |
| 3 | Acct. no. | Amount | Date due | Overdue |
| 4 | 482379 | 485,34 | 23.Nov | |
| 5 | 482380 | 7274,00 | 19.Nov | |
| 6 | 482381 | 495,20 | 14.Nov | 2 days |
| 7 | 482382 | 896,56 | 9.Nov | 7 days |
| 8 | 482383 | 4952,30 | 5.Nov | 11 days |
| 9 | 482384 | 986,60 | 31.Oct | 16 days |
| 10 | 482385 | 8593,00 | 26.Oct | 21 days |
| 11 | 482386 | 56,40 | 22.Oct | 25 days |

## 3b. Justify

You can centre, left- or right-justify text or numbers within their cells. If you do not use this command, Excel justifies all text to the left and all numbers to the right. To change this, choose the command:

**Format - Alignment**

In the example below, the header in column A is centred, while the other headers are right-justified.

| | A | B | C | D |
|---|---|---|---|---|
| 3 | Acct. no. | Amount | Date due | Overdue |
| 4 | 482379 | 485,34 | 23.Nov | |
| 5 | 482380 | 7274,00 | 19.Nov | |
| 6 | 482381 | 495,20 | 14.Nov | 2 days |
| 7 | 482382 | 896,56 | 9.Nov | 7 days |

## 3c. Font and size

You can determine the size and font in which your data is written.
Choose the command:          **Format - Font**

The different fonts possible are normal, bold, italic and bold italic.

You can alter these definitions, such as by increasing the type size,
but note that this will affect all cells defined with this same print
definition. For example, if you changed the fourth print definition,
all cells previously defined with the fourth definition would be
immediately affected.  To change a definition, select one of the four
listed, and then choose:

**Fonts**

In the example below, we have redefined the fourth definition in order
to have an enlarged bold font. Note that all cells previously defined
as Bold Italic will now become enlarged bold.

**Fonts**

| |
|---|
| 1. **Helv 10** |
| 2. **Helv 10, Bold** |
| 3. **Helv 10, Italic** |
| x  4. **Helv 10, Bold Italic** |

(before)

(after)

**Fonts**

| |
|---|
| 1. **Helv 10** |
| 2. **Helv 10, Bold** |
| 3. **Helv 10, Italic** |
| x  4. **Helv 14, Bold** |

**Fonts >>**

| Font | Size | Style |
|---|---|---|
| **Courier** | 8 | x **Bold** |
| x **Helv** | 10 | **Italic** |
| **Modern** | 12 | **Underlined** |
| **Roman** | x  14 | **Strikeout** |
| **Script** | 18 | |

In the example below, the title in A1 is formatted in enlarged bold, the headers in bold, and the actual data in normal type.

|   | A | B | C | D |
|---|---|---|---|---|
| 1 | **Accounts receivable** | | | |
| 2 | | | | |
| 3 | **acct. no.** | **amount** | **date due** | **overdue** |
| 4 | 482379 | 485,34 | 23.Nov | |
| 5 | 482380 | 7274,00 | 19.Nov | |
| 6 | 482381 | 495,20 | 14.Nov | 2 days |
| 7 | 482382 | 896,56 | 9.Nov | 7 days |

**( Excel 3.0 )**

**Choose font, size and colour**

In Excel 3.0 you can combine font, size and colour in as many varieties as you wish. Select the cells and choose:

**Format - Font**

In the example below we have chosen 10-point Helvetica bold. In the Sample box we can see how our result will look.

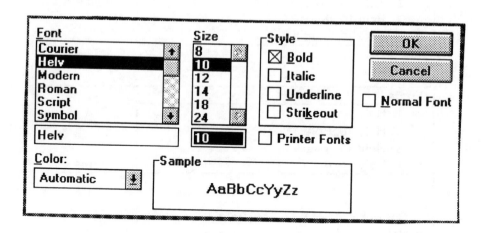

**Alignment with icons**

You can use icons to align data inside cells.

To do this, select the cells you want to align and click at:

 to left-justify

 to centre

 to right-justify

**Choose font with icon**

You can click at an icon to choose a font. Select the cells you want to format and click at:

| B | bold |

| I | italic |

For bold italic, click at both icons.
To cancel the font, click again at the icon.

## 3d. Lines, boxes and shade

**Lines and boxes**

You can draw a box around a cell or group of cells (outline), or draw a line under, over, to the left or to the right of the selected cells. Or you can shade them. To do this, choose:

**Format - Border**

In the example below, we have formatted cells A3:D3 with shade, and cells A3:D11 with righthand lines.

|   | A | B | C | D |
|---|---|---|---|---|
| 1 | **Accounts receivable** | | | |
| 2 | | | | |
| 3 | Acct. no. | Amount | Date due | Overdue |
| 4 | 482379 | 485,34 | 23.Nov | |
| 5 | 482380 | 7274,00 | 19.Nov | |
| 6 | 482381 | 495,20 | 14.Nov | 2 days |
| 7 | 482382 | 896,56 | 9.Nov | 7 days |

**Gridlines**

For lines and boxes to appear more clearly, you can get rid of the gridlines on the screen. To do this, choose:

**Options - Display**

Then choose: **Gridlines** ... and remove the X.

In addition to gridlines, you can also decide if you want formulas, row/column headings and zero values to appear on the screen.

Choose: **Options - Display** ... and then ...

**Formulas** . . . . . . . . . . . . to have formulas shown in the spreadsheet cells, instead of results.

**Row/column headings** . . to have screen headings (A,B,C,D... and 1,2,3,4...) shown on the screen.

**Zero values** . . . . . . . . . . to have zero values shown on the screen.

In the example below, we have removed gridlines as well as row and column headings.

## Accounts receivable

| Acct. no. | Amount | Date due | Overdue |
|-----------|--------|----------|---------|
| 482379 | 485,34 | 23.Nov | |
| 482380 | 7274,00 | 19.Nov | |
| 482381 | 495,20 | 14.Nov | 2 days |
| 482382 | 896,56 | 9.Nov | 7 days |

Excel 3.0

## 3e. Format styles

**Store format styles for later use**

Suppose you have formatted cells with bold type, 12-point size, left alignment and shading. You want to use this format style again later on in the spreadsheet.

| | A | B | C | D |
|---|---|---|---|---|
| 1 | Employees in Oslo | | | |
| 2 | ID | L. name | F. name | Init. |
| 3 | 4862 | Hansen | Knut | KHA |

To avoid having to define all this again the next time you want to use the same format style, you can give this format style a name. To do this, select one of the cells you have formatted and click at the down-arrow beside the box which says 'Normal' in the icon bar.

| Normal | ⬇ |

45

Type in the name you want to give to the format style. In the example below we are calling the style "Title".

Press RET.

You can now use this format style as many times as you like in the sheet. In the example below we want to format the text in row 21 with the same format style as we defined in the previous example.

|    | A | B | C | D |
|----|---|---|---|---|
| 21 | Employees in Oslo | | | |
| 22 | ID | L. name | F. name | Init. |
| 23 | 3544 | And | Anders | AA |

Select row 21 and click at the down-arrow by the box that says 'Normal' in the icon bar.

A roll-down menu appears. Click at the format style you want.

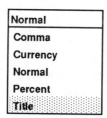

The selected cells are now formatted in the format style you chose, in this case "Title".

|    | A | B | C | D |
|----|---|---|---|---|
| 21 | **Employees in Bergen** | | | |
| 22 | ID | L. name | F. name | Init. |
| 23 | 3544 | And | Anders | AA |

**Graphic icons**

## 3f. Graphic objects

You can draw boxes, circles and lines on the spreadsheet. To do this, choose one of the following icons:

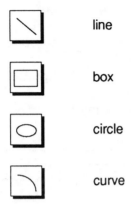

line

box

circle

curve

Then, to draw these figures on the spreadsheet, click and drag with the mouse. The cursor resembles a little cross.

Afterwards you can edit by clicking at the figure. The cursor changes to an arrow. You can move the figure by clicking and dragging.

To change size or shape, move the mouse so that the cursor resembles a little cross again. Now you can click and drag at the edges of the figure.

**Colour
and pattern**

To choose colour and pattern for your graphic object, choose:

**Format - Patterns**

To choose options, click at the arrow beside the desired list box:

For colour of the object, choose the arrow beside:     **Foreground**
For pattern, choose the arrow beside:     **Pattern**
For colour of the pattern, choose the arrow beside:     **Background**

In the lower right corner of the dialogue box you see the 'Sample' box.
This shows how your choice will appear.

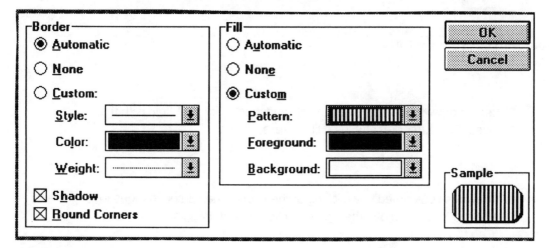

**Excel 3.0**

**Draw circles
and boxes
around data**

If you want to draw a box or circle around data, click at 'None' under
the 'Fill' box.

|   | A | B | C | D |
|---|---|---|---|---|
| 1 | Cust no. | Inv. no. | Balance | Overdue |
| 2 | 5233 | 1123311 | 4525 | 5 days |
| 3 | 8655 | 1135221 | 15240 | 35 days |
| 4 | 3564 | 2155432 | 540 | 2 days |

**Draw an arrow**

To draw an arrow, click at the icon:
Draw a line and choose:

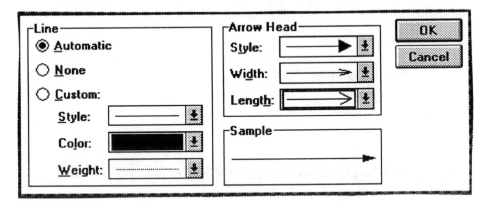

**Format - Patterns**

Under 'Arrow Head', click at the up- and down-arrows to choose style and width of the arrow. You get a visual preview in the 'Example' box.

**Create a text box**

To create a text box for help information, click at:

Draw a box on the sheet by clicking and dragging with the mouse, and write your text in the box. Format the box with Format - Patterns and the text with Format - Font. Note that here you can format individual letters within the text.

**Copy and move graphic objects**

To copy or move graphic objects such as circles, lines and text boxes, move the cursor beside the object so that the cursor changes to an arrow.

Click and drag to move the object, or choose Edit - Cut or Edit - Copy and Edit - Paste at your destination.

**Select
several
objects**

To select several objects at the same time, click at:

Draw a box around the objects you want to select by clicking and dragging.

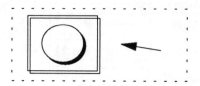

## 3g. Row height and column width

To alter the height of a row, place the cursor underneath the row number on the lefthand side of the screen and drag up or down.
For column width, place the cursor on the right of the column letter on the top of the screen, and drag back or to the right.

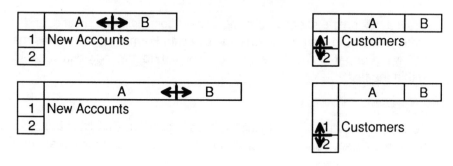

If you want to adjust row height or column width for several rows/columns, choose:

**Format Row Height** ... or ...
**Format Column Width**

To regain normal height/width, choose: **Standard**

The pictures below show our accounts before and after row height has been adjusted.

| | A | B | C | D | |
|---|---|---|---|---|---|
| 1 | **Accounts receivable** | | | | |
| 2 | | | | | |
| 3 | Acct. no. | Amount | Date due | Overdue | (before) |
| 4 | 482379 | 485,34 | 23 Nov | | |
| 5 | 482380 | 7274,00 | 19.Nov | | |
| 6 | 482381 | 495,20 | 14 Nov | 2 days | |
| 7 | 482382 | 896,56 | 9.Nov | 7 days | |

| | A | B | C | D | |
|---|---|---|---|---|---|
| 1 | **Accounts receivable** | | | | |
| 2 | | | | | |
| 3 | Acct. no. | Amount | Date due | Overdue | (after) |
| 4 | 482379 | 485,34 | 23.Nov | | |
| 5 | 482380 | 7274,00 | 19.Nov | | |
| 6 | 482381 | 495,20 | 14.Nov | 2 days | |
| 7 | 482382 | 896,56 | 9.Nov | 7 days | |

**Automatic column width**

You can have column width automatically adjusted to the width of the data the cells in the column contain.

To do this, select the columns you want to adjust and choose:

**Format - Column Width**

and click at:     **Best Fit**

In the example below we are adjusting the columns to get more room on the spreadsheet.

|   | A | B | C | D |
|---|---|---|---|---|
| 1 | ID | L. name | F. name | Init. |
| 2 | 1524 | And | Anders | AA |
| 3 | 3548 | Poirot | Hercule | HEP |
| 4 | 5244 | Corleone | Vito | VIC |

Below is the result after 'Best Fit' has been chosen.

|   | A | B | C | D |
|---|---|---|---|---|
| 1 | ID | L. name | F. name | Init |
| 2 | 1524 | And | Anders | AA |
| 3 | 3548 | Poirot | Hercule | HEP |
| 4 | 5244 | Corleone | Vito | VIC |

**Hide a row/ column**

To hide a row or column, choose Format - Row Height or Format - Column Width, and click at:

**Hide**

To reveal the row/column, click at:     **Unhide**

**Word wrap**    You can have word wrap in Excel. This means that when you are typing in text, the text will be automatically arranged in lines of desired width. If you afterwards insert or delete words, the text will adjust in the lines automatically. This is a feature common to word processing programs, but new to spreadsheets.

To use word wrap, select the column you will type your text in, and choose:

**Format - Alignment**

Click then at the check box for Wrap text:　　　X | **Wrap text**

Your text column is now formatted for word wrap. You can now type in your text in the same way as with a word processor. Adjust the width of the text lines simply by adjusting the width of the column.

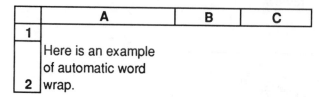

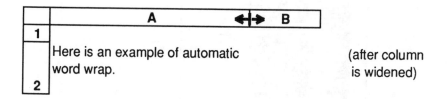

(after column
is widened)

53

# 4. Printing out

To print out your spreadsheet, choose the command:

**File - Print**

A dialogue box appears. You can choose here if you want to just print out a few pages of the document, or the entire document (default).
In the example below we are just printing out the first page.

| X | | **From :** | 1 | | **To :** | 1 | |

**Preview**

To see what the printout will look like before you actually send it to the printer, choose:

**Preview**

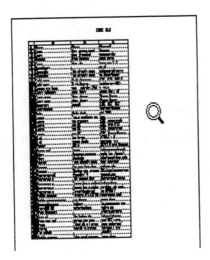

**Select
printer and
dimensions**

To select printer and printout dimensions (such as horizontal or vertical), choose:

**File - Printer Setup**

A dialogue box then appears. Select a printer from the list box.

If you are using a 2x version of Excel, you can choose horizontal/vertical printout by choosing:

**Setup**

Another dialogue box appears. Here you can choose horizontal (landscape) or vertical (portrait) printout.

| Orientation: | O  Portrait | O  Landscape |
|---|---|---|

For Excel 3x versions, see the following section.

**Gridlines
Row/
column
headings**

To make page layout adjustments, such as headers, footers, or whether you want gridlines and row/column headings in the printout, choose:

**File - Page Setup**

To remove gridlines or row/column headings from the printout, remove the X from the appropriate box. In the example below, we are removing gridlines from the printout.

| X | **Row /column headings** | | **Gridlines** |
|---|---|---|---|

**( Excel 3.0 )**

**Horizontal
Printout**

In Excel 3x, choose horizontal/vertical printout with the File - Page Setup command. The options Portrait and Landscape will appear in the dialog box.

**Headers
Footers**

For headers and footers, simply type in the appropriate boxes what you want to appear on the top (header) and the bottom (footer) of each page in your spreadsheet.

You can also use the following codes for headers and footers:

| | | | |
|---|---|---|---|
| &L | left-justify | &D | current date |
| &C | centre | &T | current time |
| &R | right-justify | &F | file name |
| &B | bold type | &P | page number |
| &I | italic type | &P+number | add number to page number |
| | | &P-number | subtract number from page no. |

In the example below, we are printing out without gridlines and row/column headings. There will be no header, and the footer will display, centred and in italic type, page numbers starting with page 20, preceded by the text "page".

**Page Setup**

Header :  [                    ]          [ OK ]

Footer :  [ &C &I page &P+19 ]

☐ Row /column headings          ☐ Gridlines

**Page breaks**

To set page breaks, place the cursor in the cell above or to the left of where you want a page break. Then choose the command:

**Options - Set Page Break**

To remove a page break set by Set - Page Break, select the cell where the page break was set, and choose:

**Options - Remove Page Break**

If the Remove Page Break command does not appear, it means no page break was set in this cell. To avoid trouble finding page breaks, it is best to:

- set vertical page breaks from a cell in column A
- set horizontal page breaks from a cell in row 1

**Print part of sheet**     You can also print a part of the worksheet by selecting the part you want printed out, and choosing:

**Options - Set Print Area**

When you print out, just this defined area will be printed.

**Cancel print area**     To cancel this defined print area, choose:

**Formula - Define Name**

A dialogue box will appear. Select "Print Area" from the list box, and choose:

**Delete**

**Display formulas**     You can print out your spreadsheet with all formulas displayed, instead of the formulas' results. To do this, choose:

**Options Display**

A dialogue box will appear. Select the box beside:     **Formulas**

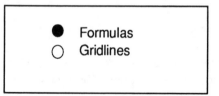

This can be useful for documentation purposes.

# 5. Built-in spreadsheet formulas

You can use built-in Excel formulas to make mathematical, financial, statistical and logical calculations. These built-in formulas are called functions.

**Paste function**

If you forget the exact name of a function, or what parameters the function requires, go to the cell where you want to write the function and choose:

**Formula Paste Function**

A dialog box will then appear. Choose the function you want.
To get parameter descriptions, click at the box at:

**Paste Arguments**

You can then edit the formula directly in the formula bar.

## 5a. Mathematical functions

**Sum**

To add figures, type:          **=SUM(**

Then select the range of figures you want to add. The easiest way to do this is to drag over the range with the mouse. The range then gets written into the formula.

**B2:B5**

Finish the formula then by typing:          **)**

And finally RET. The complete formula then looks like this:

**=SUM(B2:B5)**

**Autosum**     You can generate a SUM formula automatically by using the SUM icon (resembles a Greek sigma). Select the cell you want your SUM-formula in and click at:

Autosum suggests a SUM formula. You can then edit, or confirm with RET.

In the example below, autosum's suggestion for the formula in B7 was right. In cell E2 we had to edit.

E2     =SUM(B2:D2)

|   | A | B | C | D | E |
|---|---|---|---|---|---|
| 1 |   | Free-stand. | Block | Other | Total |
| 2 | 1986 | 9155 | 2466 | 7544 | 19165 |
| 3 | 1987 | 7825 | 2855 | 7822 |   |
| 4 | 1988 | 6522 | 3488 | 6488 |   |
| 5 | 1989 | 3522 | 3755 | 6855 |   |
| 6 | 1990 | 3466 | 5144 | 7924 |   |
| 7 | Total | 30490 |   |   |   |

**Average,
count, min,
max**

The functions for average, count, smallest and largest are written in exactly the same way as the SUM function.

| | |
|---|---|
| (averages) | **=AVERAGE(B2:B5)** |
| (finds smallest) | **=MIN(B2:B5)** |
| (finds largest) | **=MAX(B2:B5)** |
| (counts numbers) | **=COUNT(B2:B5)** |

( Excel 3.0 ) (counts numbers and text) **=COUNTA(B2:B5)**

In the example below, we have used functions to find the sum, average, smallest and largest of the figures in columns B, C and D, and the total count. Note that count finds the number of cells in a given range which have numbers. Thus a cell with text, or blank, wouldn't be counted. With counta (Excel 3x), text would be counted, but not blanks.

| B7 | | =SUM(B2:B5) | | |
|---|---|---|---|---|
| | A | B | C | D |
| 1 | | January | February | March |
| 2 | | 6565,00 | 782,40 | 456,20 |
| 3 | | 34,35 | 798,21 | 789,50 |
| 4 | | 48,20 | 154,00 | 243,70 |
| 5 | | 872,00 | 53,00 | 879,20 |
| 6 | | ---------- | ---------- | ---------- |
| 7 | Sum | 7519,55 | 1787,61 | 2368,60 |
| 8 | Average | 1879,89 | 446,90 | 592,15 |
| 9 | Largest | 6565,00 | 798,21 | 879,20 |
| 10 | Smallest | 34,35 | 53,00 | 243,70 |
| 11 | Count | 4 | | |

**Today's
date**

To get today's date, use the function:

**=NOW()**

Note that if you get a number like 32989.56, this merely means you need to change the cell to a date format with the Format - Number command.

## 5b. Conditional result

A result can depend on certain conditions. Let us say you go into a shop and want to buy an expensive watch. The question then is: do you have your credit card on you? If yes, then the watch is yours. If not, then no watch for you today. The situation can be expressed in this way: IF VISA, WATCH, OTHERWISE NOTHING DOING.

IF

In a spreadsheet, the necessary information factors would be placed in one or more cells. In the above example, you could have in cell A2, 'YES' (if you have your VISA) or 'NO' (if you don't). In cell A3 you could have 'WATCH', and in cell A4, 'NOTHING DOING'.

Then you could write the formula like this: **=IF(**

Inside the parentheses you type the first condition: **A2="YES"**
Note that quotation marks (") must be used with text.

Next comes the result if the condition is met: **A3**
Finally comes the result if the condition is not met: **A4**

The three information types which lie inside the parentheses are called 'parameters', and are separated from each other by a comma (,). The entire formula then looks like this:

**=IF(A2="YES",A3,A4)**

In the above example, equals (=) is used as operand in the first parameter. The operands >, <, >= and <= can also be used. Let us say you would buy the watch if the price is under 500 pounds. With the actual price located in cell A5, the formula would look like this:

**=IF(A5<500,A3,A4)**

Note that in the above formula, 500 is a number, so quotation marks (") are not used.

| D2 | | =IF(A5<500,A3,A4) | |
|---|---|---|---|
| | A | B | C | D |
| 2 | YES | (visa) | Answer: | **WATCH** |
| 3 | WATCH | | | |
| 4 | NOTHING DOING | | | |
| 5 | 499,00 | (watch's price) | | |

In the example below, we are testing to see if our savings are more than 500. If they are, we get 11% interest. Otherwise, we only get 6% interest. Note that we have named cell A1 "Interest_1" and cell A5 "Interest_2". Excel replaced the blank in the names with underline ( _ ). Afterwards we have copied the formula down (Edit - Fill Down).

| C6 | =IF(D2>5000,Interest_1*D5,Interest_2*D5) | | |
|---|---|---|---|
| | A | B | C | D |
| 1 | Interest 1 | | Interest | Savings |
| 2 | 11% | 1990 | | 450,00 |
| 3 | | 1991 | 27,00 | 477,00 |
| 4 | Interest 2 | 1992 | 28,62 | 505,62 |
| 5 | 6% | 1993 | 55,62 | 561,24 |
| 6 | | 1994 | 61,74 | 622,97 |

**Nested IF**

Sometimes a result is based on several conditions. You can buy the expensive watch if you have a credit card, but also if you have enough money in the bank. Then you can go to the bank and take out the money. The situation now could be expressed like this:
IF VISA, BUY WATCH, IF MONEY IN BANK, GO TO BANK, OTHERWISE NOTHING DOING

| D2 | =IF(A2="yes",A5,IF(A3>A4,A6,A7) | | |
|---|---|---|---|
| | A | B | C | D |
| 2 | no | (visa) | Answer: | **GO TO BANK** |
| 3 | 542 | (bank balance) | | |
| 4 | 540 | (watch's price) | | |
| 5 | BUY WATCH | | | |
| 6 | GO TO BANK | | | |
| 7 | NOTHING DOING | | | |

To write this formula, start with:     **=IF(A2="yes",A5,**

If 'yes' is in cell A2, the result will be A5 (buy watch).
Otherwise, the next test comes:

**IF(A3>A4,A6,**

If the bank balance (A3) is greater than the price of the watch (A4),
then you go to the bank (A6). Otherwise:

**A7))**

Otherwise forget buying the watch (A7). Finish your formula with a
parenthesis for the second IF and another parenthesis for the main
IF test. The entire formula then looks like this:

**=IF(A2="yes",A5,IF(A3>A4,A6,A7))**

Note that the IF-formula's 3-parameter structure remains the same,
even though there are several levels. In the above example, the
main IF can be broken down as follows:

1) test ...     A2="yes"
2) if yes ...   A5
3) if no ...    IF(A3>A4,A6,A7)

For the second IF, the three parameters are:

1) test ...     A3>A4
2) if yes ...   A6
3) if no ...    A7

There can be up to seven IF phrases inside a single formula.

In the example below, we are using profit margin as a condition for bonus. If the branch's profit margin is greater than 20%, then the branch leaders get Bonus 1. If the margin is 10%, they get Bonus 2. And otherwise, no bonus.

| D2 | | | =IF(C2>20%,Bonus1,IF(C2>10%,Bonus2,0)) | |
|---|---|---|---|---|
| | A | B | C | D |
| 1 | Bonus1 | | P.Margin | Bonus |
| 2 | 5000 | Blofeld | 14,7% | 3000 |
| 3 | | Poirot | -2,5% | 0 |
| 4 | Bonus2 | Wong | 18,4% | 3000 |
| 5 | 3000 | Mays | 23,8% | 5000 |
| 6 | | Wayne | 6,1% | 0 |

# 5c. Financial functions

**Financial functions**

EXCEL has a number of functions which are especially designed for financial planning and analysis. Four of these are:

PMT, which shows how much must be paid each period in an annuity (identical periodic payments), either to pay off a loan, or to save up a specific amount   (Payment)

PV, which shows how much you can loan, if you pay a specific amount periodically.    (Present Value)

RATE, which shows the interest amount per period which one either  a) receives in a savings account or b) pays in a loan.

FV, which shows the amount you get in the future if you pay a specific amount periodically.   (Future Value)

IRR, which shows the interest amount per period which one either  a) receives from an investment or  b) pays in a loan. This differs from the RATE function in that IRR takes into account extra fees, and the payments do not have to be identical.

**PMT**
**Annuity**

Suppose that you are buying a car, and want to take out a loan for 9000. The loan consists of monthly instalments spread over 4 years, at 12% interest. To find out how much you will pay per month, type:

**=PMT**

Inside the parentheses come the following parameters:

1. interest per period -    **12%/12**
2. number of payments -   **12*4**
3. PV (loan amount) -       **9000**

The entire formula then is:

**=PMT(12%/12,12*4,9000)**

PMT returns a negative result, because it is an outgoing payment.

Two formulas related to PMT are IPMT and PPMT. IPMT finds the interest part of an annuity payment for a specific period, and PPMT finds the principal part. This can be helpful for tax purposes.

**Payment on interest**

To figure out the interest part of our car loan annuity for the first period, we type:

**=IPMT(12%/12,1,12*4,9000)**

**Payment on principal**

Note that period number is the second parameter. To find the payment on principal for the first period, the PPMT parameters are identical:

**=PPMT(12%/12,1,12*4,9000)**

In the examples below, we have used the same car loan example as above, but have set up variables at the top left of the screen. The formulas, instead of containing fixed values, refer to these variables, so that we can easily change these variables and achieve a what-if effect. The table shows a breakdown of repayments by interest and principal, using IPMT and PPMT.

**B1**     =PMT(Interest/Periods,Periods*Years,Loan)

|   | A | B | C | D | E | F |
|---|---|---|---|---|---|---|
| 1 | Annuity | -237 | Interest | Principal | Balance | Per. |
| 2 | Loan | 9000 | -90 | -147 | 8853 | 1 |
| 3 | Interest | 12% | -89 | -148 | 8705 | 2 |
| 4 | Periods | 12 | -87 | -150 | 8555 | 3 |
| 5 | Years | 4 | -86 | -151 | 8403 | 4 |
| 6 |  |  | -84 | -153 | 8250 | 5 |

**C2**     =IPMT(Interest/Periods,F2,Periods*Years,Loan)

|   | A | B | C | D | E | F |
|---|---|---|---|---|---|---|
| 1 | Annuity | -237 | Interest | Principal | Balance | Per. |
| 2 | Loan | 9000 | -90 | -147 | 8853 | 1 |
| 3 | Interest | 12% | -89 | -148 | 8705 | 2 |

**D3**     =PPMT(Interest/Periods,F3,Periods*Years,Loan)

|   | A | B | C | D | E | F |
|---|---|---|---|---|---|---|
| 1 | Annuity | -237 | Interest | Principal | Balance | Per. |
| 2 | Loan | 9000 | -90 | -147 | 8853 | 1 |
| 3 | Interest | 12% | -89 | -148 | 8705 | 2 |

**Naming several cells at once**

Note that in the previous example we have named all the cells containing variables. A quick way to name several cells at once is, instead of the Formula - Define Name command, you select all the cells you want to name AND the cells containing labels. In the example below, we chose our PMT variables in cells A2:B5.

|   | A | B | C | D |
|---|---|---|---|---|
| 1 | Annuity | -237 | Interest | Principal |
| 2 | Loan | 9000 | -90 | -147 |
| 3 | Interest | 12% | | |
| 4 | Periods | 12 | | |
| 5 | Years | 4 | | |

Then choose:     **Formula - Create names**

A dialog box appears. Choose left if the labeling cells are on the left side (as in the example above), top if they are on top, etc. Confirm with RET, and then choose:

**Formula - Apply names**

This example shows the formula before Formula - Apply Names:

B1          =PMT(B3/B4,B4*B5,B2)

|   | A | B | C | D | E | F |
|---|---|---|---|---|---|---|
| 1 | Annuity | -237 | Interest | Principal | Balance | Per. |
| 2 | Loan | 9000 | -90 | -147 | 8853 | 1 |
| 3 | Interest | 12% | -89 | -148 | 8705 | 2 |
| 4 | Periods | 12 | -87 | -150 | 8555 | 3 |
| 5 | Years | 4 | -86 | -151 | 8403 | 4 |
| 6 | | | -84 | -153 | 8250 | 5 |

... and afterwards:

B1          =PMT(Interest/Periods,Periods*Years,Loan)

|   | A | B | C | D | E | F |
|---|---|---|---|---|---|---|
| 1 | Annuity | -237 | Interest | Principal | Balance | Per. |
| 2 | Loan | 9000 | -90 | -147 | 8853 | 1 |
| 3 | Interest | 12% | -89 | -148 | 8705 | 2 |
| 4 | Periods | 12 | -87 | -150 | 8555 | 3 |
| 5 | Years | 4 | -86 | -151 | 8403 | 4 |
| 6 | | | -84 | -153 | 8250 | 5 |

**Loan amount**   Suppose that you want to buy a house, but aren't sure how big a loan you can manage. You know you can afford regular repayments of 500 a month, and you know you can get a 9% interest rate on a 25-year loan. To find out how much you could lend, type:

$$=PV$$

Inside the parentheses come the following parameters:

1. interest per period -     **9%/12**
2. number of payments -      **12*25**
3. PMT (payment amount) -    **-500**

The entire formula then is:

$$=PV(9\%/12,12*25,-500)$$

PV returns a positive value, since a loan amount is incoming.
Note that PMT must be expressed as a negative number, since it is an outgoing payment.

In the example below, we have used the same house loan case, but now with variables instead of fixed values in the formula.

| B2 | | =PV(Interest/Periods, Periods*Years, Annuity) | | | |
|---|---|---|---|---|---|
| | A | B | C | D | E | F |
| 1 | Annuity | -500 | Interest | Principal | Balance | Per. |
| 2 | Loan | 59581 | -447 | -53 | 59528 | 1 |
| 3 | Interest | 9% | -446 | -54 | 59474 | 2 |
| 4 | Periods | 12 | -446 | -54 | 59420 | 3 |
| 5 | Years | 25 | -446 | -54 | 59366 | 4 |
| 6 | | | -445 | -55 | 59311 | 5 |

**Interest rate**   Suppose that you are considering alternative investment plans. One
investment plan promises a final return of 50000 over 20 years. You
would need to pay 250 twice a year. What would be your interest?
To figure this out, type:

### =RATE

Inside the parentheses come the following parameters:

| | |
|---|---|
| 1. number of payments - | **2*20** |
| 2. PMT (payment amount) - | **-250** |
| 3. PV (present value) - | **0** |
| 4. FV (future value) - | **50000** |
| 5. type - | **1** (means interest pd. at end of |
| And for annual interest ... | **\*2**          each period) |

The entire formula then is:

### =RATE(2*20,-250,0,50000,1)*2

In the example below, we have used the same investment plan, but
now with variables instead of fixed values in the formula.

| B1 | =RATE(Periods*Years,Annuity,0,Return,1)*Periods | | |
|---|---|---|---|
| **A** | **B** | **C** | **D** |
| 1 Interest | 13,5% | | |
| 2 Periods | 2 | | |
| 3 Years | 20 | | |
| 4 Annuity | -250 | | |
| 5 Return | 50000 | | |
| 6 | | | |

**Savings return**

Suppose that you would like to save 750 each quarter for 10 years. At 11.4% annual interest, how much would you end up with? To find this out, type:

=FV

Inside the parentheses come the following parameters:

1. interest per period -      **11.4%/4**
2. number of payments -      **4*10**
3. PMT (payment amount) -      **-750**
4. PV (present value) -      **0**
5. type -      **1** (means interest pd. at end of each period)

The entire formula then is:

**=FV(11.4%/4,4*10,-750,0,1)**

FV returns a positive value, since the return is incoming.

In the example below, we have used the same savings plan, but now with variables instead of fixed values in the formula.

| B5 | | =FV(Interest/Periods,Periods*Years,Annuity,0,1) | | |
|---|---|---|---|---|
| | A | B | C | D |
| 1 | Interest | 11,4% | | |
| 2 | Periods | 4 | | |
| 3 | Years | 10 | | |
| 4 | Annuity | -750 | | |
| 5 | Return | 56224 | | |
| 6 | | | | |

**Internal interest**

Suppose you have taken out a housing loan with varying repayments twice a year over 25 years at a nominal interest rate of 9%. What would be the actual interest rate you would end up paying, including rental fees. To find out, type:

**=IRR**

Inside the parentheses, select an area which includes the loan amount followed by loan repayments. If loan amount is expressed as a negative number, then the loan repayments must be positive. If the loan repayments are expressed as negative numbers, then the loan amount must be positive.

In the example below, the loan amount is entered in D2, and the loan repayments in cells D3 to D53. Inside the parentheses of our formula would then come:

**(D2:D53)**

The entire formula would then be: **=IRR(D2:D53)**

| B5 | =IRR(D2:D53) | | |
|---|---|---|---|
| | A | B | C | D |
| 1 | Loan | 59581 | | Repayment |
| 2 | Interest | 9% | | 59581 |
| 3 | Periods | 2 | | -2252 |
| 4 | Years | 25 | | -2252 |
| 5 | Int. interest | 11% | | -3052 |
| 6 | | | | -3052 |

# 5d. Protect your spreadsheet and formulas

If people other than yourself use your spreadsheets, you may wish to take measures to secure your data and formulas.

**Protect spreadsheet**

To protect a spreadsheet, you do the following:

1. Go to the spreadsheet you wish to protect.
2. Choose:      **File - Save as**
3. Choose:      **Options**
4. Type in a password.

Password [        ]

5. Press RET.

Hereafter, Excel will ask for a password before opening the file.

**Protect window**

To protect a window so that no one can change its size, do the following:

1. Go to the window you wish to protect. If you want to hide its contents, first reduce the size of the window so that the contents are no longer visible.

2. Choose:      **Options - Protect Document**

3. Select the box by:      **Windows**

[X] Windows

4. If you wish, type in a password.

Password [        ]

5. Press RET.

Now the size of the protected window cannot be changed.

**Hide**
**Window**

To hide a window, choose:     **Window - Hide**

The window will be hidden from view and no longer listed in the menu under Window. This can be useful for hiding a macro or other supporting document which you don't want users to see.

To save the file as a hidden window, simply go out of Excel. You will be asked if you want to save the hidden file. Answer 'Yes'.

To view the hidden file, open it and choose:     **Window - Unhide**


**Protect**
**cells**

To protect individual cells, you do the following:

1. Select the entire spreadsheet (click in the upper lefthand corner)

2. Choose:     **Format - Cell Protection**

3. Remove the cross in the box by:     **Locked**
   Press RET. By default, all cells are locked when the spreadsheet is protected. This unlocks them.

   ☐ Locked

4. Now select the cells you wish to protect (press CTRL while you click).

5. Choose:     **Options - Protect Document**

6. Select the box by:     **Contents**

   ☒ Contents

7. If you wish, type in a password.

   Password ☐

8. Press RET.


Now the protected cells cannot be edited, moved or deleted.

## 5e. Outline

You can create an automatic outline on your spreadsheet. To do this, select the range you want to outline and choose:

**Formula - Outline**
and: **Create**

Some symbols appear to the left of your range. A minus-symbol indicates a row of higher priority. A line from this row goes around the rows which are subordinate.

**Reduce to an outline**

To reduce the range of cells to an outline, click at the minus-symbol.

The subordinate rows will then be hidden.

In the example below we have selected the cells we want to outline.

|    | A | B | C | D |
|----|-----------|------------|-------------|----------|
| 1  | Building started by the end of the year | | | |
| 2  | Year | Housing | Rural hous. | Total |
| 3  | 1986 | 12500 | 16000 | 19600 |
| 4  | 1987 | 13000 | 16500 | 20100 |
| 5  | 1988 | 13500 | 17000 | 20600 |
| 6  | 1989 | 17000 | 20500 | 24100 |
| 7  | 1990 | 24000 | 27500 | 31100 |
| 8  | sum | 80000 | 97500 | 115500 |
| 9  | | | | |
| 10 | Homes divided by type | | | |
| 11 | | Free-stand. | Block | Other |
| 12 | 1986 | 12050 | 4500 | 9800 |
| 13 | 1987 | 9854 | 4622 | 9765 |
| 14 | 1988 | 9900 | 4487 | 9255 |
| 15 | 1989 | 9544 | 4211 | 9912 |
| 16 | 1990 | 9233 | 4388 | 9466 |
| 17 | sum | 50581 | 22208 | 48198 |

Next we choose Formula - Outline - Create.

|   | A | B | C | D |
|---|---|---|---|---|
| 1 | **Building started by the end of the year** | | | |
| 2 | Year | Housing | Rural hous. | Total |
| 3 | 1986 | 12500 | 16000 | 19600 |
| 4 | 1987 | 13000 | 16500 | 20100 |
| 5 | 1988 | 13500 | 17000 | 20600 |
| 6 | 1989 | 17000 | 20500 | 24100 |
| 7 | 1990 | 24000 | 27500 | 31100 |
| 8 | **sum** | 80000 | 97500 | 115500 |
| 9 | | | | |
| 10 | **Homes divided by type** | | | |
| 11 | | Free-stand. | Block | Other |
| 12 | 1986 | 12050 | 4500 | 9800 |
| 13 | 1987 | 9854 | 4622 | 9765 |
| 14 | 1988 | 9900 | 4487 | 9255 |
| 15 | 1989 | 9544 | 4211 | 9912 |
| 16 | 1990 | 9233 | 4388 | 9466 |
| 17 | **sum** | 50581 | 22208 | 48198 |

Finally we click at the minus-symbol to create an outline.

|   | A | B | C | D |
|---|---|---|---|---|
| 1 | **Building started by the end of the year** | | | |
| 2 | Year | Housing | Rural hous. | Total |
| 8 | **sum** | 80000 | 97500 | 115500 |
| 9 | | | | |
| 10 | **Homes divided by type** | | | |
| 11 | | Free-stand. | Block | Other |
| 17 | **sum** | 50581 | 22208 | 48198 |

**Select visible rows only**

The subordinate rows are now hidden, but they have not gone. If you select all the rows for copying or creating a chart, all the hidden rows will also be selected.

To select only the visible rows in the outline, select the rows and click at:

When a subordinate row is hidden, the minus-symbol by the main row changes to plus.

**Expand the spreadsheet**

To expand the spreadsheet, click at the plus-symbol. The hidden rows then appear once again.

In the example below we clicked at the plus-symbols so that the hidden rows would reappear.

|    | A | B | C | D |
|----|---|---|---|---|
| 1  | Building started by the end of the year | | | |
| 2  | Year | Housing | Rural hous. | Total |
| 3  | 1986 | 12500 | 16000 | 19600 |
| 4  | 1987 | 13000 | 16500 | 20100 |
| 5  | 1988 | 13500 | 17000 | 20600 |
| 6  | 1989 | 17000 | 20500 | 24100 |
| 7  | 1990 | 24000 | 27500 | 31100 |
| 8  | sum | 80000 | 97500 | 115500 |
| 9  | | | | |
| 10 | Homes divided by type | | | |
| 11 | | Free-stand. | Block | Other |
| 12 | 1986 | 12050 | 4500 | 9800 |
| 13 | 1987 | 9854 | 4622 | 9765 |
| 14 | 1988 | 9900 | 4487 | 9255 |
| 15 | 1989 | 9544 | 4211 | 9912 |
| 16 | 1990 | 9233 | 4388 | 9466 |
| 17 | sum | 50581 | 22208 | 48198 |

**Excel 3.0**

**Remove outline symbols**

To remove the plus and minus outline symbols, click at:

Note that the outline is still functioning, even though the symbols have disappeared.

**Excel 3.0**

**Remove outline**

To remove the outline itself from the spreadsheet, select the cells you have outlined and click at the left-arrow icon up in the icon-bar.

# 5f. Optimising results

**Adjust variable to achieve desired result**

If a result is based on certain variables, you can have the variables adjusted so that you achieve a specified result. To do this, select the cell where you want a specified result and choose:

**Formula - Goal Seek**

A dialogue box appears.
For 'To value', type in your desired result.
For 'By changing cell', click at the variable you want adjusted.

In the example below, number of periods is to be adjusted so that our annuity is 3500.

Set cell: $B$1

To value: -3500

By changing cell: $B$4

B1   =PMT(B3/B4;B4*B5;B2)

|   | A | B | C |
|---|---|---|---|
| 1 | pmt | -3500 | |
| 2 | loan | 40000 | |
| 3 | interest | 17,5% | |
| 4 | periods | 4 | |
| 5 | years | 4 | |

**Excel 3.0**

**Adjust
more than
one variable**

You can have several variables adjusted automatically for an optimum result. To do this, select the cell where you want your optimum result and choose:

**Formula - Solver**

A dialogue box appears.

For 'Equal to', click at 'Max' or 'Min' depending on whether you want a maximum or minimum result. Alternatively, you can specify a result in 'Value'.

For 'By changing cells', select the cells you want adjusted to achieve your optimum result.

**Excel 3.0**

**Add
constraints**

To limit how much your variable can be adjusted, click at:

**Add**

Select the variable in the sheet, choose '>=','>=' or '=' and type a value. In the example below, we have set the limitation that cell A6 not be greater that 500.

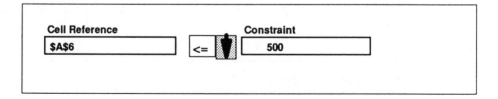

You can continue setting limitations on other variables in the same way. When you have finished, click at OK, and then:

**Solve**

**Excel 3.0**

**Keep
solution**

When the problem is solved, a dialogue box appears.
Choose whether to keep the solution or restore original values. Click at OK.

In the example below we are adjusting marketing outlays so that we may achieve maximum profit.

| | A | B | C | D | E | F |
|---|---|---|---|---|---|---|
| 1 | Quarter | Q1 | Q2 | Q3 | Q4 | Total |
| 2 | Season var. | 0,5 | 1,1 | 0,7 | 1,7 | |
| 3 | | | | | | |
| 4 | No. sold | 1.992 | 4.383 | 2.789 | 6.774 | 15.939 |
| 5 | Sales | 19.014.729 | 41.832.404 | 26.620.621 | 64.650.079 | 152.117.833 |
| 6 | Var. exp. | 18.395.117 | 40.469.257 | 25.753.163 | 62.543.397 | 147.160.934 |
| 7 | Gross profit | 619.612 | 1.363.147 | 867.457 | 2.106.682 | 4.956.899 |
| 8 | | | | | | |
| 9 | Commissions | 96.000 | 96.000 | 108.000 | 108.000 | 408.000 |
| 10 | Marketing | 120.000 | 120.000 | 120.000 | 120.000 | 480.000 |
| 11 | Fixed exp. | 2.852.209 | 6.274.861 | 3.993.093 | 9.697.512 | 22.817.675 |
| 12 | Total exp. | 3.068.209 | 6.490.861 | 4.221.093 | 9.925.512 | 23.705.675 |
| 13 | | | | | | |
| 14 | Net profit | -2.448.597 | -5.127.713 | -3.353.636 | -7.818.830 | -18.748.776 |
| 15 | Profit margin | -12,9% | -12,3% | -12,6% | -12,1% | -12,3% |
| 16 | | | | | | |
| 17 | Price | 480,00 | | | | |
| 18 | Cost | 300,00 | | | | |

We choose Formula - Solver from the menu and fill out the dialogue box as follows:

Set Cell: $F$14

Equal to: ●Max ○ Min ○ Value of:

By Changing Cells: $B$10:E$10

Subject to the Constraints:

Add

We click at 'Add' to add a limitation.
Our limitation is that total marketing costs not exceed 600.000.

| Cell Reference | | Constraint |
|---|---|---|
| $F$10 | <= | 600000 |

We click at OK, then at 'Solve'. The result is shown in the example below.

| | A | B | C | D | E | F |
|---|---|---|---|---|---|---|
| 1 | Quarter | Q1 | Q2 | Q3 | Q4 | Total |
| 2 | Season var. | 0,5 | 1,1 | 0,7 | 1,7 | |
| 3 | | | | | | |
| 4 | No. sold | 1.302 | 5.103 | 2.240 | 9.947 | 18.593 |
| 5 | Sales | 12.429.435 | 48.701.088 | 21.378.762 | 94.937.589 | 177.446.874 |
| 6 | Var. exp. | 12.024.410 | 47.114.119 | 20.682.116 | 91.843.960 | 171.664.605 |
| 7 | Gross profit | 405.025 | 1.586.970 | 696.647 | 3.093.628 | 5.782.269 |
| 8 | | | | | | |
| 9 | Commissions | 96.000 | 96.000 | 108.000 | 108.000 | 408.000 |
| 10 | Marketing | 39.942 | 176.199 | 68.478 | 315.381 | 600.000 |
| 11 | Fixed exp. | 1.864.415 | 7.305.163 | 3.206.814 | 14.240.638 | 26.617.031 |
| 12 | Total exp. | 2.000.357 | 7.577.362 | 3.383.293 | 14.664.020 | 27.625.031 |
| 13 | | | | | | |
| 14 | Net profit | -1.595.332 | -5.990.393 | -2.686.646 | -11.570.391 | 21.842.762 |
| 15 | Profit margin | -12,8% | -12,3% | -12,6% | -12,2% | -12,3% |

**Change constraint**

If you want to alter your constraints, choose Formula - Solver again and at the bottom of the dialogue box, click at:

**Change**

**Add constraints**

You can now edit. To add more constraints, click at:     **Add**

# 5g. Consolidating

**Consolidate information**

You can consolidate information from several spreadsheets. For example, to create a sales report you could consolidate sales figures from several districts.

In the example below we have sales data from three sheets, which we want to consolidate onto a fourth sheet.

NORDLAND.XLS

|   | A | B | C | D | E |
|---|---|---|---|---|---|
| 1 | Nordland (in mill.) | | | | |
| 2 | | sales | profit | | |
| 3 | q1 | 3654 | 256 | | |
| 4 | q2 | 7842 | 486 | | |
| 5 | q3 | 4821 | -45 | | |
| 6 | q4 | 4652 | 781 | | |

FINNMARK.XLS

|   | A | B | C | D | E |
|---|---|---|---|---|---|
| 1 | Finnmark (in mill.) | | | | |
| 2 | | sales | profit | | |
| 3 | q1 | 4216 | 54 | | |
| 4 | q2 | 3527 | -21 | | |
| 5 | q3 | 8945 | 684 | | |
| 6 | q4 | 6452 | 74 | | |

TROMS.XLS

|   | A | B | C | D | E |
|---|---|---|---|---|---|
| 1 | Troms (in mill.) | | | | |
| 2 | | sales | profit | | |
| 3 | q1 | 4654 | 111 | | |
| 4 | q2 | 2654 | 451 | | |
| 5 | q3 | 2845 | 354 | | |
| 6 | q4 | 6254 | 542 | | |

**Create area
for
consolidating**

On the sheet you want to consolidate the data, type your headings.
Select the area and choose:

**Data - Consolidate**

Then select the first source area and click at:     **Add**

Continue selecting source areas and clicking at 'Add' until you have
selected all the data you want to consolidate.

**Basis for
consolidating**

Either cell addresses or headings can be used as a basis for
consolidating. Click at the check box to consolidate by headings. If
the check box is blank, consolidation will be done by cell address.

You can consolidate by adding (default), averaging, counting etc.
Choose this in the list box.

In the example below we are consolidating the three sheets with sales
data from Northern Norway. First we select the area where we want the
consolidated data to be placed.

|   | A | B | C | D |
|---|---|---|---|---|
| | NTNORWAY.XLS | | | |
| 1 | Northern Norway (sum in mill.) | | | |
| 2 | | sales | profit | |
| 3 | q1 | | | |
| 4 | q2 | | | |
| 5 | q3 | | | |
| 6 | q4 | | | |

We select the source areas and click at 'Top row' and 'Left column' so that the information is consolidated according to headings.

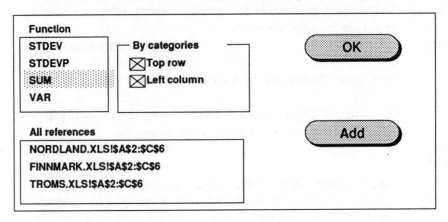

Below is the result.

| | A | B | C | D |
|---|---|---|---|---|
| | | NORDNRGE.XLS | | |
| 1 | Northern Norway (sum in mill.) | | | |
| 2 | | sales | profit | |
| 3 | q1 | 12524 | 421 | |
| 4 | q2 | 14023 | 916 | |
| 5 | q3 | 16611 | 993 | |
| 6 | q4 | 17358 | 1397 | |

# 6. Charts

Often tables of figures can be presented in a more clear and
effective way when presented graphically. You can do this easily
in Excel, choosing among 48 different styles of chart. Within the
chart you can add text and change fonts and colours. In addition
you can use shadows and boxes.

## 6a. Create a chart

To create a chart, mark your table, including headers, and press:

| ALT | | F1 |
|-----|-----|-----|

In the example below, we are marking a sales table.

|   | A | B | C | D | E | F |
|---|-----|------|------|-------|--------|---|
| 1 |          |      |      |       |        |   |
| 2 |          | Jan  | Feb  | March | 91 avg |   |
| 3 | Region 1 | 5685 | 7824 | 4562  | 5002   |   |
| 4 | Region 2 | 343  | 7982 | 7895  | 3022   |   |
| 5 | Region 3 | 482  | 1540 | 2437  | 654    |   |
| 6 | Region 4 | 8720 | 530  | 8792  | 7673   |   |

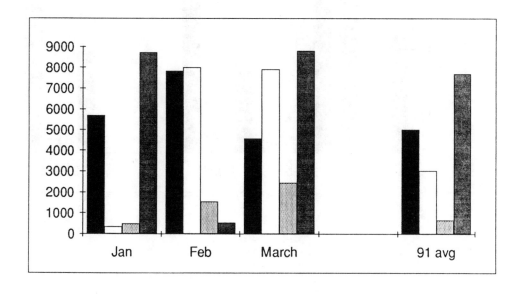

**Create chart from several ranges**  You can also create a chart from parts of several tables by marking the different areas simultaneously (press CTRL as you mark). In the example below, we have taken sales figures from two different tables. The resulting chart is the same as in the previous example.

|    | A        | B      | C      | D       | E |
|----|----------|--------|--------|---------|---|
| 1  |          |        |        |         |   |
| 2  |          | Jan    | Feb    | March   |   |
| 3  | Region 1 | 5685   | 7824   | 4562    |   |
| 4  | Region 2 | 343    | 7982   | 7895    |   |
| 5  | Region 3 | 482    | 1540   | 2437    |   |
| 6  | Region 4 | 8720   | 530    | 8792    |   |
| 7  |          |        |        |         |   |
| 8  |          | 89 avg | 90 avg | 91 avg  |   |
| 9  | Region 1 | 3201   | 4002   | 5002    |   |
| 10 | Region 2 | 4250   | 2418   | 3022    |   |
| 11 | Region 3 | 596    | 745    | 654     |   |
| 12 | Region 4 | 4152   | 3256   | 7673    |   |

A column chart is then created, as in the example below.

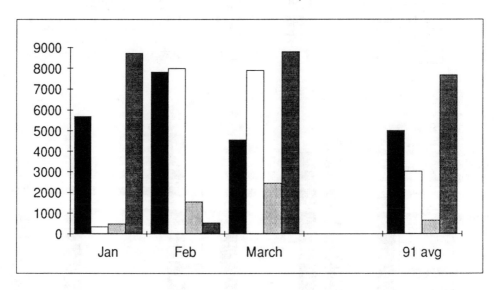

**Create a**
**chart on the**
**spreadsheet**

By using the icon bar, you can create a chart right on your spreadsheet. Select the table you are basing your chart on and click at:

The cursor will resemble a cross.      +

Click and drag to draw a box to show where you want the chart placed. Afterwards you can move, size and shape this box in the same way as with other graphic objects.

In the example below we have selected the table we will create a chart from, clicked at the chart-symbol and drawn a frame within which the chart is to be placed.

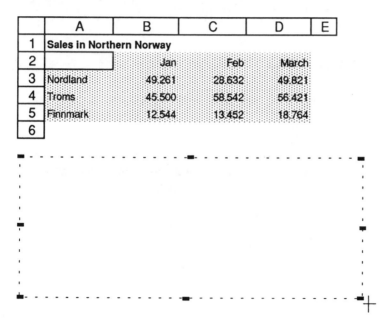

When we have finished, the chart is inserted automatically into our frame.

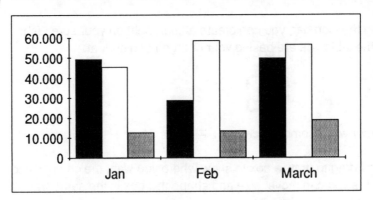

**Excel 3.0**

**Edit chart**    To edit the chart, click at the chart frame to select it, and then click at the chart-symbol. A new window is created, where you can edit the chart in the same way as in earlier versions of Excel.

## 6b. Format the chart

**Style of chart**    You can choose which style chart you want by choosing in the menu:

**Gallery**

The main chart styles are: area, bar, column, line, pie, scatter and combination. The chart comes up first as a column chart.

**3D chart**   You can also choose a 3D style when you choose Gallery.
In the example below we have chosen 3D columns.

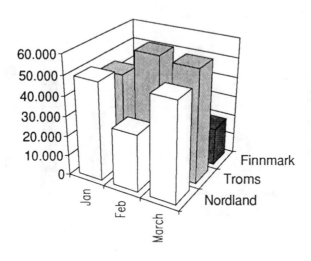

**Rotate
chart**   You can rotate a 3D chart to get the view you want. To do this, select the
chart, click at the chart icon to get the chart window up, and then choose:

**Format - 3D-View**

Click at the rotating buttons until you get the view you want.

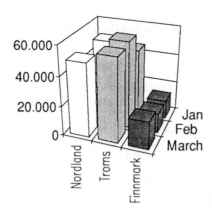

**Legend**     To create a legend for your chart, choose:

**Chart - Add legend**

We have added a legend in the example below.

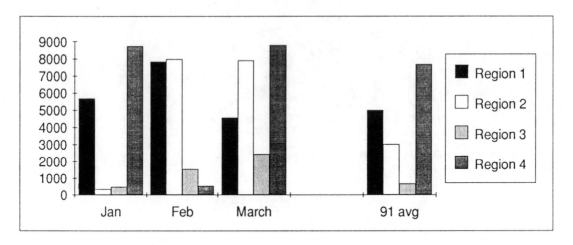

**Move**      You can move the legend to the top, bottom or corner of your
**legend**    chart. To do this, choose:

**Format - Legend**

**Add text**  You can add text to the chart. To do this:

1. click with the mouse at an empty part of the chart
2. write your text
3. press RET

The text will then appear in the chart, surrounded by little boxes.

You can now place the text where you want it on the chart. Do this
by clicking inside the little boxes with the mouse and dragging to
where you want the text on the chart.

In the example below, we have added a title.

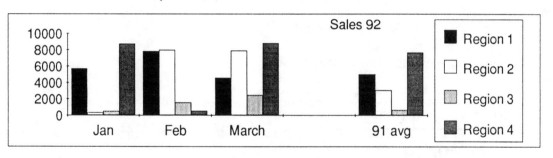

**Format text**   You can change size, font and colour of text. To do this, choose:

**Format - Font**

A dialogue box appears, where you can choose your options.

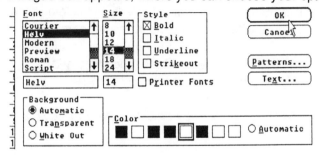

In our example below, we have chosen size 18 bold with a purple colour for our title.

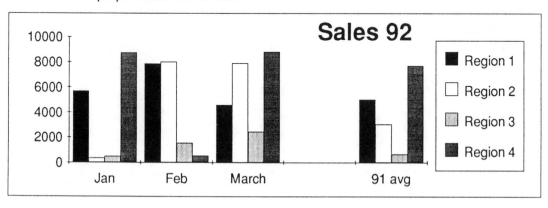

**Format graphics**

To add boxes and change colours and patterns of graphics, choose:

### Format - Patterns

A dialogue box appears as shown below.

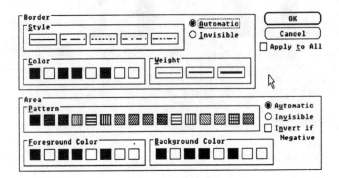

| | |
|---|---|
| **Colour** | The colour of the frame. Originally the colour of the frame is white, meaning no frame appears. |
| **Pattern** | The pattern inside the frame (such as a grid). Originally the pattern is blank. |
| **Foreground colour** | The colour inside the frame. Originally this colour is white. |
| **Background colour** | The colour of the pattern (for example of the grid). Originally this colour is black. |
| **Shadow** | Click here to give your frame a shadow. |

In the example below, the title has a shadow and blue frame.
We have given the columns different patterns so as to differentiate them
on a black and white printout.

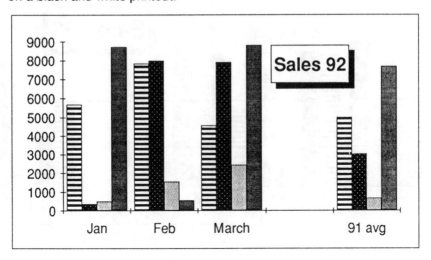

## 6c. Linking charts

**Dynamic link**

This chart is dynamically linked with the sales tables on the spreadsheet. If any figures in the sales table are adjusted, the chart will reflect these changes immediately.

In the example below, we have dramatically increased the sales figure for March in Region 3.

| | A | B | C | D | E | F |
|---|---|---|---|---|---|---|
| 1 | | | | | | |
| 2 | | Jan | Feb | March | 91 avg | |
| 3 | Region 1 | 5685 | 7824 | 4562 | 5002 | |
| 4 | Region 2 | 343 | 7982 | 7895 | 3022 | |
| 5 | Region 3 | 482 | 1540 | 9865 | 654 | |
| 6 | Region 4 | 8720 | 530 | 8792 | 7673 | |

The chart adjusts automatically.

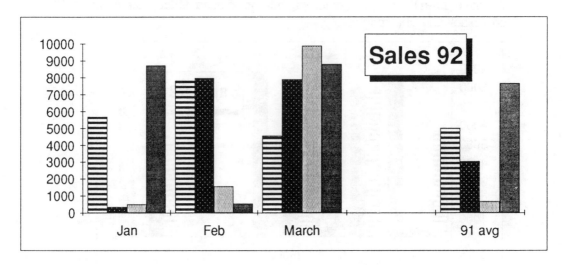

Sales 92

( Excel 3.0 )

**Change
values
graphically**

When the table the chart is based on changes, the chart also adjusts automatically. This can also go the other way. You can drag a column or line in the chart, and the numbers in the spreadsheet table will be adjusted automatically (dragging data points).

To do this, the chart must be either a 2D line, bar or column.

Click at the element you want to change, press: Ctrl and drag.

Your spreadsheet figures will be adjusted automatically.

In the example below we have increased January sales in Troms by dragging the column upwards.

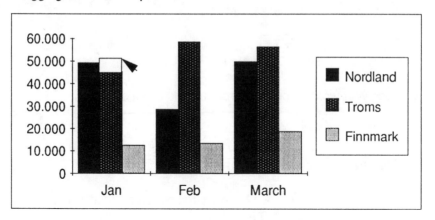

The spreadsheet table is adusted accordingly.

|   | A | B | C | D | E |
|---|---|---|---|---|---|
| 1 | **Sales in Northern Norway** | | | | |
| 2 | | January | February | March | |
| 3 | Nordland | 49.261 | 28.632 | 49.821 | |
| 4 | Troms | 54.475 | 58.542 | 56.421 | |
| 5 | Finnmark | 12.544 | 13.452 | 18.764 | |
| 6 | | | | | |

**Copy chart
to another
program**

You can copy your chart to a word processing program to include it as part of a written presentation. As long as the program runs under WINDOWS, this is what you do:

1. Press     | SHIFT |
   and choose: **Edit - Copy picture**

2. Open your word processing program and choose:

   **Edit - Paste**

   The chart will be pasted into the work area.

   In the example below, we have pasted our sales chart onto a sales report in MS-WRITE.

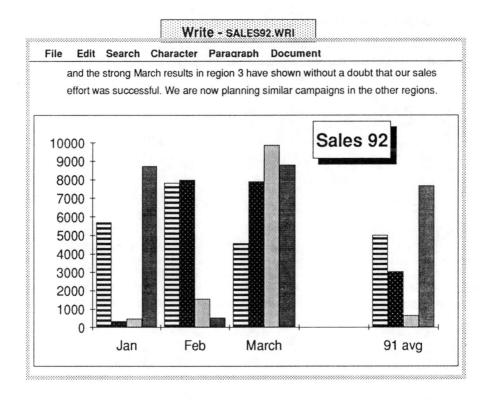

# 7. Information tables

You can use EXCEL to store tables of information, such as lists of accounts, customer addresses, employee information and an inventory.

There are a number of lookup and database query functions which make it possible to extract information quickly and generate reports or graphs.

## 7a. Lookup tables

**Lookup**

Suppose you have a customer information table, and would like to extract information quickly on a specific customer. With a LOOKUP formula, you can key in a customer number in one cell, and then write a LOOKUP formula in another cell which finds the desired information corresponding to that customer. The customer number you keyed in identifies which line in the table Excel will look for, so we call this identifying customer number the 'index key'.

**Information table**

The customer table in our example would have a row for each customer. Customer number would be in the first column. In the next column might be name, in the next address, and so on. To properly function as an information table, two conditions must be met:

1. Information in each row must be in the same order, for example customer number, then name, then address.
2. The column which is used as index key (customer number in our example) must be the first column in the table, and must be sorted in ascending order.

Below is an example of an information table.

|    | A | B | C | D |
|----|---|---|---|---|
| 6  | Cust. no. | Name | Address | City |
| 7  | 45231 | Norsk | Kongsg. 1 | Oslo |
| 8  | 45232 | Exxon | 6 Cal. St. | Dallas |
| 9  | 45233 | Dupont | G.Alle 45 | Paris |
| 10 | 45234 | Noroil | Storgt. 3 | Oslo |

**Extract information**

Suppose there are thousands of customers listed in your table. You would like to get information on one customer simply by keying in customer number. A LOOKUP function can do this for you. Every time you key in a new customer number, new information will appear immediately, replacing the previous information.

|   | A | B | C | D |
|---|---|---|---|---|
| 1 | Cust. no. | Name | Address | City |
| 2 | 45234 | Noroil | Storgt. 3 | Oslo |

|   | A | B | C | D |   |
|---|---|---|---|---|---|
| 1 | Cust. no. | Name | Address | City | (customer no. |
| 2 | 45233 | Dupont | G.Alle 45 | Paris | changed) |

**Lookup formulas**

There are two LOOKUP formulas in EXCEL, one for lookup in a horizontal table, and one for lookup in a vertical table. In a horizontal table, your information records are stored in columns, and you find your information by looking across the table. In a vertical table, your information records are stored in rows, and you find your information by looking down the table. The table in the above example is a vertical table.

## 7b. Vertical lookup

**VLOOKUP**

To extract information from a vertical table, we use a formula called VLOOKUP.

We first type in the index key, in this case customer number. In the other cells we write VLOOKUP formulas for each type of data we want, for example a VLOOKUP formula for customer name, another VLOOKUP formula for address, and so on.

|   | A | B | C | D | E |
|---|---|---|---|---|---|
| 1 | Cust. no. | Name | Address | City | Discount |
| 2 |   | (vlookup) | (vlookup) | (vlookup) | (vlookup) |
| 3 |   |   |   |   |   |
| 4 | Cust. no. | Name | Address | City | Discount |
| 5 | 45231 | Norsk | Kongsg. 1 | Oslo | 10 % |
| 6 | 45232 | Exxon | 6 Cal. St. | Dallas | 0 % |
| 7 | 45233 | Dupont | G.Alle 45 | Paris | 15 % |
| 8 | 45234 | Noroil | Storgt. 3 | Oslo | 5 % |

To write a formula in cell B2 to get customer name, we would type:

**=VLOOKUP(**

Inside the parentheses come the following parameters:

| | |
|---|---|
| 1. lookup key - | **A2** |
| 2. lookup table - | **A5:E450** |
| 3. column no. in table - | **2** |

Note that the lookup table starts with the first row of data, and does NOT include the headers. You can use the mouse to mark the table area. The table area must not include extra columns, but can and should include extra rows, in case new rows of information are later added to the table. In this case we have allowed space for 445 rows.

Note also that the column number is 2, because customer name is the type of information you want, and the names are in the 2nd column in the lookup table. Even if the lookup table began in column C instead of column A, the column number would still be 2, since that is the column number within the table.

The entire formula then is:

**=VLOOKUP(A2,A5:E450,2)**

If you then typed in a customer number in cell A2, the VLOOKUP formula we wrote in cell B2 would return the correct customer name:

B2   =VLOOKUP(A2,A5:D450,2)

| | A | B | C | D | E |
|---|---|---|---|---|---|
| 1 | Cust. no. | Name | Address | City | Discount |
| 2 | 45234 | Noroil | | | |

We can then write similar formulas in C2, D2 and E2 to get address, city and discount. The only difference is in the last parameter of the formula. Customer name is the 2nd column in the lookup table, but address is the 3rd, city the 4th and discount the 5th. Thus we type:

In cell C2: =VLOOKUP(A2,A5:E450,3)
In cell D2: =VLOOKUP(A2,A5:E450,4)
In cell E2: =VLOOKUP(A2,A5:E450,5)

The results then appear on the screen:

E2   =VLOOKUP(A2,A5:E450,5)

|   | A | B | C | D | E |
|---|---|---|---|---|---|
| 1 | Cust. no. | Name | Address | City | Discount |
| 2 | 45234 | Noroil | Storgt. 3 | Oslo | 5 % |

**Give name to table**

You can give a name to a range of cells in the same way you do to a single cell. To give a name to our lookup table, we choose:

**Formula Define Name**

In the example below, we have called our lookup table "TAB". We then moved the cursor to the box under "Refers to", cleared what was already there, and then marked the lookup table with the mouse.

In this case it is actually easiest to just mark the first few rows of the table with the mouse, so that something like "$A$5:$E$9" appears in the box. Then you can merely use the keyboard to change "$E$9" to "$E$450".

| | |
|---|---|
| | OK |
| Name: | tab |
| Refers to: | $A$5:$E$450 |

100

When giving a name to a range of cells, you don't use Formula Apply Names. Rather, you simply type the name into the formula instead of the range itself. For example, after defining our lookup table, we can write our lookup formula in cell C2 like this:

**=VLOOKUP(A2,tab,3)**

**Lookup in table on another sheet**

You can write a LOOKUP formula which uses a lookup table from another file. To do this, you give your lookup table a name with the Formula Define Name command. You do this on the same file where you are writing your LOOKUP formula.

When the dialogue box comes up, you give the lookup table a name, move to the 'Refers to' box and mark the table just as you do when the table is on the same sheet. Only this time, when marking the table, you choose Window, activate the file with the lookup table on it, and then mark it with the mouse. The table range will then be filled in automatically. Press RET, and you will be returned to the sheet you started from.

In the example below, our lookup table is located on the sheet called CUST.XLS.

| Window |
| --- |

| SHEET1 |
| --- |
| x CUST.XLS |

**Name:** tab

**Refers to:** =CUST.XLS!$A$7:$E$450

|  | A | B | C | D | E |
| --- | --- | --- | --- | --- | --- |
| | | | CUST.XLS | | |
| 6 | Cust. no. | Name | Address | City | Discount |
| 7 | 45231 | Norsk | Kongsg. 1 | Oslo | 10 % |
| 8 | 45232 | Exxon | 6 Cal. St. | Dallas | 0 % |
| 9 | 45233 | Dupont | G.Alle 45 | Paris | 15 % |
| 10 | 45234 | Noroil | Storgt. 3 | Oslo | 5 % |

Once you have named your lookup table, you can write the lookup formulas as before, using your name for the second parameter.
In the example below, the formulas refer to our defined name, "tab", as the lookup table.

**SHEET1**

D2    =VLOOKUP(A2,tab,5)

|   | A | B | C | D | E |
|---|---|---|---|---|---|
| 1 | Cust. no. | Name | Address | City | Discount |
| 2 | 45234 | Noroil | Storgt. 3 | Oslo | 5 % |

**CUST.XLS**

|    | A | B | C | D | E |
|----|---|---|---|---|---|
| 9  | 45233 | Dupont | G.Alle 45 | Paris | 15 % |
| 10 | 45234 | Noroil | Storgt. 3 | Oslo | 5 % |
| 11 | 45235 | Quantas | 4 Burke St. | Melbourne | 10 % |

**Error in VLOOKUP**

If you get an error in the formula, check that the table name is correctly defined. Do this by choosing Formula - Define Name from the menu and choosing the table name in the list box. Check that the area defined in the 'Refers to' box is correct :

1. All columns in the table (but no extra) are included.
2. Enough rows are included.
3. The row with headers is NOT included.

# 7c. Lookup in a horizontal table

**Horizontal table**

In a horizontal table, lookup occurs from left to right. In the horizontal table below, you find sales amount for the third month by search from left to right in the top row (1, 2, 3 ...)

|   | A | B | C | D |
|---|---|---|---|---|
| 4 |   | 1 | 2 | 3 |
| 5 | . | January | February | March |
| 6 | Bergen | 438144 | 255472 | 441168 |
| 7 | Oslo | 446998 | 442120 | 230832 |
| 8 | Stavanger | 86240 | 136472 | 323904 |
| 9 | Trondheim | 29680 | 492352 | 585984 |

**HLOOKUP**

To look up information in a horizontal table, use the HLOOKUP formula. In the example below, we are looking up sales in Bergen in the first month. We begin with:

**=HLOOKUP(**

Inside the parentheses come the following parameters:

1. lookup key - **C1**
2. lookup table - **B4:N15**
3. row no. in table - **3**

Now column A contains the headers, so it is not included in the table. With HLOOKUP we can include extra columns, but not extra rows.

D1  =HLOOKUP(C1,B4:N15,3)

|   | A | B | C | D |
|---|---|---|---|---|
| 1 |   | Month | 1 |   |
| 2 |   | Bergen's sales | 438144 |   |
| 3 |   |   |   |   |
| 4 |   | 1 | 2 | 3 |
| 5 |   | January | February | March |
| 6 | Bergen | 438144 | 255472 | 441168 |
| 7 | Oslo | 446998 | 442120 | 230832 |

103

## 7d. Advanced lookup

**Double lookup**

We can also use a LOOKUP formula to find data both horizontally and vertically at the same time. In the example below, we have used our formula to find sales for any given city in any given month. We then use city to find the row (first parameter) and month to find the column. Because the columns in the table begin one column before the month numbers begin, the column number is = month + 1.

C3 `=VLOOKUP(C2,B7:N25,C1+1)`

|    | B | C | D | E |
|----|-----------|--------|----------|--------|
| 1  | Month : | 3 | | |
| 2  | City : | Stavanger | | |
| 3  | Sales : | 86240 | | |
| 4  | | | | |
| 5  | | 1 | 2 | 3 |
| 6  | | January | February | March |
| 7  | Bergen | 438144 | 255472 | 441168 |
| 8  | Oslo | 446998 | 442120 | 230832 |
| 9  | Stavanger | 86240 | 136472 | 323904 |
| 10 | Trondheim | 29680 | 492352 | 585984 |

**#N/A**

If nothing is entered in the cell containing the index key, or the index key doesn't exist in the lookup table, "#N/A" (not available) will be returned in the cell. In the example below, no city is entered in C2.

C3 `=VLOOKUP(C2,tab,C1+1)`

|    | B | C | D | E |
|----|---------|------|---|---|
| 1  | Month : | | | |
| 2  | City : | | | |
| 3  | Sales : | #N/A | | |

104

**Formulas within formulas**

You can write formulas inside formulas in Excel. In the example below, we write a VLOOKUP formula inside an IF formula. The IF formula tests if C1 contains data. If yes, the VLOOKUP formula finds sales in the given month and city. If C1 contains no data, C3 remains blank ("").

| C3 | =IF(C1>0,VLOOKUP(C2,tab,C1+1),"") | | |
|---|---|---|---|
| | B | C | D | E |
| 1 | Month : | | | |
| 2 | City : | | | |
| 3 | Sales : | | | |

# 7e. Databases

**Databases**

LOOKUP functions work well if you want to extract data based on a single index key, and the table is sorted according to that index key. However, what if that is not the case? What if you want to look up data based on other index keys?

For example, with the LOOKUP function you can look up customer information based on customer number. But what if you also want to be able to:

1. Look up customer information based on the customer's name?
2. List all customers located in Oslo?
3. List all customers with a balance over 100 and overdue over 30 days?

You can do this using database commands. In order to use Excel's database commands, you need to:

1. Set aside an area for your index keys.
2. Define this area by giving it the name "criteria".
3. Define the information table as a database. You do this by giving the table the name "database".

**Define
criteria
area**

A criteria area consists of one line with headings and one line for your index keys, or criteria. The headings must be identical to the headings used in the information table.

To define the criteria area, mark the criteria headings and one cell underneath each heading, and choose:

### Data Set Criteria

This command gives the name "criteria" to the range you marked.

In the example below, we have marked a criteria area which is based on a customer information table. Note that not all headings in the information table need be used in the criteria area. However, the headings which ARE used must be identical to those in the information table.

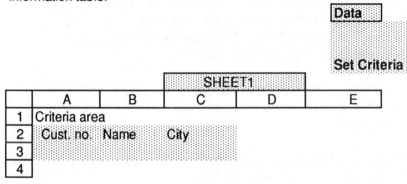

**Define
database**

You define the information table as a database in much the same way as you defined it as a lookup table. On the sheet where your criteria area is located, choose the command:

### Formula Define Name

When defining the table as a database, you type "database" in the 'Name' box. Then select the 'Refers to' box and select the database table, even if the table is located on another spreadsheet.

In the example below, we have defined the customer information table as a database.

| | | | Window |
|---|---|---|---|
| **Name:** | database | | |
| **Refers to:** | =CUST.XLS!$A$6:$E$450 | | SHEET1 |
| | | | x CUST.XLS |

CUST.XLS

| | A | B | C | D | E |
|---|---|---|---|---|---|
| 6 | Cust. no. | Name | Address | City | Discount |
| 7 | 45231 | Norsk | Kongsg. 1 | Oslo | 10 % |
| 8 | 45232 | Exxon | 6 Cal. St. | Dallas | 0 % |
| 9 | 45233 | Dupont | G.Alle 45 | Paris | 15 % |
| 10 | 45234 | Noroil | Storgt. 3 | Oslo | 5 % |

**Database on same sheet**

If your information table is on the same sheet as your criteria area, you can define it in the same way as you did the criteria area, namely:

1. Mark the information table, including headers.
2. Choose:     **Data - Set Database**

**Extract data from database**

To extract data from the database (information table) according to your criteria, you need to:

1. Fill in criteria (index keys) under the criteria headers.
2. Set aside an area for your results. This area must have the same headers as your database has.
3. Mark the result area, including headers and enough lines underneath for the results to fit.
4. Choose:     **Data Extract**
5. A dialogue box appears. Press RET.
   Your results will then appear in your result area.

In the example below, we are extracting rows from the customer information table. The criteria is that the customer name begins with 'N', and the discount is more than 5%.

Data

Extract

|   | A | B | C | D | E |
|---|---|---|---|---|---|
| 1 | Criteria area | | | | |
| 2 | Cust. no. | Name | Discount | | |
| 3 | | n | >5% | | |
| 4 | | | | | |
| 5 | Result area | | | | |
| 6 | Cust. no. | Name | Address | City | Discount |
| 7 | | | | | |
| 8 | | | | | |

Note that in the criteria:

1.  Excel doesn't distinguish between upper and lower case.
2.  Abbreviations are allowed.
3.  < and > can be used with arithmetic criteria.

## Excel 3.0

**Define extract range**

You can define your extract range in the same way as your criteria range. In this way you avoid having to select the extract range each time you use the Data - Extract command. Define the extract range by selecting the area and choosing:

**Data - Set Extract**

The extract range is given the name 'Extract'. Now you can use the Data - Extract command without having to select any area beforehand.

Alternatively, if you haven't defined any extract range, it is enough now to simply select the headers for the extract range and then choose Data - Extract.

Below is the result of the Data Extract command.

| | A | B | C | D | E |
|---|---|---|---|---|---|
| | | | SHEET1 | | |
| 1 | Criteria area | | | | |
| 2 | Cust. no. | Name | Discount | | |
| 3 | | N | >5% | | |
| 4 | | | | | |
| 5 | Result area | | | | |
| 6 | Cust. no. | Name | Address | City | Discount |
| 7 | 45231 | Norsk | Kongsg. 1 | Oslo | 10 % |
| 8 | 45235 | Northrop | 5 Stuart St. | Harwich | 15 % |

| | A | B | C | D | E |
|---|---|---|---|---|---|
| | | | CUST.XLS | | |
| 5 | Database area | | | | |
| 6 | Cust. no. | Name | Address | City | Discount |
| 7 | 45231 | Norsk | Kongsg. 1 | Bergen | 10 % |
| 8 | 45232 | Exxon | 6 Cal. St. | Dallas | 0 % |
| 9 | 45233 | Dupont | G.Alle 45 | Lyons | 15 % |
| 10 | 45234 | Noroil | Storgt. 3 | Oslo | 5 % |
| 11 | 45235 | Northrop | 5 Stuart St. | Harwich | 15 % |

**Error with Data Extract**

If you get an error message:

1. Check that your database and criteria area are correctly defined. Do this by choosing Formula Define Name and choosing "Database" and "Criteria" in the name box. Then look at the box under "Refers to" to see if the range is correct. Perhaps there is one too many columns, or the headers aren't included, or there is one too many rows in the criteria area.

2. Check that the headers in your criteria and result areas are identical with those in the database.

**New queries**     You can now continue performing queries on the database by filling in new data in the criteria area, marking the result table and choosing Data Extract. Since the criteria and database areas are already defined, you don't need to redefine them.

**Adding data to the database**

You can add data to the database without having to redefine the database, as long as there is enough space in the database.

For example, if you defined the database as A6:E450, then as long as your data doesn't go beyond row 450, you are fine.

If new data goes beyond row 450, then you need to extend the defined database. You do this by:

1. Choosing:    **Formula Define Name**
2. Choosing the name of your database in the list box on the left.
3. Adjusting the range which is in the box under "Refers to".

In the example below, we have extended the database to include 300 more rows.

| | |
|---|---|
| **Name:**    database | |
| **Refers to:**    =CUST.XLS!$A$6:$E$450 | (before) |

| | |
|---|---|
| **Name:**    database | |
| **Refers to:**    =CUST.XLS!$A$6:$E$750 | (after) |

**External**
**databases**

You can retrieve information from external databases such as text files, Dbase, SQL Server, Oracle and OS/2 Extended Edition.

You do this via Q+E, a database interface program which is included in the Excel package.

**Link Excel**
**to an**
**external**
**database**

To link an Excel spreadsheet to an external database file, do the following:

1. Open Q+E.
2. Choose: **File - Open**
3. Choose the desired database file.
4. Choose: **Edit - Copy Special**
   To include headings, check: **Include Column Headings**
   To include all rows in the database, check: **Entire Window**
   To include the SQL select statement, check: **Formula link**
   at: **SQL text**
5. Activate Excel and select the cells to be linked to the database file.
6. Choose: **Edit - Paste Link**

If the query file in Q+E were called 'Query1', and if you had NOT chosen 'SQL text', the formulas in the linked cells would look like this:

**{=QE|Query1!'ALL/HEADERS'}**

If you DID choose 'SQL text', the formulas would look like this:

**{=QE|'SELECT NR,NAME,ADDR FROM C:\QE\QUERY1'!ALL/HEADERS}**

**Edit**
**SQL-**
**SELECT**

You can now edit the SQL query in Excel. To do this, choose one of the linked cells, edit the formula and press:

All the formulas in the array will then be changed.
You can also type a formula referring to an external database directly
into Excel.

Once the cells are linked to the external database, you can manipulate
these cells in Excel exactly as if they were a local database.

**Define
an external
database**

Another way to link a spreadsheet to an external database is to define
the external database as a database in Excel. To do this, choose
in Excel:

**Data - Set Database**

and click at: **External database**

Q+E is activated. This takes a little time.
Finally a dialogue box appears. Choose database file from the list box.
If you are using several database files, click at:

**Add**

... and choose the next database file from the list box.

**Create a
criteria
range**

To create a criteria range, move the cursor to where you want your
criteria area and choose:

**Data Paste Fieldnames**

If you are using all the columns in the database, choose: **Paste all**

If you are using some of the columns, choose the ones you want from
the list box (Shift and click) and choose: **Paste**

If you want the columns in a different sequence, choose: **Order fields**
Choose from the list box the column you want first and choose: **Add**
Repeat until you have chosen all the columns you want. Click at: **OK**

Column headings (field names) will be pasted into the spreadsheet.
Type in criteria in the normal way underneath the criteria headings.

Select the criteria range and choose: **Data - Set criteria**

**Join**    To fetch data from more than one database, you include a 'join' in the criteria area. First you find a column (field) in each database file which contains similar information. For example, one file is called 'EMPLOYEE' and another is called 'PROJECT'. The field in common is employee number, called NO in the employee table and EMP_ID in the project table. To define a join, you would type the following in the criteria area:

**EMPLOYEE.NO**
**=PROJECT.EMP_ID**

**Execute**    To retrieve the data from the database, choose:    **Data - Extract**
This can take a little time.

**SQL**    Instead of creating a criteria area, you can write or edit the SQL-SELECT
**SELECT**    text. To do this, choose:

**Data - SQL Query**

Here you can type in or edit the query text.
Execute by choosing:                **Run**

# 7f. Database functions

You can perform mathematical operations on data which follow given criteria. For example, you might want to get a sum total of sales for all customers in a certain region. To do this, you use a function called DSUM.

**DSUM**

To use DSUM:

1. Give a name to your information table. The name doesn't have to be "database", but remember to include headers when marking the table.
2. Set aside a criteria area. This time you don't have to give it a name. If you choose to give it a name, the name doesn't have to be "criteria".

In the example below, we have given the area A6:D100 on the SALES sheet (SALES.XLS!$A$6:$D$100) the name "sales".

| | A | B | C | D | E |
|---|---|---|---|---|---|
| | | | SHEET1 | | |
| 1 | | | | | |
| 2 | Region | Sales | | | |
| 3 | EEC | | | | |
| 4 | | | | | |

| | A | B | C | D | E |
|---|---|---|---|---|---|
| | | | SALES.XLS | | |
| 5 | Database area | | | | |
| 6 | Cust. no. | Name | Region | Sales to date | |
| 7 | 45231 | Norsk | Scand | 26941,00 | |
| 8 | 45232 | Exxon | USA | 49706,00 | |
| 9 | 45233 | Dupont | EEC | 4987,00 | |

Then, in the cell you want your result, in our case B3, type:

**=DSUM(**

Inside the parentheses come the following parameters:

1. Database area -    **sales**
2. Column no. -       **4**
3. Criteria area -    **A2:A3**

We are totalling figures in the 4th column of the database, so column number is 4.

We give the criteria area as A2:A3, which includes the heading and one cell underneath for criteria.

Below we see the result of our formula, which adds all sales totals which fit the criteria given in cells A2:A3 ... in this case, sales in the European Common Market (EEC) region.

SHEET1

| B3 | =DSUM(sales,4,A2:A3) | | | |
|---|---|---|---|---|
| | A | B | C | D | E |
| 1 | | | | | |
| 2 | Region | Sales | | | |
| 3 | EEC | 564.025 | | | |
| 4 | | | | | |

SALES.XLS

| | A | B | C | D | E |
|---|---|---|---|---|---|
| 5 | Database area | | | | |
| 6 | Cust. no. | Name | Region | Sales to date | |
| 7 | 45231 | Norsk | Scand | 26941,00 | |
| 8 | 45232 | Exxon | USA | 49706,00 | |
| 9 | 45233 | Dupont | EEC | 4987,00 | |
| 10 | 45234 | Noroil | Scand | 51248,00 | |
| 11 | 45235 | Northrop | EEC | 12478,00 | |

Along with the DSUM formula to add figures which follow criteria, you can use:

1. DAVERAGE to average figures which follow criteria.
2. DMAX to find highest among figures which follow criteria.
3. DMIN to find smallest among figures which follow criteria.
4. DCOUNT to count number of fields which contain data and follow the criteria.

**DAVERAGE**   In the example below, we are using DAVERAGE to get average sales in the Scandinavian region.

C3 | **=DAVERAGE(sales,4,A2:A3)**

|   | A | B | C | D | E |
|---|---|---|---|---|---|
| 1 |  | Total | Average |  |  |
| 2 | Region | Sales | Sales |  |  |
| 3 | Scand | 78189,00 | 39094,50 |  |  |
| 4 |  |  |  |  |  |

**DMAX**   In the example below, we are using DMAX to get the highest sales figure in the Scandinavian region.

D3 | **=DMAX(sales,4,A2:A3)**

|   | A | B | C | D | E |
|---|---|---|---|---|---|
| 1 |  | Total | Average | Highest |  |
| 2 | Region | Sales | Sales | Sales |  |
| 3 | Scand | 78189,00 | 39094,50 | 51248,00 |  |
| 4 |  |  |  |  |  |

**DMIN**   In the example below, we are using DMIN to get the lowest sales figure in the Scandinavian region.

E3 | **=DMIN(sales,4,A2:A3)**

|   | A | B | C | D | E |
|---|---|---|---|---|---|
| 1 |  | Total | Average | Highest | Lowest |
| 2 | Region | Sales | Sales | Sales | Sales |
| 3 | Scand | 78189 | 39095 | 51248 | 12478 |
| 4 |  |  |  |  |  |

**DCOUNT**    In the example below, we are using DCOUNT to find out the number of sales figures listed for the Scandinavian region.

E3 | =DCOUNT(sales,4,A2:A3)

|   | A | B | C | D | E | F |
|---|---|---|---|---|---|---|
| 1 |  | Total | Average | Highest | No. of |  |
| 2 | Region | Sales | Sales | Sales | Offices |  |
| 3 | Scand | 78189,00 | 39094,50 | 51248,00 | 21 |  |

( **Excel 3.0** )

**DGET**    This function fetches a value from the database according to your criteria. The formula is written as follows:

=DGET(database range,column no.,criteria range)

In the example below we have used DGET in cell B2 to fetch the last name corresponding to the initials in cell A2.

B2    =DGET(A4:D3000,2,A1:A2)

|   | A | B | C | D |
|---|---|---|---|---|
| 1 | Init. | L. name |  |  |
| 2 | JB | Bond |  |  |
| 3 |  |  |  |  |
| 4 | ID | L. name | F. name | Init. |
| 5 | 1524 | And | Anders | AA |
| 6 | 1853 | Bond | James | JB |
| 7 | 4862 | Hansen | Knut | KHA |

## 7g. Useful lookup aids

Two functions, MATCH and INDEX, can be useful when used as part of a formula to extract information from a table.

**MATCH**

To find a data item's relative location within a row or column, use MATCH. For example, if the data item were the 3rd item in a row, MATCH would return 3. Or if the item were the 4th row in a column, MATCH would return 4.

In the example below, we are writing a MATCH formula to find Noroil's relative location in the customer name column. In cell C4, first type:

**=MATCH(**

Inside the parentheses come the following parameters:

1. Column (row) area -     **C7:C100**
2. Data item -     **C3**
3. Type of match -     **0**
   (0 means exact match)

So the entire formula would be:

**=MATCH(C7:C100,C3,0)**

... and the result in this case would be 4.

|    | A | B | C | D | E |
|----|---|---|---|---|---|
| 3  | Customer name : | | Noroil | | |
| 4  | | Row no. : | 4 | | |
| 5  | | | | | |
| 6  | | Cust. no. | Name | Sales to date | |
| 7  | | 45231 | Norsk | 26941,00 | |
| 8  | | 45232 | Exxon | 49706,00 | |
| 9  | | 45233 | Dupont | 4987,00 | |
| 10 | | 45234 | Noroil | 51248,00 | |
| 11 | | 45235 | Northrop | 12478,00 | |

Below is an example of how MATCH could be used within an information formula. Here you want a LOOKUP formula to find sales of any customer the user specifies. This would be fine if customer number is used as the lookup key. But here, customer name is the lookup key.

This creates two problems:
1) customer names are not sorted and
2) they aren't in the first column of the table.

To resolve this, we add a column to the left of the table with sequence numbers, and redefine the sales table to include this new column (Formula Define Name).

Next, we use a match formula to find the sequence (in this case row) number of our customer name. The first parameter in the VLOOKUP formula is row number, so we include the match formula as the first parameter in our lookup formula.

In the example below, the result of MATCH is 3, so VLOOKUP uses 3 as the index key to find the correct row.

| C4 | =VLOOKUP(MATCH(C7:C100,C3,0),sales,4) | | | | |
|------|--------------|-----------|----------|---------------|-----|
|      | A            | B         | C        | D             | E   |
| 3    | Customer name : |        | Noroil   |               |     |
| 4    |              | Sales :   | 51248,00 |               |     |
| 5    |              |           |          |               |     |
| 6    |              | Cust. no. | Name     | Sales to date |     |
| 7    | 1            | 45231     | Norsk    | 26941,00      |     |
| 8    | 2            | 45232     | Exxon    | 49706,00      |     |
| 9    | 3            | 45233     | Noroil   | 51248,00      |     |
| 10   | 4            | 45234     | Dupont   | 4987,00       |     |
| 11   | 5            | 45235     | Northrop | 12478,00      |     |

**INDEX**

To find the value contained in a cell, use INDEX.
For column 3, row 2 within the sales table in the example below,
INDEX would return 49706.

|     | A | B | C | D | E |
|-----|---|---|---|---|---|
| 3   |   |   | Index column : | 3 |   |
| 4   |   |   | Index row : | 2 |   |
| 5   |   |   | Value : | 49706,00 |   |
| 6   |   |   |   |   |   |
| 7   |   | Cust. no. | Name | Sales to date |   |
| 8   |   | 45231 | Norsk | 26941,00 |   |
| 9   |   | 45232 | Exxon | 49706,00 |   |
| 10  |   | 45233 | Dupont | 4987,00 |   |
| 11  |   | 45234 | Noroil | 51248,00 |   |
| 12  |   | 45235 | Northrop | 12478,00 |   |

To attain this result in cell D5, we first type:     **=INDEX(**

Inside the parentheses come the following parameters:

1. Table area -        **B8:D100**
2. Column number -     **D3**
3. Row number -        **D4**

So the entire formula would be:        **=INDEX(B8:D100,D3,D4)**

Let us say we wanted to find a value within column D. We then only need
specify the row number. The formula would then look like this:

**=INDEX(D8:D100,D4)**

The same goes if we want to find a value within a row, for example row 2.
We then only need specify the column number. The formula would then
look like this:

**=INDEX(B9:D9,D3)**

The example below shows a practical use of the INDEX formula.

We wish to compare sales to date this year with last year's corresponding sales to date.

In this case, we have sales figures up to and including March. Thus, the month in cell B2 is 3 (this could be arrived at automatically with the COUNT formula). In column N, we use SUM to get the totals for each customer.

In column O, we use SUM again to get last year's totals for each customer. From cell B2 we know that we want to sum from January 1990 to the 3rd month (March 1990). To find which cell the third month's sale is located in, we use INDEX. The area in the first formula in cell O5 is SALES.XLS!B3:M3 (sales for 'Norsk' in 1990). The cell's position is acquired from the month number in cell B2. Then we can copy the formula down.

### SALES91.XLS

O5 | =SUM(SALES.XLS!B3:INDEX(SALES.XLS!B3:M3,$B$2))

| | A | B | ........ | N | O |
|---|---|---|---|---|---|
| 1 | 1991 | | | | |
| 2 | Month : | 3 | | | |
| 3 | | | | | **1990** |
| 4 | Name | January | ........ | Total | **Sales to date** |
| 5 | Norsk | 79590 | | 194658 | 180710 |
| 6 | Exxon | 4809 | | 137246 | 162206 |
| 7 | Dupont | 6748 | | 56342 | 44590 |
| 8 | Noroil | 122080 | | 164785 | 180420 |

### SALES90.XLS

| | A | B | C | D | E |
|---|---|---|---|---|---|
| 1 | 1990 | | | | |
| 2 | Name | January | February | March | April |
| 3 | Norsk | 56850 | 78240 | 45620 | 50182 |
| 4 | Exxon | 3435 | 79821 | 78950 | 86845 |
| 5 | Dupont | 4820 | 15400 | 24370 | 26807 |
| 6 | Noroil | 87200 | 5300 | 87920 | 96712 |

# 8. Macros

Suppose you have a procedure, a series of commands that must be repeated again and again, such as to extract information from the database. Each time, you have to:
1) select the result area
2) choose Data - Extract and press RET
3) return the cursor to the criteria area

Instead of having to go through these 3 steps every time you run a new query, you can write a program to do this. Then every time you want to run a new query, you merely start the program, and the program does it for you. In Excel, this program is called a macro.

## 8a. Macro recorder

A macro is a series of instructions. In Excel you can write the instructions yourself, or you can let Excel do it for you. To let Excel do it for you, you:

1. Give your new macro a shortcut key.
2. Start a built-in recorder.
3. Carry out the tasks you want included in your macro.
4. Stop the built-in recorder.
5. Save the newly-created macro.

Now, when you want to run the macro, you press CTRL and the shortcut key.

**Create macro**
In the example below, we are creating a macro to run a database query. First we define our macro and give it a shortcut key. To do this we activate the sheet we want the macro to start from and choose:
### Macro - Record

Then we type in a name for our macro and a shortcut key. In the example below, we are calling our macro "query" and are giving it the shortcut key "q". Note that Excel distinguishes between higher and lower case letters.

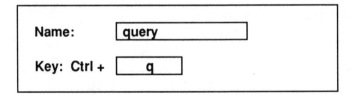

Now the macro recorder is switched on. Every action we take in Excel will now be recorded and included as part of our macro. In this case we want to do the following:

1. Select the result area.
2. Choose Data - Extract and press RET.
3. Move the cursor to the criteria area.

Stop the macro recorder by choosing:

**Macro - Stop Recorder**

**Test macro**

Next, we test our macro with a trial run. In the example below, we have changed the criteria. Now we want all customers listed who get 15% discount.

C3

|   | A | B | C | D |
|---|---|---|---|---|
| 1 | Criteria area | | | |
| 2 | Cust. no. | Name | Discount | |
| 3 | | | 15% | |
| 4 | | | | |

We gave our macro the shortcut key "q". So to start the macro, you would press:

| CTRL | | q |

In the example below, the macro worked, and the new query was run.

A3

|   | A | B | C | D | E |
|---|---|---|---|---|---|
| 1 | Criteria area | | | | |
| 2 | Cust. no. | Name | Discount | | |
| 3 | | | 15% | | |
| 4 | | | | | |
| 5 | Result area | | | | |
| 6 | Cust. no. | Name | Address | City | Discount |
| 7 | 45233 | Dupont | G.Alle 45 | Lyons | 15 % |
| 8 | 45235 | Northrop | 5 Stuart St | Harwich | 15 % |

If a dialog box with the text 'HALT!' appears on the screen, then there is an error in the macro. If this happens, it is best to cancel and check the macro, or create the macro again.

**User instructions**

Once you know the macro works, you can write instructions on the sheet so that whoever uses the macro next will know what to do:

|   | A | B | C | D | E |
|---|---|---|---|---|---|
| 1 | Criteria area | | | To run new query, | |
| 2 | Cust. no. | Name | Discount | fill in criteria (A3:C3) | |
| 3 | | | 15% | and press CTRL q | |
| 4 | | | | (lower case q) | |
| 5 | Result area | | | | |
| 6 | Cust. no. | Name | Address | City | Discount |
| 7 | 45233 | Dupont | G.Alle 45 | Lyons | 15 % |
| 8 | 45235 | Northrop | 5 Stuart St | Harwich | 15 % |

124

**Save macro**   Finally, you go to Macro1, the macro sheet created by Excel. In the example below, you can see the macro instructions written by Excel.

| | A | B |
|---|---|---|
| | **Macro1** | |
| 1 | Query | |
| 2 | =SELECT("R6C1:R10C5") | |
| 3 | =EXTRACT(FALSE) | |
| 4 | =SELECT("R3C1") | |
| 5 | =RETURN() | |
| 6 | | |

Now you can save the macro with the command:   **File Save**

The macro will be saved with the file type:   **.XLM**

**Excel 3.0**

**Macro**   You can draw a macro button on the spreadsheet, and use it to run a
**button**   macro. First create the macro. Then click to the right on the icon-bar at:

A dialog box appears. Choose the macro from the list box which you want to be started by your button.

You can write text in the button and manipulate the button in the same way as any other graphic object.

In the example below we have created a macro button. When the user clicks at the 'Transfer' button, our macro is started.

| | A | B | C | D | E |
|---|---|---|---|---|---|
| 1 | ALLOCATION OF FUNDS | | | | |
| 2 | | | | | |
| 3 | **Transfer** | | | D | K |
| 4 | 1.Jan | Available funds | | | 150.000 |
| 5 | 20.Jan | Energy proj. | | 25.000 | |
| 6 | 21.Jan | Envir. proj. | | | 10.000 |

| **Start another macro** | To start another macro, choose the command: **Macro - Record** |
|---|---|

Proceed as before, but give your new macro a different name and shortcut key. This new macro will be created on the same macro sheet as the previous one.

| **Add to existing macro** | To add more steps to an existing macro, choose: |
|---|---|

**Macro - Start Recorder**

## 8b. Write and edit macros

You can go into the macro file and make adjustments to your macros.

If you want to start writing your own macro on the same sheet, do this:

1. Choose:     **Macro - Set Recorder**
2. Choose:     **Macro - Record**
   Give a name and shortcut key to the new macro.
3. Choose:     **Macro - Stop Recorder**

Now you can start writing statements in the area this new macro was created.

| **Change name of existing macro** | To change the name of an existing macro, choose: |
|---|---|

**Formula - Define Name**

Here you can select the old name, change it to a new name (in the 'Refers to' box) and delete the old one (select it from the list box and choose Delete).

**Cell references**

Note that with recorded macros, cell addresses are written differently. Cell A1 is for example written "R1C1", which means row 1, column 1.

cell B3 =    "R3C2"
cell E1 =    "R1C5"
A5:F35 =    "R5C1:R35C6"

When you write cell references yourself within a macro, precede the cell reference with "!". For example:

cell A1 is written as:              !A1
the range B3:D9 is written as:      !B3:D9

You can also use a reference relative to the active cell. An example of the relative reference form: if C4 were the active cell, R[1]C[2] would be one row down, 2 columns, over, or cell E5.

With C4 as the active cell:

cell B3 can be written as:         "R[-1]C[-1]"
cell E1 can be written as:         "R[-3]C[2]"
cells A5:F35 can be written as:    "R[1]C[-2]:R[31]C[3]"

## 8c. Macro commands

A number of command statements correspond directly to menu commands. For example:

**=PRINT()** - - - - - - **File - Print**
**=COPY()** - - - - - - **Edit - Copy**
**=FORMAT.FONT()** - - **Format - Font**

To generate the above types of statements, it is best to use the macro recorder.

A number of command statements also correspond directly to worksheet functions, such as VLOOKUP, SUM, PMT and INDEX. For these types of statements, it is normally best to write the corresponding functions on the worksheet itself.

Here are some macro statements that are useful to know:

**Activate**      =ACTIVATE() - - - - activates sheet
**sheet**          for example, to activate the sheet CUST.XLS:

**=ACTIVATE("CUST.XLS")**

**Move**        =SELECT() - - - - - selects cell or range of cells
**cursor**        for example to select the range B6:F26

**=SELECT("R6C2:R26C6")**

**Type in data/ formula**   =FORMULA() - - - - enters data or formula into selected cell
for example to enter the text "out of stock" into cell G5:

**=SELECT("R5C7")**
**=FORMULA("out of stock")**

or to enter a LOOKUP formula into cell B4:

**=SELECT("R4C2")**
**=FORMULA("=VLOOKUP(RC[-1],tab,2)")**

Note that the RC reference form (e.g. RC[-1]) MUST be used
in the FORMULA statement.


**End macro**   =RETURN() - - - - - ends the macro

**=RETURN()**


## 8d. Interactive statements

Here are some useful statements for making your macro more
interactive.

**Message**   =ALERT() - - - - displays dialogue box with message to user
To write this statement, type:

**=ALERT(**

Inside the parentheses comes the following information:

1. Your message to the user
2. Type of dialogue box: 1 = offers choice (OK or Cancel)
                         2 = message
                         3 = error message

Below are examples of the 3 types of ALERT statements:

**1...  =ALERT("Are you sure you want to do that?",1)**

The following dialogue box will then appear:

```
?        Are you sure you want to do that?

      [   OK   ]              [ Cancel ]
```

**2 ...  =ALERT("All rows are now updated",2)**

The following dialogue box will then appear:

```
*        All rows are now updated

              [   OK   ]
```

**3 ...  =ALERT("Number must be between 1 and 10",3)**

The following dialogue box will then appear:

```
!        Number must be between 1 and 10

              [   OK   ]
```

**User**
**choice**

=STATEMENT?() - - - if you want the macro to choose a menu command, but allow the user to choose options within the command, or cancel the command entirely. For example, to choose the File Print command and display the dialogue box so that the user can choose options or cancel, you would write:

**=PRINT?()**

**Input**

=FORMULA(INPUT()) - gives cue to user to type something.
To write this statement, type:

**=FORMULA(INPUT(**

Inside the parentheses comes the following information:

1. cue - your message to the user
2. type of input:  0 = formula, 1 = number, 2 = text

For example, if you want the user to type an invoice number into cell F5:

**=SELECT("R5C7")**
**=FORMULA(INPUT("Type in invoice number",1))**

The following dialogue box will then appear:

```
┌─────────────────────────────────────────────────────────┐
│                                                           │
│  Type in invoice number:              ┌──────────┐        │
│                                        │    OK    │        │
│                                        └──────────┘        │
│                                        ┌──────────┐        │
│                                        │  Cancel  │        │
│                                        └──────────┘        │
│     ┌──────────────────────────────────┐                  │
│     │                                  │                  │
│     └──────────────────────────────────┘                  │
│                                                           │
└─────────────────────────────────────────────────────────┘
```

## 8e. Program statements

Here are some useful statements for navigating and testing inside
your macro.

**Active cell**     ACTIVE.CELL() - - - - refers to the active cell on the worksheet
from which the macro is being run.

**Remember**     =SET.NAME() - - - - gives name to specified cell.
**cell**     This name can be used in later macro statements to identify the cell.
In the example below, the active cell is remembered with the name
"total". Later on in the macro, the cell named as "total" is selected
again.

> **=SET.NAME("total",ACTIVE.CELL())**
> - - - -
> - - - -
> **=SELECT(total)**

**Select with**     =SELECT(INDEX(range,column no./row no.)) - - - selects the
**INDEX**     cell returned by the index function. In the example below, we are
selecting the appropriate cell to enter the current month's sales.

> **=SELECT(INDEX(!B4:M4,!B1))**

|   | A | B | C | D | E |
|---|---|---|---|---|---|
| 1 | Month | 3 | | | |
| 2 | | | | | |
| 3 | | January | February | March | April |
| 4 | Denmark | 4685 | 6091 | | |
| 5 | Finland | 4321 | 5617 | | |
| 6 | Iceland | 1564 | 2033 | | |

Note: the RC reference does NOT work with INDEX statements. Use instead
the direct reference form (e.g. !B1).

| **Go to** | =GOTO()  -  - move to another line in macro |
|---|---|
| | For example, to move to the statement in A3 in the macro sheet and start carrying out instructions from there: |

$$=GOTO(A3)$$

| **If** | =IF()  -  -  -  if certain conditions are met, do one thing, otherwise do another thing. For example, if the active cell is blank, move to A3 in the macro; otherwise move to A13: |
|---|---|

$$=IF(ACTIVE.CELL()="",GOTO(A3),GOTO(A13))$$

| **Submacro** | =submacro()  -  -  -  -  -  -  -  -  -  - calls another macro. When the other macro is finished, control is returned to the statement following the submacro call. The submacro must be defined using Formula - Define name. In the example below, cell D14 is defined with the name 'cleanup'. The macro in column A calls the submacro CLEANUP. After 'cleanup' is finished, control returns to the next macro statement in cell A15. |
|---|---|

(main macro)                          (submacro)

|    | A | B | C | D | E |
|----|---|---|---|---|---|
| 14 | =cleanup() ⟶ | | | cleanup | |
| 15 | =SELECT(!G5) ⟵ | | | - - - - | |
| 16 | - - - - | | | - - - - | |
| 17 | - - - - | | | =RETURN() | |
| 18 | | | | | |

| **While** | =WHILE() ....=NEXT()  -  if certain conditions are met, continue with |
|---|---|
| **Next** | the macro statements up to NEXT(). Then return to WHILE() again. |
| | If the condition in WHILE isn't met, skip to the first statement after NEXT() |

The macro in the example below deletes empty rows on a sheet:

| | |
|---|---|
| =WHILE(ACTIVE.CELL()="") | if the active cell is blank, continues - otherwise skips to RETURN |
| =SELECT("R") | selects the same row |
| =EDIT.DELETE() | deletes the row |
| =NEXT() | returns to the WHILE test |
| =RETURN() | ends the macro |

**For**       =FOR() ......=NEXT() - executes all macro statements between FOR
**Next**      and NEXT for a desired number of times.

The FOR statement contains three parts.
1. the name of a counter. This can be "counter".
2. the number the counter begins counting from (usually 1).
3. the number the counter counts to. This (minus the start-number) determines how many times the statements between FOR and NEXT will be executed.

The macro in the example below tests the next 250 rows in the sheet and runs a delete-row submacro for each row that is empty.

```
=FOR("counter",1,250)          'counter' starts at 1 - continues to 250
=IF(ACTIVE.CELL()=""),del-row(),SELECT("R[1]C"))
                               if active cell is blank, runs 'del-row'
                               submacro, otherwise selects next row
=NEXT()                        adds one to counter
=RETURN()                      ends macro
```

**Step**      =STEP() - stops the macro and displays a dialogue box. You can choose to let the macro continue, stop it or step through the macro statement by statement. This can be useful when testing the macro.

```
=STEP()
```

**ESC**      To stop the macro while it is in progress, press:

```
ESC
```

**Echo**      To cause a macro to run faster, you can turn off screen updating.

```
=ECHO(FALSE)          turns off visual screen updating
=ECHO(TRUE)           turns visual screen updating
                      back on
```

Screen updating will automatically be turned back on again at the end of your macro.

**Calculation**    To cause a macro to run faster, you can turn off automatic calculation of formulas.

>    **=CALCULATION(3)**          turns off automatic calculation
>    **=CALCULATION(1)**          turns automatic calculation
>                                 back on

**Wait**    To cause your macro to operate at a given time, type the following:

>    **=WAIT(**

Inside the parentheses, type a time you want your macro to be run:

>    **"23:00"**

The entire formula :         **=WAIT("23:00")**

WAIT can also be used to cause your macro to wait a specified time before continuing, which can be useful in demos.  1 second = .00001 The following formula would make your macro wait for 2 seconds:

>    **=WAIT(NOW()+.00002)**

## 8f. Macros for customizing menus

You can add a command to the menu, so that when the user chooses this command, your macro is started automatically.

**Add command**    Let us say you want to include the macro below as a command under "Data" in the normal worksheet menu.

MACRO1.XLS

| | A | B |
|---|---|---|
| 1 | DBQuery | |
| 2 | =SELECT("R6C1:R10C5") | |
| 3 | =EXTRACT(FALSE) | |
| 4 | =SELECT("R3C1") | |
| 5 | =RETURN() | |
| 6 | | |

First we go to the macro sheet and define our new command, and the name of the corresponding macro.

| | A | B |
|---|---|---|
| 7 | | |
| 8 | DBQuery | MACRO1.XLS!DBQuery |
| 9 | | |

Next, somewhere else on the macro sheet, we type:

**=ADD.COMMAND(**

Within the parentheses come the following parameters:

1. menu ID -          **1**
   (1 = normal worksheet menu bar, 2 = chart menu bar,
    3 = no menu bar, and 4 = information menu bar)
2. menu pos.-          **5**          (the fifth item in the top menu - Data)
3. menu ref -          **A8:B8**     (address on the macro sheet where
                                                    new command and macro names are given)

The entire statement then would be:

**=ADD.COMMAND(1,5,A8:B8)**

When you run this macro, your new command will be added as the last command under "Data" in the menu.

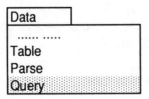

```
Data
...... ......
Table
Parse
Query
```

| **Delete command** | To delete this command from the menu, you would type first: |
| --- | --- |

=DELETE.COMMAND(

Within the parentheses come the falling parameters:

1. menu ID -        1
2. menu pos.-        5
3. command -    **"Query"**
         (the entire name must be typed out)

The entire statement then would be:        =DELETE.COMMAND(1,5,"Query")

When you run this macro, your new command "Query" will be deleted from the menu.


**Add menu item and command**

You can also add a new menu item and include your new command under the new menu item.

To do this, first go to the macro sheet and type the new menu item on top of the command name.

In the example below, we are calling our menu item "Finance".

|   | A | B |
| --- | --- | --- |
| 7 | Finance | |
| 8 | Query | MACRO1.XLS!DBQuery |
| 9 | | |

Next, instead of our ADD.COMMAND statement, we type first:

=ADD.MENU(

Within the parentheses come the falling parameters:

1. menu ID -        1
3. menu ref -    **A7:B8**    (includes menu, command and macro name)

The entire statement then would be:     **=ADD.MENU(1,A7:B8)**

When you run this macro, your new menu item will be added as the last item in the worksheet menu.

| Options | Window | Finance |
|---------|--------|---------|
|         |        | Query   |

**Rename command**

To rename a command, you type first:               **=RENAME.COMMAND(**

Within the parentheses come the falling parameters:

1. menu ID -          **1**
2. menu item-         **9**      (or "Finance")
3. command -          **1**      (or "Query")
4. new name -     **"Report"**

The entire statement then would be:

   **=RENAME.COMMAND(1,9,1,"Report")**

When you run this macro, your new command will be renamed from "Query" to "Report".

**Delete command from own menu item**

To delete this command from a custom menu item, you would type first:
   **=DELETE.COMMAND(**

Within the parentheses come the falling parameters:

1. menu ID -           **1**
2. menu item-    **"Finance"**           (the name must be typed out)
3. command -    **"Query"**

The entire statement then would be:

   **=DELETE.COMMAND(1,"Finance","Query")**

When you run this macro, the command "Query" will be deleted from the menu.

**Delete menu item and command**

To delete this menu item, and the attached command as well, you would type first:

    **=DELETE.MENU(**

Within the parentheses come the falling parameters:

1. menu ID -        **1**
2. menu item -   **"Finance"**
                (the entire name must be typed out)

The entire statement then would be:     **=DELETE.MENU(1,"Finance")**

When you run this macro, your new command "Query" plus your new menu item "Finance" will be deleted from the menu.


**Start macro when file is opened**

To start your menu automatically when the macro sheet is opened, do the following:

1. select the top cell in the macro.
2. choose:     **Formula - Define Name**
3. For 'Name', type a name that begins with:     **Auto open**
   For example, 'Auto open menu'.


**Open macro when Excel is opened**

To automatically open the macro sheet (or a worksheet) every time Excel is opened, save the sheet in the catalogue:

    **c:\excel\xlstart**


**Save a hidden macro**

You may want to hide your macro sheet so the user doesn't see it. To hide the macro sheet and save the macro as a hidden sheet, do the following:

1. Edit the macro in some way.
2. Choose:     **Window - Hide**
3. Close Excel by choosing:     **File - Exit**
4. A dialog box will appear asking if you want to save the macro.
   Select:     **Yes**

**Customizing dialogue boxes**

To create your own customized dialogue box, you first select an unused area on your macro sheet. Here you define your dialogue box.

The following must be defined for your dialogue box:
- item (such as OK button or list box). These are identified by numbers from 1 to 20.
- x position - horizontal position in points from the left of your dialogue box to the left edge of your item (0 means centered)
  When positioning your dialogue box, x position is measured from the left of your screen to the left edge of your dialogue box.
  8 points = one character
- y position - vertical position in points from the top of your dialogue box to the top edge of your item (0 means centered)
  When positioning your dialogue box, y position is measured from the top of your screen to the top edge of your dialogue box.
  12 points = one line
- width in x points
- height in y points
- text to be included in the box
- a place for the data which the user inputs

In the first line of the definition, you give the size and position of your dialogue box.

Below is an example of a dialogue box definition.

|   | B | C | D | E | F | G | H | I |
|---|---|---|---|---|---|---|---|---|
| 1 | item | x | y | width | height | text | init/suit | gram |
| 2 |  |  |  | 540 | 190 |  |  | handful |
| 3 | 1 | 460 | 6 | 72 | 21 | OK |  | kilo |
| 4 | 13 | 385 | 30 | 147 | 21 | &Recipe finished | TRUE | cup |
| 5 | 5 | 8 | 6 | 140 | 12 | &Recipe |  | litre |
| 6 | 6 | 8 | 30 | 140 | 18 |  | cinnamon toa | slice |
| 7 | 16 | 8 | 55 | 140 | 120 | COST.XLS!R5C2:R21C2 | 6 | T-spoon |
| 8 | 5 | 160 | 6 | 100 | 12 | &Ingredient |  | piece |
| 9 | 6 | 160 | 30 | 100 | 18 |  | ginger | t-spoon |
| 10 | 16 | 160 | 55 | 100 | 120 | FOOD.XLS!R4C2:R18C2 | 8 |  |
| 11 | 5 | 272 | 6 | 100 | 12 | &Unit |  |  |
| 12 | 6 | 272 | 30 | 100 | 18 |  | handful |  |
| 13 | 16 | 272 | 55 | 100 | 120 | COST.XLM!R1C9:R9C9 | 2 |  |
| 14 | 5 | 385 | 60 | 60 | 12 | &Amount |  |  |
| 15 | 8 | 385 | 80 | 60 | 18 |  | 1 |  |
| 16 |  |  |  |  |  |  |  |  |

To call this dialogue box in your macro, type:     **=DIALOG.BOX(**

Inside the parentheses, fill in the area of your dialogue box definition:

**B2:H15**

Based on our definition, the following dialogue box would appear.

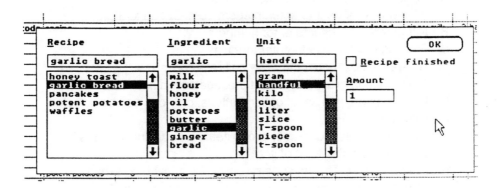

The user input data is placed in the init/suit column of your dialog definition. These cells can then be referred to further on in the macro.

**Items**　　　　The items are identified by numbers from 1 to 20. They are as follows:

1　OK button, default (chosen by pressing RET)
2　Cancel button
3　OK button
4　Cancel button, default (chosen by pressing RET or ESC)
5　Text. Type '&' before the letter you want underlined.
6　Input box for user to enter information
7　Integer box for user to enter integers from -32768 to 32767
8　Number box for user to enter numbers
9　Formula box for user to enter formulas
10　Reference box for user to enter cell references
11　Option button group. This must precede option buttons
12　Option button. In a set of option buttons, only one can be selected
13　Check box
14　Group box. Used to visually group items within your dialogue box
15　List box. Contains a list of items.
16　Linked list box. This must be preceded by a text box. When an item is chosen here, it is also automatically entered in the text box
17　Icon. Displays a question mark (?), asterisk (*) or exclamation point (!)
18　Linked file list box. Lists files in a directory, and must be preceded by a text box and followed by a linked drive and directory list box
19　Linked drive and directory list box. This must follow a linked file list box If this is followed by a text box, the current drive and directory will be automatically entered here.
20　Directory box. Displays the name of the current directory.

## 8h. Version 2.1 and 3 graphic definition

In Excel version 2.1 and up, you define your dialogue box graphically. Instead of filling in details on your macro sheet, you go into a graphic editor and 'draw' your box and its contents. This is then converted automatically to the type of definition as shown above.

First, open the file:　　　　**EXCELDE.EXE**

A dialogue box will appear on your screen.
Click and drag to move and size your dialogue box.

Choose from the menu:     **Item**

Then proceed to choose the items you want in your dialogue box.
Size and move then by clicking and dragging.

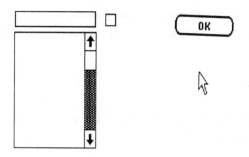

To include options, do the following:

1. Choose:     **Group Box**
2. Type in your text for the group box.
3. An option button appears. Type in your text for the option button.
4. The next option button appears. Type in text.
   When you don't want any more options, click outside the group box.

In the example below, we have typed in "Finish recipe" for our group box text
and defined three options.

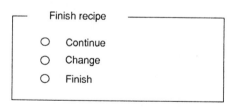

When you have finished with your design, choose:

**Edit - Select All Items**

Then choose:

**Edit - Copy**

Exit EXCELDE and return to your macro sheet.
Place the cursor where you want your dialogue definition area
and choose:

**Edit - Paste**

The dialogue definition created in EXCELDE will be converted to the
format useable by the Excel macro.

| item | x | y | width | height | text | init/suit |
|------|-----|----|-------|--------|-------------|-----------|
|      |     |    | 516   | 186    |             |           |
| 1    | 436 | 6  | 72    | 21     | OK          |           |
| 2    | 436 | 30 | 72    | 21     | Cancel      |           |
| 5    | 8   | 6  | 120   | 12     | Choose Item |           |

# 9. Error messages

The following occurs when there is not enough space in the
cell for the number:

#######

Remedy: increase cell width or change number format.
This error message can occur when the number is formatted
in a more lengthy format (such as with a currency sign, or  in %).

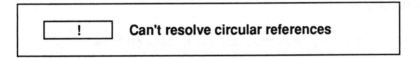

This indicates an error in the formula, usually a misplaced
comma, period or parenthesis.

Remedy: correct the formula

---

| ! | **Can't resolve circular references** |

This occurs when you have written a formula which contains
a reference to the same cell the formula is written in, for example
you have written '=A3+B3' in cell B3.

Remedy: change the cell reference

## #REF!

This occurs when you refer to a cell or range that is no longer available. Often the cell or range is on a sheet which is not open.

Remedy: make the cell/range availiable, for example by opening the appropriate worksheet. Or alternatively, change the formula.

## #N/A

This occurs when an item of data is not available. Often this happens in connection with a LOOKUP function.

Remedy: If this occurs in connection with a LOOKUP or database function, it can be because the entire table is not included in the defined area. In this case, redefine the table. Other possibilities are to add data to the database, or change the formula.

## #NAME?

This occurs when your formula refers to a name which has not been defined.

Remedy: use the Formula - Define Name command to define the name used in the formula. Alternatively, check that the name isn't spelled differently in your formula and in Formula - Define Name.

**The following error messages occur specifically in connection with database commands.**

| ! | **Database range is not defined.** |

This occurs if no database has been defined.

If this comes after using the Data - Extract command, it could also mean that your database wasn't defined with the name 'database'.

Remedy: define the database with the name 'database'.

| ! | **Criteria range is not defined.** |

This occurs if no criteria range has been defined.

If this comes after using the Data - Extract command, it could also mean that your criteria wasn't defined with the name 'criteria'.

Remedy: define the criteria range with the name 'criteria'.

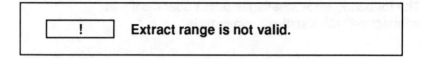

| ! | **Extract range is not valid.** |

This ocurs if there is something wrong either with the criteria range, the database range or the extract range. The columns may not agree, or the headings may be slightly different.

Remedy: check headings and definitions of the database, criteria and extract range. These must be correct, and columns and headings must correspond. If not, correct them.

| ! | **Extract range is full.** |

This occurs if there isn't enough room in the result area for the extracted data.

Remedy: Press RET to carry out the command.
Then define a larger result area, or change your criteria.

# Part 2 | Exercises

## Accounts

Fee: [          ]     Date: [          ]

| Total | Due | Paid | Balance | Fee | Bal.+fee | Overdue |
|-------|-----|------|---------|-----|----------|---------|
| 5220,00 | 5.Jun | 0,00 | | | | |
| 4788,00 | 2.Jun | 0,00 | | | | |
| 8035,20 | 30.May | 6000,00 | | | | |
| 11437,20 | 28.May | 11437,20 | | | | |
| 9007,40 | 25.May | 0,00 | | | | |
| 8424,00 | 23.May | 8424,00 | | | | |
| 1146,00 | 20.May | 1000,00 | | | | |
| 9261,00 | 18.May | 9261,00 | | | | |

## Exercise 1a - employee register

You have six employees in your department. Type out a list with name, hours worked per week and hourly wage. Calculate weekly wage for each employee, based on hours worked and hourly wage.
Save with the name "employee".

|          | hours | hr.wage | wk.wage |
|----------|-------|---------|---------|
| Andersen | 40    | 120     |         |
| Bond     | 35    | 100     |         |
| Caudillo | 40    | 130     |         |
| Colombo  | 50    | 60      |         |
| Corleone | 25    | 80      |         |
| Greer    | 38    | 85      |         |

## Exercise 1b - accounts receivable

You have eight customers who have ordered goods. Make a debtor
list containing customer no., total amount purchased and amount already
paid. Calculate balance due based on amount purchased and amount
paid. Save with the name "accounts".

| Cust.no. | Total | Paid | Balance |
|---|---|---|---|
| 1112 | 9261 | 9261 | |
| 1120 | 1146 | 1000 | |
| 1116 | 8424 | 8424 | |
| 1117 | 9007 | 0 | |
| 1119 | 11437 | 11437 | |
| 1113 | 8035 | 6000 | |
| 1115 | 4788 | 0 | |
| 1121 | 5220 | 0 | |

## Exercise 1c - tax return

Make a form for a tax return, using Excel. Type out the text for items 1 to 5.
Then fill out name, tax classification and age, as well as items 1-5.
You can use a tax return information pamphlet to help you fill out the form.
Calculate the sums for items 1d to 5. Save with the name "taxcalc".

TAX RETURN

| name | Kuliyakin | classif. | 1 | age | 35 |
|------|-----------|----------|---|-----|----|

INCOME

| Item 1a | Salary | 250000 |
|---------|--------|--------|
| | Social security | |
| | Loan advantage | 2000 |
| | Company car | 15000 |
| Item 1d | Other income | 5600 |
| | Total income | |
| | | |
| Item 3b | Other benefits | 0 |
| Item 5 | SUM (basis for min. deduction) | |

## Exercise 2a - deleting, moving, copying

Two departments have been merged, with you as department leader! To the
right of the original employees, write the names of the six new employees
in your department, together with hours worked and hourly wage (headings, too).

Use Edit - Cut to move the new information (headings included) down under the
original list, so that the two lists are merged into one. Select the row with the
superfluous headings and use Edit - Delete to delete the row. Weekly wages
also have to be calculated for the new staff. Instead of writing new formulas
for these, use Edit - Fill down to copy down the formula in the last line in the original
list (Greer).

| | hours | hr.wage | wk.wage | | hours | hr.wage |
|---|---|---|---|---|---|---|
| Andersen | 40 | 120 | 4800 | Marple | 40 | 185 |
| Bond | 35 | 100 | 3500 | Jones | 40 | 120 |
| Caudillo | 40 | 130 | 5200 | Blofeld | 25 | 80 |
| Colombo | 50 | 60 | 3000 | Solo | 40 | 130 |
| Corleone | 25 | 80 | 2000 | Syse | 35 | 100 |
| Greer | 38 | 85 | 3230 | Iacocca | 25 | 95 |

# Exercise 2b - editing, deleting, copying

Use Edit - Clear (DEL RET) to remove the formulas for balance.

Write the first formula again, and copy down with Edit - Fill down.

Use Edit - Insert to insert a new column for invoice no.

Insert the column to the left of customer no.

| Inv. no. | Cust.no. | Total | Paid | Balance |
|---|---|---|---|---|
| | 1112 | 9261 | 9261 | 0 |
| | 1120 | 1146 | 1000 | 146 |
| | 1116 | 8424 | 8424 | 0 |
| | 1117 | 9007 | 0 | 9007,2 |
| | 1119 | 11437 | 11437 | 0 |
| | 1113 | 8035 | 6000 | 2035,2 |
| | 1115 | 4788 | 0 | 4788 |
| | 1121 | 5220 | 0 | 5220 |

## Exercise 2c - tax table

On a new sheet, make a table which shows federal and local tax for
classification 1 and 2, for yearly income from 175000 to and including 375000.
As income increases by 1000, local tax increases by 210, federal tax by 246.
Use the figures below when writing the first line in the table.

| classification 1 | | | classification 2 | |
|---|---|---|---|---|
| income | local tax | fed. tax | local tax | fed. tax |
| 175000 | 33012 | 17053 | 29274 | 10806 |

In the second line of the table come the following formulas:

| income | local tax | fed. tax | | local tax | fed. tax |
|---|---|---|---|---|---|
| 175000 | 33012 | 17053 | | 29274 | 10806 |
| ( + 1000 ) | ( + 210 ) | ( + 246 ) | | ( + 210 ) | ( + 246 ) |

Then use Edit - Fill to copy down in all columns so that the
table continues on to where income is 375000.

**Tax tables**

| classif. 1 | | | classif. 2 | |
|---|---|---|---|---|
| income | local tax | fed. tax | local tax | fed. tax |
| 175000 | 33012 | 17053 | 29274 | 10806 |
| 176000 | 33222 | 17299 | 29484 | 11052 |
| 177000 | 33432 | 17545 | 29694 | 11298 |
| 178000 | 33642 | 17791 | 29904 | 11544 |
| 179000 | 33852 | 18037 | 30114 | 11790 |
| 180000 | 34062 | 18283 | 30324 | 12036 |
| 181000 | 34272 | 18529 | 30534 | 12282 |
| 182000 | 34482 | 18775 | 30744 | 12528 |
| 183000 | 34692 | 19021 | 30954 | 12774 |
| 184000 | 34902 | 19267 | 31164 | 13020 |
| 185000 | 35112 | 19513 | 31374 | 13266 |
| 186000 | 35322 | 19759 | 31584 | 13512 |
| 187000 | 35532 | 20005 | 31794 | 13758 |

# Exercise 3a - locking, linking and mass copying

Your department has shown good results. All employees will therefore get
a bonus of 500. Add two rows on the top of the employee list. In the top row,
type 'Bonus', and in the next cell, '500'. Add columns for weekly wage + bonus.

Write a formula to calculate weekly wage + bonus for the first employee. Use
cell references in the formula instead of numbers. Copy down with Edit - Fill down.
But first lock the appropriate cell reference in the formula with $.

Bonus          500

| emp.no. | name | hours | hr.wage | wk.wage | + bonus |
|---|---|---|---|---|---|
| 1111 | Andersen | 40 | 120 | 4800 | 5300 |
| 1119 | Blofeld | 25 | 80 | 2000 | |
| 1112 | Bond | 35 | 100 | 3500 | |
| 1113 | Caudillo | 40 | 130 | 5200 | |
| 1114 | Colombo | 50 | 60 | 3000 | |
| 1115 | Corleone | 25 | 80 | 2000 | |
| 1116 | Greer | 38 | 85 | 3230 | |
| 1122 | Iacocca | 25 | 95 | 2375 | |
| 1118 | Jones | 40 | 120 | 4800 | |
| 1117 | Marple | 40 | 185 | 7400 | |
| 1120 | Solo | 40 | 130 | 5200 | |
| 1121 | Syse | 35 | 100 | 3500 | |

# Exercise 3b - naming cells, linking and mass copying

The boss has decided that a fee of 50 will be instituted for overdue invoices.
Add two lines at the top of the debtor list. In the top line, type 'Fee', and in the
next line, '50'. Add another column for balance + overdue fee.

Write a formula to calculate balance + fee for the first invoice. Use cell
references instead of numbers. Copy down with Edit - Fill down. But first
lock the appropriate cell reference in the formula. This time, however, don't
use $ to lock the reference, but instead give the cell (where the new fee is)
a name (using Formula - Define name).

Then delete the fee in the rows where balance is nil.

Fee                  50

| Inv. no. | Cust.no. | Total | Paid  | Balance | + fee |
|----------|----------|-------|-------|---------|-------|
| 24207    | 1121     | 5220  | 0     | 5220    | 5270  |
| 24206    | 1115     | 4788  | 0     | 4788    |       |
| 24205    | 1113     | 8035  | 6000  | 2035,2  |       |
| 24204    | 1119     | 11437 | 11437 | 0       |       |
| 24203    | 1117     | 9007  | 0     | 9007,2  |       |
| 24202    | 1116     | 8424  | 8424  | 0       |       |
| 24201    | 1120     | 1146  | 1000  | 146     |       |
| 24200    | 1112     | 9261  | 9261  | 0       |       |

Tax class and age will be used in subsequent formulas in the tax return.
Give these cells names using Formula - Define name, so that these names
can be used later on in formulas, instead of cell references.

TAX RETURN

| name | Kuliyakin | class | 1 | age | 35 |
|------|-----------|-------|---|-----|-----|

INCOME

| Item 1a | Salary | 250000 |
|---------|--------|--------|
| | Social security | |
| | Loan advantage | 2000 |
| | Company car | 15000 |
| Item 1d | Other income | 5600 |
| | Total income | 272600 |
| | | |
| Item 3b | Other benefits | 1000 |
| Item 5 | SUM (basis for min. deduction) | 273600 |

## Exercise 4a - number series and sorting

Use Edit - Insert to insert a new column for employee no. to the left
of employee name. Use Data - Series to generate employee numbers.
The first number is 1111, which you simply type in, and then the numbers
increase by 1.

Use Data - Sort to sort alphabetically by name.

| emp.no. | name | hours | hr.wage | wk.wage |
|---|---|---|---|---|
| 1111 | Andersen | 40 | 120 | 4800 |
| | Bond | 35 | 100 | 3500 |
| | Caudillo | 40 | 130 | 5200 |
| | Colombo | 50 | 60 | 3000 |
| | Corleone | 25 | 80 | 2000 |
| | Greer | 38 | 85 | 3230 |
| | Marple | 40 | 185 | 7400 |
| | Jones | 40 | 120 | 4800 |
| | Blofeld | 25 | 80 | 2000 |
| | Solo | 40 | 130 | 5200 |
| | Syse | 35 | 100 | 3500 |
| | Iacocca | 25 | 95 | 2375 |

# Exercise 4b - number series and sorting

Use Data - Series to generate invoice numbers. Type in the first number: 24200. Afterwards, this increases by 1.

Use Data - Sort to sort the debtor list by invoice number in descending order.

| Inv. no. | Cust.no. | Total | Paid | Balance |
|----------|----------|-------|------|---------|
| 24200 | 1112 | 9261 | 9261 | 0 |
| | 1120 | 1146 | 1000 | 146 |
| | 1116 | 8424 | 8424 | 0 |
| | 1117 | 9007 | 0 | 9007,2 |
| | 1119 | 11437 | 11437 | 0 |
| | 1113 | 8035 | 6000 | 2035,2 |
| | 1115 | 4788 | 0 | 4788 |
| | 1121 | 5220 | 0 | 5220 |

# Exercise 5a - linking spreadsheets

On another sheet, make a form for information about a single employee.
The form should include name, employee number, hourly wage, hours worked,
weekly wage, bonus and total wage paid out.

Retrieve information from the employee register, using linking
(formulas with =, not copying information)

| | | | *Uke 42* |
|---|---|---|---|
| **Andersen, Jaques** | | *Employee no.* | 1111 |
| *Rate* | 120 | *Salary* | 4800 |
| *Hours* | 40 | *Bonus* | 500 |
| | | *Total* | 5300 |

## Exercise 6a - formatting

Format the employee list so that headings appear in italic type.
One of the employees, Caudillo, has mentioned to you that actually his name is
"El Caudillo". Change this. As a result, the column will have to be widened.

Centre and put a box around the cell at the top of the sheet containing bonus
of 500. Right-justify the headings, except for name which can stay as it is, and
employee number. Centre the latter along with the rest of its column.

Add two lines at the top of the sheet and write the name of the department in
bold type, with 18-pt. size, and in grey (shadow). Remove gridlines from the
screen.

Give a name to the cell containing bonus amount. Insert the name in all formulas
which contain references to bonus.

**EDB Service**

Bonus      500

| emp.no. | name | hours | hr.wage | wk.wage | + bonus |
|---|---|---|---|---|---|
| 1111 | Andersen | 40 | 120 | 4800 | 4800 |
| 1119 | Blofeld | 25 | 80 | 2000 | 2000 |
| 1112 | Bond | 35 | 100 | 3500 | 3500 |
| 1113 | El Caudillo | 40 | 130 | 5200 | 5200 |
| 1114 | Colombo | 50 | 60 | 3000 | 3000 |
| 1115 | Corleone | 25 | 80 | 2000 | 2000 |
| 1116 | Greer | 38 | 85 | 3230 | 3230 |
| 1122 | Iacocca | 25 | 95 | 2375 | 2375 |
| 1118 | Jones | 40 | 120 | 4800 | 4800 |
| 1117 | Marple | 40 | 185 | 7400 | 7400 |
| 1120 | Solo | 40 | 130 | 5200 | 5200 |
| 1121 | Syse | 35 | 100 | 3500 | 3500 |

## Exercise 6b - formatting

Format the debtor list so that headings appear in italic type.
Format the amounts so that they appear with no decimals, and "$" before.
You will have to widen some of the columns.

Centre and put a box around the cell at the top of the sheet containing the fee
of 50. Right-justify the headings, except for invoice and customer number,
which should be centred along with the rest of their columns.

Insert a new column to the right of 'Total', and give it the heading 'Due'.
Write in due dates similar to the example below.

Add two lines at the top of the sheet and write "Invoice List" in bold type,
with 18-pt. size, and in grey (shadow). Write today's date in the top righthand
corner of the sheet. Remove gridlines from the screen.

## Invoice List

Date:    8.Oct.90

Fee :    | 50 |

| *Inv. no.* | *Cust.no.* | *Total* | *Due* | *Paid* | *Balance* | *+ fee* |
|:---:|:---:|---:|---:|---:|---:|---:|
| 24207 | 1121 | $5220 | 7.Oct | $0 | $5220 | $5270 |
| 24206 | 1115 | $4788 | 5.Oct | $0 | $4788 | $4838 |
| 24205 | 1113 | $8035 | 3.Oct | $6000 | $2035 | $2085 |
| 24204 | 1119 | $11437 | 1.Oct | $11437 | $0 | $50 |
| 24203 | 1117 | $9007 | 30.Sep | $0 | $9007 | $9057 |
| 24202 | 1116 | $8424 | 28.Sep | $8424 | $0 | $50 |
| 24201 | 1120 | $1146 | 26.Sep | $1000 | $146 | $196 |
| 24200 | 1112 | $9261 | 25.Sep | $9261 | $0 | $50 |

# Exercise 6c - formatting

Format your tax form with boxes, grey fields (shadow), justifying and fonts as shown in the example below. Remove gridlines.

|  | TAX RETURN |  |  |
|---|---|---|---|

| name | Kuliyakin | class | 1 | age | 35 |
|---|---|---|---|---|---|

| INCOME |
|---|

| Item 1a | Salary | 250000 |
|---|---|---|
|  | Social security |  |
|  | Loan advantage | 2000 |
|  | Company car | 15000 |
| Item 1d | Other income | 5600 |
|  | Total income | 272600 |

| Item 3b | Other benefits | 1000 |
|---|---|---|
| Item 5 | SUM (basis for min. deduction) | 273600 |

## Exercise 7a - printout

Use File - Printer setup to select printer.

Use File - Page setup to remove gridlines and row/column headings
(A, B, C ... and 1, 2, 3 ...) from the printout.

Use File - Page setup to remove page headings,
and to change the footer to "p." instead of "Page".
Cause the footer to be written in italic font.

Print out, but first look at Preview.


**EDB Service**

Bonus | 500

| emp.no. | name | hours | hr.wage | wk.wage | + bonus |
|---------|------|-------|---------|---------|---------|
| 1111 | Andersen | 40 | 120 | 4800 | 4800 |
| 1119 | Blofeld | 25 | 80 | 2000 | 2000 |
| 1112 | Bond | 35 | 100 | 3500 | 3500 |
| 1113 | El Caudillo | 40 | 130 | 5200 | 5200 |
| 1114 | Colombo | 50 | 60 | 3000 | 3000 |
| 1115 | Corleone | 25 | 80 | 2000 | 2000 |
| 1116 | Greer | 38 | 85 | 3230 | 3230 |
| 1122 | Iacocca | 25 | 95 | 2375 | 2375 |
| 1118 | Jones | 40 | 120 | 4800 | 4800 |
| 1117 | Marple | 40 | 185 | 7400 | 7400 |
| 1120 | Solo | 40 | 130 | 5200 | 5200 |
| 1121 | Syse | 35 | 100 | 3500 | 3500 |

## *Exercise 7b - printout*

Use File - Printer setup and then Setup to get a horizontal printout.

Use File - Page setup to remove gridlines and row/column headers
(A, B, C ... and 1, 2, 3 ...) from the printout.

Use File - Page setup to remove page headings,
and to change the footer to "p." instead of "Page".
Cause the footer to be written in italic font.

Print out, but first look at Preview.

## Invoice List

Date:   8.Oct.90

Fee :       50

| Inv. no. | Cust.no. | Total | Due | Paid | Balance | + fee |
|---|---|---|---|---|---|---|
| 24207 | 1121 | $5220 | 7.Oct | $0 | $5220 | $5220 |
| 24206 | 1115 | $4788 | 5.Oct | $0 | $4788 | $4788 |
| 24205 | 1113 | $8035 | 3.Oct | $6000 | $2035 | $2035 |
| 24204 | 1119 | $11437 | 1.Oct | $11437 | $0 | $0 |
| 24203 | 1117 | $9007 | 30.Sep | $0 | $9007 | $9007 |
| 24202 | 1116 | $8424 | 28.Sep | $8424 | $0 | $0 |
| 24201 | 1120 | $1146 | 26.Sep | $1000 | $146 | $146 |
| 24200 | 1112 | $9261 | 25.Sep | $9261 | $0 | $0 |

## Exercise 7c - printout

Use File - Printer setup to select printer.

Use File - Page setup to remove gridlines and row/column headings
(A, B, C ... and 1, 2, 3 ...) from the printout.

Use File - Page setup to remove page headings,
and to change the footer to "p." instead of "Page".
Cause the footer to be written in italic font.

Print out, but first look at Preview.

| | TAX RETURN | |
|---|---|---|

| name | Kuliyakin | **class** | 1 | age | 35 |
|---|---|---|---|---|---|

**INCOME**

| Item 1a | Salary | 250000 |
|---|---|---|
| | Social security | |
| | Loan advantage | 2000 |
| | Company car | 15000 |
| Item 1d | Other income | 5600 |
| | Total income | 272600 |

| Item 3b | Other benefits | 1000 |
|---|---|---|
| Item 5 | SUM (basis for min. deduction) | 273600 |

## Exercise 8a - mathematical functions

Use the SUM-function to add the figures in each column.
Use the AVERAGE-function to average the figures in each column.
Use the MAX-function to get the highest number in each column.
Use the MIN-function to get the lowest number in each column.
Use Edit - Fill right to copy the formulas to the right.
Use the COUNT-function to count the number of employees.
Use the NOW-function to get the day's date.
(Format - Number to get date format)

**EDB Service**                                                    (now)

Bonus        | 500 |

| emp.no. | name | hours | hr.wage | wk.wage | + bonus |
|---------|------|-------|---------|---------|---------|
| 1111 | Andersen | 40 | 120 | 4800 | 4800 |
| 1119 | Blofeld | 25 | 80 | 2000 | 2000 |
| 1112 | Bond | 35 | 100 | 3500 | 3500 |
| 1113 | El Caudillo | 40 | 130 | 5200 | 5200 |
| 1114 | Colombo | 50 | 60 | 3000 | 3000 |
| 1115 | Corleone | 25 | 80 | 2000 | 2000 |
| 1116 | Greer | 38 | 85 | 3230 | 3230 |
| 1122 | Iacocca | 25 | 95 | 2375 | 2375 |
| 1118 | Jones | 40 | 120 | 4800 | 4800 |
| 1117 | Marple | 40 | 185 | 7400 | 7400 |
| 1120 | Solo | 40 | 130 | 5200 | 5200 |
| 1121 | Syse | 35 | 100 | 3500 | 3500 |

|         |           |           |           |           |
|---------|-----------|-----------|-----------|-----------|
| Sum | (sum) | (sum) | (sum) | (sum) |
| Average | (average) | (average) | (average) | (average) |
| Highest | (max) | (max) | (max) | (max) |
| Lowest | (min) | (min) | (min) | (min) |
| Count | (count) | | | |

## Exercise 8b - mathematical functions

Use the SUM-function to add the figures in each column.
Use the AVERAGE-function to average the figures in each column.
Use the MAX-function to get the highest number in each column.
Use the MIN-function to get the lowest number in each column.
Use Edit - Fill right to copy the formulas to the right.
Press DEL and RET to clear away sum, average, etc. for due date.
Use the COUNT-function to count the number of invoices.
Use the NOW-function to get the day's date.
(Format - Number to get date format)

**Invoice List**

Date:   8.Oct.90

Fee :       50

| Inv. no. | Cust.no. | Total | Due | Paid | Balance | + fee |
|---|---|---|---|---|---|---|
| 24207 | 1121 | $5220 | 7.Oct | $0 | $5220 | $5220 |
| 24206 | 1115 | $4788 | 5.Oct | $0 | $4788 | $4788 |
| 24205 | 1113 | $8035 | 3.Oct | $6000 | $2035 | $2035 |
| 24204 | 1119 | $11437 | 1.Oct | $11437 | $0 | $0 |
| 24203 | 1117 | $9007 | 30.Sep | $0 | $9007 | $9007 |
| 24202 | 1116 | $8424 | 28.Sep | $8424 | $0 | $0 |
| 24201 | 1120 | $1146 | 26.Sep | $1000 | $146 | $146 |
| 24200 | 1112 | $9261 | 25.Sep | $9261 | $0 | $0 |
| | Sum | (sum) | (sum) | (sum) | (sum) | |
| | Average | (average) | (average) | (average) | (average) | |
| | Highest | (max) | (max) | (max) | (max) | |
| | Lowest | (min) | (min) | (min) | (min) | |
| | Count | (count) | | | | |

# Exercise 8c - SUM

Use the SUM function now to calculate total income in item 1d and the sum in item 5.

|  | TAX RETURN |  |  |
|---|---|---|---|

| name | Kuliyakin | class | 1 | age | 35 |
|---|---|---|---|---|---|

## INCOME

| Item 1a | Salary | 250000 |
|---|---|---|
|  | Social security |  |
|  | Loan advantage | 2000 |
|  | Company car | 15000 |
| Item 1d | Other income | 5600 |
|  | Total income | 272600 |

| Item 3b | Other benefits | 1000 |
|---|---|---|
| Item 5 | SUM (basis for min. deduction) | 273600 |

## Exercise 9a - IF

Insert a column to the left of '+ bonus'. Give it the heading 'bonus'.
Use the IF-function to test if hours worked is more than 20.
If it is, than the employee gets a bonus, and if not, forget it (0).
Use Edit - Fill down to copy the formulas down, and Edit - Fill right
to copy the formulas on the bottom line, to the right.

**EDB Service**

Bonus     500

| emp.no. | name | hours | hr.wage | wk.wage | bonus | + bonus |
|---|---|---|---|---|---|---|
| 1111 | Andersen | 40 | 120 | 4800 | (if) | |
| 1119 | Blofeld | 25 | 80 | 2000 | (if) | |
| 1112 | Bond | 40 | 100 | 4000 | (if) | |
| 1113 | El Caudillo | 40 | 130 | 5200 | (if) | |
| 1114 | Colombo | 40 | 60 | 2400 | (if) | |
| 1115 | Corleone | 25 | 80 | 2000 | (if) | |
| 1116 | Greer | 10 | 85 | 850 | (if) | |
| 1122 | Iacocca | 25 | 95 | 2375 | (if) | |
| 1118 | Jones | 40 | 120 | 4800 | (if) | |
| 1117 | Marple | 40 | 185 | 7400 | (if) | |
| 1120 | Solo | 10 | 130 | 1300 | (if) | |
| 1121 | Syse | 25 | 100 | 2500 | (if) | |
| | Sum | 360 | 1285 | 39625 | (sum) | (sum) |
| | Average | 30 | 107 | 3302 | (average) | (average) |
| | Highest | 40 | 185 | 7400 | (max) | (max) |
| | Lowest | 10 | 60 | 850 | (min) | (min) |
| | Count | 12 | | | | |

# Exercise 9b - IF

Insert a column to the left of '+ fee'. Give it the heading 'Fee'.
Use the IF-function to test if balance is higher than 100.
If it is, the customer is charged a fee, and otherwise, the cell remains empty.
Use already-defined cell names, and adjust the formulas for '+ fee'.

Insert a column after '+ fee'. Give it the heading 'overdue'.
Write a formula to find number of days overdue. Use IF first to test
if balance is nil, and if so, the cell can remain empty (""). Otherwise,
a formula calculates days overdue (today's date minus due date).
Write this formula as the third parameter inside of the IF-function.

Use Edit - Fill down to copy the formulas down, and
Edit - Fill right to copy the formulas on the bottom line, to the right.

**Invoice List**

Date:    8.Oct.90

Fee :          50

| Total | Due | Paid | Balance | Fee | + fee | Overdue |
|-------|-----|------|---------|-----|-------|---------|
| 5220 | 7.Oct | 0 | 5220 | (if) | (bal.+fee) | (if) |
| 4788 | 5.Oct | 0 | 4788 | (if) | (bal.+fee) | (if) |
| 8035,2 | 3.Oct | 6000 | 2035,2 | (if) | (bal.+fee) | (if) |
| 11437,2 | 1.Oct | 11437,2 | 0 | (if) | (bal.+fee) | (if) |
| 9007,2 | 30.Sep | 0 | 9007,2 | (if) | (bal.+fee) | (if) |
| 8424 | 28.Sep | 8424 | 0 | (if) | (bal.+fee) | (if) |
| 1146 | 26.Sep | 1000 | 146 | (if) | (bal.+fee) | (if) |
| 9261 | 25.Sep | 9261 | 0 | (if) | (bal.+fee) | (if) |
| | Sum | 36122 | 21196 | (sum) | (sum) | |
| | Average | 4515 | 2650 | (average) | (average) | |
| | Highest | 11437 | 9007 | (max) | (max) | |
| | Lowest | 0 | 0 | (min) | (min) | |

# Exercise 9c - cell naming and IF

Type in the following variables on the top of the sheet, and define with
Formula - Define name:
1. Tax free limit for shares (class 1 and 2)
2. Standard deduction (minimum and maximum limits)
3. Travel amount that cannot be deducted

Tax free amount in item 11 is 3000 in class 1, 6000 in class 2.
Use IF to test for tax class.
Sum of federal tax is the sum of item 10a, 10b and stock dividend, minus tax-free amount.
Sum of local tax is the sum of item 10a and 10b minus tax-free amount.
However, you don't want any negative numbers in these cells, and that is exactly
what you would get if the tax-free amount is higher than the sum of the other items.
So you will need to include an IF to test if this is the case, and if so, make the result 0.

As for standard deduction, it is = the low limit (mindeduct) if income * 13% is lower
than the low limit. If income * 13% is higher than the high limit (maxdeduct), then
the result would be the high limit. For example:
If income = 200000, 200000*13%=26000, so standard deduction would be 7000.
If income is 18000, 18000*13%=2340, so standard deduction would be 3000.

Sum of deductibles can't be a negative number either, so here an IF needs to
Sum of deductibles can't be a negative number either, so here an IF needs to
be included, in the same way as with sum of federal and local tax.

| | | |
|---|---|---|
| freediv1 | 3000 | item 11 |
| freediv2 | 6000 | |
| mindeduct | 3000 | item 21a |
| maxdeduct | 7000 | |
| mintravel | 5000 | item 24b |

| TAX RETURN |
|---|

**name** Kuliyakin  **class** [ 1 ] **age** [ 35 ]

| INCOME |
|---|

| | | |
|---|---|---|
| Item 1a | Salary | 250000 |
| | Social security | |
| | Loan advantage | 2000 |
| | Company car | 15000 |
| Item 1d | Other income | 5600 |
| | Total income | 272600 |

| | | |
|---|---|---|
| Item 3b | Other benefits | 1000 |
| Item 5 | SUM (basis for min. deduction) | 273600 |

| | | |
|---|---|---|
| Item 10a | Interest | 5000 |
| Item 10b | Insurance, savings div. | 3000 |
| Item 11 | Stock dividend | 4000 |
| | Tax-free allowance (for p. 10/11) | (if) |
| | Sum federal tax | (if) |
| | Sum local tax | (if) |
| Item 12-19 | Other income | 2500 |

| | | |
|---|---|---|
| Item 20 | SUM gross income | |

## INCOME DEDUCTION

| | | | |
|---|---|---|---|
| Item 21a | Standard deduction | | (if) |
| Item 24a | Travel to/from work | 14000 | |
| Item 24b | Travel exp . for home visit | 0 | |
| | Min. amount - NOT to be deducted | | |
| | SUM deductible travel exp. | (if) | |
| Item 26a | Parent's deduction | | |
| Item 26b | Single parent deduction | | |
| Item 29 | Entertainment | | |
| Item 30 | Pension | | |
| Item 31a | Interest on debt | | |
| Item 31b | Deficit portion in real estate co. | | |
| Item 32 | Other deduction | | |
| Item 33 | Sum deductions | | |

## Calculation of net income

| | | |
|---|---|---|
| Item 37 | Special deduction | |
| item 38 | Net income local (p.20 minus 33) | |
| item 39 | Stock dividend (p.10b) | |
| item 40 | Net income federal (p.38 + 39a) | |

# Exercise 10 - PMT

You are considering buying a car for 80000.
The finance plan is as follows:
- 35% down payment
- monthly loan repayments for 3 years
- at 15,9% interest

Use the PMT-function to calculate the amount of each repayment.
Make some variables at the top of the sheet for annuity, interest,
number of years, periods per year, amount of loan, price of car, % financing
and down payment. Use simple formulas to calculate price and down payment.
Use Formula - Create Names to define names for the cells containing variables.

Make a table on the same sheet which shows a breakdown of repayments
into payments on principal, interest repayments and resulting balance for
each period. Use the PPMT and IPMT functions.

Use Formula - Apply Names to replace cell references in the formulas
with the newly-defined names.

| | | | period | interest | principal | balance |
|---|---|---|---|---|---|---|
| Annuity | 2809 | | 1 | 1060 | 1749 | 78251 |
| Interest | 15,9% | | 2 | 1037 | 1772 | 76480 |
| Number of yrs. | 3 | | 3 | 1013 | 1795 | 74684 |
| Periods | 12 | | 4 | 990 | 1819 | 72865 |
| Loan amount | 52000 | | 5 | 965 | 1843 | 71022 |
| Price | 80000 | | 6 | 941 | 1868 | 69155 |
| Financing | 65% | | 7 | 916 | 1892 | 67262 |
| Down payment | 28000 | | 8 | 891 | 1917 | 65345 |
| | | | 9 | 866 | 1943 | 63402 |
| | | | 10 | 840 | 1969 | 61434 |
| | | | 11 | 814 | 1995 | 59439 |
| | | | 12 | 788 | 2021 | 57418 |
| | | | 13 | 761 | 2048 | 55370 |
| | | | 14 | 734 | 2075 | 53295 |
| | | | 15 | 706 | 2102 | 51193 |
| | | | 16 | 678 | 2130 | 49062 |
| | | | 17 | 650 | 2159 | 46904 |
| | | | 18 | 621 | 2187 | 44717 |

# Exercise 11 - PV

You have decided to buy a house, but need to find out which price range
you can afford. What you know is that you can afford repayments of 5000 per
month, and have 100000 in savings which can be used as down payment.

The finance plan is as follows:
- 15% down payment
- monthly loan repayments for 30 years
- at 12,4% interest

Use the PV-function to calculate the loan amount you could handle.
Make some variables at the top of the sheet for annuity, interest,
number of years, periods per year, amount of loan, price of car, % financing
and down payment. Use simple formulas to calculate price and down payment.
Use Formula - Create Names to define names for the cells containing variables.

Make a table on the same sheet which shows a breakdown of repayments
into payments on principal, interest repayments and resulting balance for
each period. Use the PPMT and IPMT functions.

Use Formula - Apply Names to replace cell references in the formulas
with the newly-defined names.

| | | period | interest | principal | balance |
|---|---|---|---|---|---|
| Annuity | 5000 | 1 | 4876 | 124 | 471795 |
| Interest | 12,4% | 2 | 4875 | 125 | 471671 |
| Number of yrs. | 30 | 3 | 4874 | 126 | 471545 |
| Periods | 12 | 4 | 4873 | 127 | 471417 |
| Loan amount | 471919 | 5 | 4871 | 129 | 471288 |
| Price | 555199 | 6 | 4870 | 130 | 471158 |
| Financing | 85% | 7 | 4869 | 131 | 471027 |
| Down payment | 83280 | 8 | 4867 | 133 | 470894 |
| | | 9 | 4866 | 134 | 470760 |
| | | 10 | 4865 | 135 | 470625 |
| | | 11 | 4863 | 137 | 470488 |
| | | 12 | 4862 | 138 | 470350 |
| | | 13 | 4860 | 140 | 470210 |
| | | 14 | 4859 | 141 | 470069 |
| | | 15 | 4857 | 143 | 469926 |

# Exercise 12 - RATE

You are considering several savings plans.
Use the RATE function to compare interest rates of the different plans.

Plan 1: you receive 800000 after 20 years if you deposit 5000 twice a year.
Plan 2: you receive 500000 after 20 years if you deposit 7000 once a year.
Plan 3: you receive 50450 after 20 years if you make a one-time deposit of 5000.

| | |
|---|---|
| Interest | |
| Future amount | 800000 |
| 1-time deposit | |
| Annuity | 5000 |
| Number of yrs. | 20 |
| No. of periods | 2 |

| | |
|---|---|
| Interest | |
| Future amount | 500000 |
| 1-time deposit | |
| Annuity | 7000 |
| Number of yrs. | 20 |
| No. of periods | 1 |

| | |
|---|---|
| Interest | |
| Future amount | 50450 |
| 1-time deposit | 5000 |
| Annuity | |
| Number of yrs. | 20 |
| No. of periods | 1 |

# Exercise 13 - FV

You are thinking of saving 750 each quarter for 10 years.
Interest is 11,4%. Use the FV-function to calculate how much you will
have saved up after 10 years.

Make some variables at the top of the sheet for annuity, interest,
number of years, periods per year and total amount saved.
Use Formula - Create Names to define names for the cells containing variables.

Make a table on the same sheet which shows a breakdown of repayments
into payments on principal, interest repayments and resulting balance for
each period. Use the PPMT and IPMT functions.

Use Formula - Apply Names to replace cell references in the formulas
with the newly-defined names.

|  |  |
|---|---|
| Annuity | 750 |
| Interest | 11,4% |
| Number of yrs. | 10 |
| Periods | 4 |
| Savings | |

| Period | Interest | Balance |
|---|---|---|
| 1 | 21 | 771 |
| 2 | 43 | 1565 |
| 3 | 66 | 2381 |
| 4 | 89 | 3220 |
| 5 | 113 | 4083 |
| 6 | 138 | 4971 |
| 7 | 163 | 5884 |
| 8 | 189 | 6823 |
| 9 | 216 | 7789 |
| 10 | 243 | 8782 |
| 11 | 272 | 9804 |
| 12 | 301 | 10855 |
| 13 | 331 | 11935 |
| 14 | 362 | 13047 |
| 15 | 393 | 14190 |
| 16 | 426 | 15366 |
| 17 | 459 | 16575 |
| 18 | 494 | 17819 |
| 19 | 529 | 19098 |
| 20 | 566 | 20414 |
| 21 | 603 | 21767 |
| 22 | 642 | 23159 |

## Exercise 14 - IRR

You are considering an investment which involves providing 50000 in capital.
You have estimated your investment return each year for 10 years. Use the
IRR function to calculate the actual interest return on your investment.

| | |
|---|---|
| Investment | -50000 |
| Interest return | 7,8% |
| Number of yrs. | 10 |

| | | |
|---|---|---|
| Investment: | | -50000 |
| Return: | Year 1 | -1000 |
| | Year 2 | 1000 |
| | Year 3 | 2500 |
| | Year 4 | 6500 |
| | Year 5 | 8000 |
| | Year 6 | 10000 |
| | Year 7 | 12000 |
| | Year 8 | 14000 |
| | Year 9 | 16000 |
| | Year 10 | 18000 |

## Exercise 15 - charts

Type in the sales information shown in the example below.
Present this information in the form of a readable, self-explanatory chart.

**Sales in Northern Norway**

| District | Sales 86 | Sales 87 | Sales 88 | Sales 89 | Sales 90 |
|----------|----------|----------|----------|----------|----------|
| Troms | 69320 | 90116 | 135174 | 202761 | 185263 |
| Nordland | 13900 | 18070 | 27105 | 32154 | 48231 |
| Finnmark | 8630 | 11219 | 9588 | 9642 | 10254 |

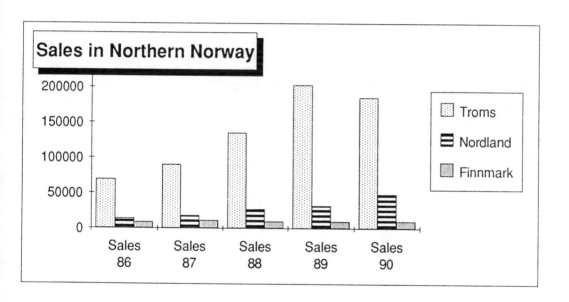

## Exercise 16a - VLOOKUP

Use the employee form you made in exercise 5a.
Use VLOOKUP-formulas to look up name, hourly rate, hours worked,
weekly wage, bonus and total wages corresponding to the employee
number which is input.

|  |  |  | **Week 42** |
|---|---|---|---|
| **Andersen, Jaques** |  | *Emp. no.* | 1111 |
| *Rate* | 120 | *Wage* | 4800 |
| *Hours* | 40 | *Bonus* | 500 |
|  |  | *Total* | 5300 |

# Exercise 16b - VLOOKUP

On a new sheet, make a form for information about a single invoice.
Use VLOOKUP-formulas to find customer no., invoice no., due date,
amount paid, balance, penalty fee and total payable. These should
correspond to the invoice number which is input.

| | | | | |
|---|---|---|---|---|
| *Inv. no.* | 24205 | *Cust.no.* | 1113 | |
| | | | | |
| *Inv. total* | 8035 | *Balance* | 2035 | |
| *Due date* | 3.Oct | *Penalty fee* | 50 | |
| *Paid* | 6000 | **Total payable** | **2085** | |

# *Exercise 16c - VLOOKUP*

Add some variables to the list at the top of the sheet, using Formula - Define name:

1. Welfare
2. Taxfree amount for special state tax (class 1 and 2)
3. Special tax %

Welfare is 7,9% of gross income (p. 1d)
The taxfree amount for special state tax is 195000 for class 1 and 235000 for class 2.
Special tax is 8,5% of above amount.

## Special state tax

Sum salary and pension is taken from the sum in item 1d.
Stock dividend is taken from item 39.
For taxfree amount, use IF to test for tax class (1 or 2).
The basis for calculating special tax is the sum of 'sum salary and pension'
and 'stock dividend' minus 'taxfree amount'. An IF-function will be needed
here to avoid negative numbers in the results.
Special tax is special tax % (8,5%) of 'amount for special tax'.

## Income tax to state, city and district

Net income local is taken from item 38.
For 'local and district tax", use the VLOOKUP-function. The lookup key is
net income local. The tax table you made in exercise 2c is the lookup table.
Column number depends on whether tax class is 1 or 2.
So in the last parameter of the VLOOKUP-formula, you'll need IF.
Net income state is taken from item 40.
For state tax, use the VLOOKUP-function. The lookup key is net income
local. The tax table here is also the lookup table, and the column number
also depends on whether tax class is 1 or 2 (IF).

*(example on following page)*

| | | |
|---|---|---|
| freediv1 | 3000 | item 11 |
| freediv2 | 6000 | |
| mindeduct | 3000 | item 21a |
| maxdeduct | 7000 | |
| mintravel | 5000 | item 24b |
| welfare | 7,9% | |
| freespec1 | 195000 | |
| freespec2 | 235000 | |
| spectax | 8,5% | |

| TAX RETURN |
|---|

| name | Kuliyakin | class | 1 | age | 35 |
|---|---|---|---|---|---|

## INCOME

| | | | |
|---|---|---|---|
| Item 1a | Salary | 250000 | |
| | Social security | | |
| | Loan advantage | 2000 | |
| | Company car | 15000 | |
| Item 1d | Other income | 5600 | |
| | Total income | 272600 | |
| | | | |
| Item 3b | Other benefits | 1000 | |
| Item 5 | SUM (basis for min. deduction) | 273600 | 273600 |
| | | | |
| Item 10a | Interest | 5000 | |
| Item 10b | Insurance, savings div. | 3000 | |
| Item 11 | Stock dividend | 4000 | |
| | Taxfree allowance (for p. 10/11) | 3000 | |
| | Sum state tax | 9000 | 9000 |
| | Sum local tax | 5000 | |
| Item 12-19 | Other income | 2500 | 2500 |
| | | | |
| Item 20 | SUM gross income | | 285100 |

## INCOME DEDUCTION

| Item 21a | Standard deduction | | | 7000 |
|----------|--------------------|---|---|------|
| Item 24a | Travel to/from work | 14000 | | |
| Item 24b | Travel exp . for home visit | 0 | | |
| | Min. amount - NOT to be deducted | -5000 | | |
| | SUM deductible travel exp. | 9000 | 9000 | |
| Item 26a | Parent's deduction | | | |
| Item 26b | Single parent deduction | | | |
| Item 29 | Entertainment | | | |
| Item 30 | Pension | | | |
| Item 31a | Interest on debt | | | |
| Item 31b | Deficit portion in real estate co. | | | |
| Item 32 | Other deduction | | | |
| Item 33 | Sum deductions | | | 16000 |

## Calculation of net income

| Item 37 | Special deduction | |
|---------|-------------------|---|
| item 38 | Net income local (p.20 minus 33) | 285100 |
| item 39 | Stock dividend (p.10b) | 4000 |
| item 40 | Net income fed. (p.38 + 39a) | 289100 |

## Life insurance

| Item 41a | Group life insurance | 0 |
|----------|----------------------|---|
| Item 41b | Individual life insurance | 1000 |

**Welfare**
7,9% of gross income (P.1)

**Special federal tax**
Sum salary and pension (P.1-2)
Stock dividend (P.39)
Tax-free amount
Basis for calculation of special tax
Special tax, 8,5% of above

(if)
(if)

**Income tax to fed., city, district**
Net income local (P.38)
Local and district tax
Net income fed. (P.40)
Federal tax

(vlookup)

(vlookup)

# Exercise 17a - database

On a new sheet, make a criteria and result area, and use Data - Extract to generate a list with name, hours worked and salary + bonus for all employees that worked 40 hours.

**EDB Service**

Date:    8.Oct.90

CRITERIA

| emp.no. | name | hours | hr.wage | wk.wage | bonus | + bonus |
|---------|------|-------|---------|---------|-------|---------|
|         |      | 40    |         |         |       |         |

RESULT

| name | hours | hr.wage |
|------|-------|---------|
| Andersen | 40 | 5300 |
| Bond | 40 | 4500 |
| El Caudillo | 40 | 5700 |
| Colombo | 40 | 2900 |
| Jones | 40 | 5300 |
| Marple | 40 | 7900 |

## Exercise 17b - database

On a new sheet, make a criteria and result area, and use Data - Extract to generate a list with invoice number, customer number, balance and overdue for all outstanding invoices (overdue and with remaining balance).

**Invoice List**

Date:      8.Oct.90

CRITERIA

| Inv. no. | Cust.no. | Balance | Overdue |
|----------|----------|---------|---------|
|          |          | >0      | >0      |

RESULT

| Inv. no. | Cust.no. | Total | Due | Paid | Balance | Overdue |
|----------|----------|-------|-----|------|---------|---------|
| 24207 | 1121 | 5220 | 7.Oct | 0 | 5220 | 1 day |
| 24206 | 1115 | 4788 | 5.Oct | 0 | 4788 | 3 day |
| 24205 | 1113 | 8035 | 3.Oct | 6000 | 2035 | 4 day |
| 24203 | 1117 | 9007 | 30.Sep | 0 | 9007 | 8 day |
| 24201 | 1120 | 1146 | 26.Sep | 1000 | 146 | 11 day |

# *Exercise 18a - database functions*

On a new sheet, make two criteria areas, one for those who work over 35 hours,
and one for those who work 35 hours or less.

Use DSUM to calculate total weekly wages and DAVERAGE to find average
weekly wages and hourly rate.

**EDB Service**

Date:    8.Oct.90

|                  | *hours*      | *rate*       |
|------------------|--------------|--------------|
|                  | >35          | <36          |
| Total wk. wages  | *(dsum)*     | *(dsum)*     |
| Avg. wk. wages   | *(daverage)* | *(daverage)* |
| Avg. rate        | *(daverage)* | *(daverage)* |

# Exercise 18b - database functions

On a new sheet, make three criteria areas, one for all overdue invoices,
one for all invoices more than 7 days overdue, and one for more than 10 days
overdue.

Use DSUM to calculate total balance and DAVERAGE to find average
balance.

**Invoice List**

Date:       8.Oct.90

|  | Overdue >0 | Overdue >7 | Overdue >10 |
|---|---|---|---|
| Total balance | (dsum) | (dsum) | (dsum) |
| Avg. balance | (daverage) | (daverage) | (daverage) |

## Exercise 19a - macros

On the same sheet you made criteria and result areas (exercise 16),
create a macro to:

1. Select the result area.
2. Choose Data - Extract and OK.
3. Move the curser back to the criteria area.

Write some instructions to future users of the macro.

**EDB Service**

Date:     8.Oct.90

Type in criteria and press CTRL A to get your information.

CRITERIA

| emp.no. | name | hours | hr.wage | wk.wage | bonus | + bonus |
|---------|------|-------|---------|---------|-------|---------|
|         |      | 40    |         |         |       |         |

RESULT

| | name | hours | hr.wage |
|---|------|-------|---------|
| | Andersen | 40 | 5300 |
| | Bond | 40 | 4500 |
| | El Caudillo | 40 | 5700 |
| | Colombo | 40 | 2900 |
| | Jones | 40 | 5300 |
| | Marple | 40 | 7900 |

## Exercise 19b - macros

On the same sheet you made criteria and result areas (exercise 16),
create a macro to:

1. Select the result area.
2. Choose Data - Extract and OK.
3. Move the curser back to the criteria area.

Write some instructions to future users of the macro.

**Invoice List**

Date:     8.Oct.90

Type in criteria and press CTRL D to get your information.

CRITERIA

| Inv. no. | Cust.no. | Balance | Overdue |
|----------|----------|---------|---------|
|          |          | >0      | >0      |

RESULT

| Inv. no. | Cust.no. | Total | Due | Paid | Balance | Overdue |
|----------|----------|-------|------|------|---------|---------|
| 24207 | 1121 | 5220 | 7.Oct | 0 | 5220 | 1 day |
| 24206 | 1115 | 4788 | 5.Oct | 0 | 4788 | 3 day |
| 24205 | 1113 | 8035 | 3.Oct | 6000 | 2035 | 4 day |
| 24203 | 1117 | 9007 | 30.Sep | 0 | 9007 | 8 day |
| 24201 | 1120 | 1146 | 26.Sep | 1000 | 146 | 11 day |

# Part 3 | Models

## Deviation from budget: September

| Periode 9 | Accumulated | | | Deviation from | |
|---|---|---|---|---|---|
| | To date | Budgeted | Last yr. | Budgeted | Last yr. |
| Gross income | 15378723 | 13050000 | 17835115 | 2328723 | -2456393 |
| Variable expenses | 6527014 | 4567500 | 6169552 | 1959514 | 357462 |
| Marketing expenses | 171091 | 162000 | 218823 | 9091 | -47732 |
| Operational expenses | 7948485 | 7626600 | 9546239 | 321885 | -1597754 |
| | | | | | |
| Total expenses | 14646590 | 12356100 | 15934614 | 2290490 | -1288024 |
| | | | | | |
| Operational profit/loss (sum gross income minus var. and fixed expenses) | 732133 | 693900 | 1900501 | 38233 | -1168368 |

# Model A

# Financial analysis

*This model consists of five linked spreadsheets and a macro.*

**1** a monthly budget

**2** a daily ledger

**3** a monthly accounts book

**4** a macro to transfer ledger accounts to the monthly accounts book

**5** last year's accounts

**6** an analysis of the year's accounts compared with the year's budget, and with the previous year's accounts

| | | | | | |
|---|---|---|---|---|---|
| **Monthly Budget** | In the monthly budget, income and expenses are entered under January for each post. Fill right for the remaining months. | | | | |

Formulas then:
1. Calculate totals for each of the main categories (e.g. gross income).
2. Calculate operational profit.
3. Calculate yearly totals for each post.

| | A | B | C | D | E | F |
|---|---|---|---|---|---|---|
| 1 | | | *1991 Budget* | | | |
| 2 | | | | | | |
| 3 | | | January | February | March | April |
| 4 | | Gross income | 1.450.000 | 1.450.000 | 1.450.000 | 1.450.000 |
| 5 | | Variable expenses | 507.500 | 507.500 | 507.500 | 507.500 |
| 6 | | Marketing expenses | 18.000 | 18.000 | 18.000 | 18.000 |
| 7 | | Operational expenses | 847.400 | 847.400 | 847.400 | 847.400 |
| 8 | | | | | | |
| 9 | | Total expenses | 1.372.900 | 1.372.900 | 1.372.900 | 1.372.900 |
| 10 | | | | | | |
| 11 | | Operational profit/loss | 77.100 | 77.100 | 77.100 | 77.100 |
| 12 | | (sum gross income minus | | | | |
| 13 | | var. and fixed expenses) | | | | |
| 14 | | | | | | |
| 15 | Gross income | Sales | 1.450.000 | 1.450.000 | 1.450.000 | 1.450.000 |
| 16 | | Rent income | 0 | 0 | 0 | 0 |
| 17 | | Investment | 0 | 0 | 0 | 0 |
| 18 | Variable expenses | Raw mat. | 500.000 | 500.000 | 500.000 | 500.000 |
| 19 | | Misc. | 0 | 0 | 0 | 0 |
| 20 | | Freight | 7.500 | 7.500 | 7.500 | 7.500 |
| 21 | Marketing expenses | Marketing | 5.000 | 5.000 | 5.000 | 5.000 |
| 22 | | Printing | 2.000 | 2.000 | 2.000 | 2.000 |

### KEY FORMULAS

| Cell | Formula | Comments |
|---|---|---|
| O15 | =SUM(C15:N15) | This calculates total sales. Fill down. |
| C4 | =SUM(C15:C17) | This calculates gross income. |
| C5 | =SUM(C18:C20) | This calculates variable expenses. |
| C6 | =SUM(C21:C24) | This calculates marketing expenses. |
| C7 | =SUM(C25:C41) | This calculates operation expenses. |
| C9 | =SUM(C5:C7) | This calculates total expenses. |
| C11 | =C4-C9 | This calculates operational profit. Fill right all January calculations. |

**Daily Ledger**

In the daily ledger, day, description, code and amount are entered for each item.

Formulas then:
1. Place the amount under the correct column according to its code.
2. Total each column, so that the last row contains totals.
3. Retrieve the row of totals into a column at the far right of the sheet.

| | A | B | C | D | E | F | G | H |
|---|---|---|---|---|---|---|---|---|
| 1 | | | September accounts ledger | | | | | |
| 2 | | | Press CTRL a to transfer figures to yearly account book. | | | | | |
| 3 | Month | | | | | Code | | |
| 4 | 9 | | | | | 1 | 2 | 3 |
| 5 | | | | | | Gross income | | |
| 6 | Day | Description | Code | Amount | | Sales | Rent income | Investment |
| 7 | 1 | mail | 17 | 1250 | | | | |
| 8 | 1 | invno. 12445 | 1 | 222040 | | 222040 | | |
| 9 | 2 | mail brochures | 9 | 12480 | | | | |
| 10 | 5 | 500 k. cinammon | 4 | 244410 | | | | |
| 11 | 5 | invno. 12450 | 1 | 308490 | | 308490 | | |
| 12 | 6 | freight invno. 12477 | 6 | 2560 | | | | |
| 13 | 6 | paper | 16 | 3500 | | | | |
| 14 | 7 | invno. 12449 | 1 | 160290 | | 160290 | | |
| 15 | 8 | invno. 12448 | 1 | 320840 | | 320840 | | |
| 16 | 9 | plastic bags | 4 | 2680 | | | | |
| 17 | 9 | invno. 12439 | 1 | 123240 | | 123240 | | |
| 18 | 9 | mail | 17 | 960 | | | | |
| 19 | 12 | 100 k. ginger,nr.2876 | 4 | 95460 | | | | |
| 20 | 13 | mail | 17 | 7850 | | | | |
| 21 | 14 | invno. 12465 | 1 | 48540 | | 48540 | | |
| 22 | 15 | freight invno. 12478 | 6 | 1560 | | | | |
| 23 | 15 | mail | 17 | 760 | | | | |
| 24 | 16 | 500 k. cardamon,nr.283! | 4 | 296140 | | | | |
| 25 | 19 | invno. 12434 | 1 | 356480 | | 356480 | | |
| 26 | 20 | salary - adm | 11 | 474108 | | | | |
| 27 | 20 | salary - op. | 12 | 342080 | | | | |
| 28 | 21 | invno. 12315 | 1 | 184990 | | 184990 | | |
| 29 | 22 | rent | 13 | 26500 | | | | |
| 30 | 23 | invno. 12445 | 1 | 407290 | | 407290 | | |
| 31 | 23 | freight invno. 12479 | 6 | 3560 | | | | |
| 32 | 26 | invno. 12457 | 1 | 147940 | | 147940 | | |
| 33 | 26 | 500 k. cloves,nr.7633 | 4 | 313450 | | | | |
| 34 | 27 | freight invno. 12480 | 6 | 4780 | | | | |
| 35 | 28 | credit card fee | 23 | 5200 | | | | |
| 36 | 29 | travel | 21 | 35200 | | | | |
| 37 | 30 | bank fees | 24 | 2300 | | | | |
| 38 | 30 | interest | 27 | 6540 | | | | |
| 39 | TOTAL | | | | | 2280140 | 0 | 0 |

| | AG | AH | AI | AJ | AK |
|---|---|---|---|---|---|
| 1 | Total | | | | |
| 2 | Gross income | Sales | 2280140 | 1 | January |
| 3 | | Rent income | 0 | 2 | February |
| 4 | | Investment | 0 | 3 | March |
| 5 | Variable expenses | Raw mat. | 952140 | 4 | April |
| 6 | | Misc. | 0 | 5 | May |
| 7 | | Freight | 12460 | 6 | June |
| 8 | Marketing expenses | Marketing | 0 | 7 | July |
| 9 | | Printing | 0 | 8 | August |
| 10 | | Mail | 12480 | 9 | September |
| 11 | | PR | 0 | 10 | October |
| 12 | Fixed expenses | Salary - adm. | 474108 | 11 | November |
| 13 | | Salary - oper. | 342080 | 12 | December |
| 14 | | Rental exp | 26500 | 13 | |
| 15 | | Insurance | 0 | 14 | |
| 16 | | Phone/Telex | 0 | 15 | |
| 17 | | Supplies | 3500 | 16 | |
| 18 | | Mail | 10820 | 17 | |
| 19 | | Equipment | 0 | 18 | |
| 20 | | Samples | 0 | 19 | |
| 21 | | Legal/acc. | 0 | 20 | |
| 22 | | Travel | 35200 | 21 | |
| 23 | | Training | 0 | 22 | |
| 24 | | Credit card | 5200 | 23 | |
| 25 | | Bank fees | 2300 | 24 | |
| 26 | | Tax/fees | 0 | 25 | |
| 27 | | Misc. | 0 | 26 | |
| 28 | | Interest | 6540 | 27 | |
| 29 | | | | | |

## DEFINED NAMES

| Name | Area |
|---|---|
| month | $AJ$4:$AK$13 |

## KEY FORMULAS

| Cell | Formula | Comments |
|---|---|---|
| F7 | =IF($C7=F$4,$D7,"") | This causes the amount to be entered if the code agrees. Fill down and right. |
| F39 | =SUM(F7:F38) | Fill right. |
| AI2 | =INDEX($F$39:$AF$39,AJ2) | This causes the first total in row 39 to be retrieved. We can then fill down, so that the rest of the totals are retrieved as a column of figures, for later use in the monthly accounts. |
| C1 | =VLOOKUP(A4,month,2) | This looks up the name of the month. |

**Monthly Accounts**

In the monthly accounts, income and expenses are entered under January for each post. Fill right for the remaining months.

Formulas then:
1. Calculate totals for each of the main categories (e.g. gross income).
2. Calculate operational profit.
3. Calculate yearly totals for each post.

|  | B | C | D | E | F | | N | O |
|---|---|---|---|---|---|---|---|---|
| **1** | | *1991 accounts through ...* | | | | | | |
| **2** | | | | | | | | |
| **3** | | January | February | March | April | | December | TOTAL |
| **4** | Gross income | 1.755.244 | 1.627.224 | 1.712.867 | 1.324.500 | | 0 | 15.378.723 |
| **5** | Variable expenses | 573.593 | 766.942 | 635.560 | 669.011 | | 0 | 6.527.014 |
| **6** | Marketing expenses | 12.299 | 17.255 | 34.815 | 15.287 | | 0 | 171.091 |
| **7** | Operational expenses | 815.769 | 793.536 | 796.448 | 926.081 | | 0 | 7.948.485 |
| **8** | | | | | | | | |
| **9** | Total expenses | 1.401.662 | 1.577.733 | 1.466.823 | 1.610.379 | | 0 | 14.646.590 |
| **10** | | | | | | | | |
| **11** | Operational profit/loss | 353.582 | 49.490 | 246.044 | -285.879 | | 0 | 732.133 |
| **12** | (sum gross income minus | | | | | | | |
| **13** | var. and fixed expenses) | | | | | | | |
| **14** | | | | | | | | |
| **15** | Sales | 1.755.244 | 1.627.224 | 1.712.867 | 1.324.500 | | | 15.378.723 |
| **16** | Rent income | 0 | 0 | 0 | 0 | | | 0 |
| **17** | Investment | 0 | 0 | 0 | 0 | | | 0 |
| **18** | Raw mat. | 565.327 | 758.241 | 626.401 | 659.370 | | | 6.434.872 |
| **19** | Misc. | 0 | 0 | 0 | 0 | | | 0 |
| **20** | Freight | 8.266 | 8.701 | 9.159 | 9.641 | | | 92.142 |
| **21** | Marketing | 0 | 0 | 0 | 0 | | | 0 |
| **22** | Printing | 0 | 0 | 25.641 | 0 | | | 50.161 |

### KEY FORMULAS

| Cell | Formula | Comments |
|---|---|---|
| O15 | =SUM(C15:N15) | This calculates total sales. Fill down. |
| C4 | =SUM(C15:C17) | This calculates gross income. |
| C5 | =SUM(C18:C20) | This calculates variable expenses. |
| C6 | =SUM(C21:C24) | This calculates marketing expenses. |
| C7 | =SUM(C25:C41) | This calculates operation expenses. |
| C9 | =SUM(C5:C7) | This calculates total expenses. |
| C11 | =C4-C9 | This calculates operational profit. Fill right all January calculations. |

**End of month macro**

This macro does the following:
1. Copies the totals in the last column of the daily ledger over to the appropriate column in the monthly accounts spreadsheet.
2. Stores both the daily ledger and the updated monthly accounts.
3. Clears the daily ledger and readies it for next month's accounts.

| STATEMENTS | EXPLANATION |
|---|---|
| =OPEN("ACCOUNTS.XLS") | opens monthly accounts file |
| =SELECT("R1C15") | selects O1 |
| =FORMULA("=LEDGER.XLS!R4C1") | links to A4 on daily ledger |
| =COPY() | copies O1 |
| =PASTE.SPECIAL(3,1,FALSE,FALSE) =CANCEL.COPY() | converts formula to straight value |
| =ACTIVATE("LEDGER.XLS") | activates daily ledger |
| =SELECT("R2C35:R28C35") | selects totals in column AI |
| =COPY() | copies totals |
| =ACTIVATE("ACCOUNTS.XLS") | activates monthly accounts |
| =SELECT(INDEX(!C15:N15,!O1)) | selects column for current month |
| =PASTE.SPECIAL(3,1,FALSE,FALSE) =CANCEL.COPY() | pastes in totals in straight values (no formulas) |
| =SELECT("R1C1") | selects A1 |
| =CALCULATE.NOW() | calculates |
| =SAVE.AS?() | saves if desired |
| =ACTIVATE("LEDGER.XLS") | activates daily ledger |
| =SELECT("R4C1") | selects A4 |
| =SAVE.AS?() | saves if desired |
| =SELECT("R7C1:R38C4") | selects ledger area |
| =CLEAR(3) | clears last month's figures |
| =SELECT("R4C2") | |
| =increment() | increases month number by 1 (subroutine) |
| =CALCULATE.NOW() | calculates |
| =SAVE.AS?() =RETURN() | saves if desired |

## SUBMACRO TO INCREASE VALUE BY 1

| STATEMENTS | EXPLANATION |
|---|---|
| increment<br>=FORMULA("=RC[-1]+1") | sets number 1 more than cell on left |
| =COPY()<br>=SELECT("RC[-1]") | copies to cell on left ... |
| =PASTE.SPECIAL(3,1,FALSE,FALSE)<br>=CANCEL.COPY() | ... without the formula |
| =SELECT("RC[1]")<br>=FORMULA("") | clears the formula in the cell on the right |
| =SELECT("RC[-1]")<br>=RETURN() | selects the cell on the left |

**Last year's Accounts**  The layout and formulas used for the previous year's accounts are identical to those used for the current year's accounts.

| | A | B | C | D | E | F |
|---|---|---|---|---|---|---|
| 1 | | | *1990 Accounts* | | | |
| 2 | | | | | | |
| 3 | | | January | February | March | April |
| 4 | | Gross income | 1.435.320 | 1.165.462 | 1.396.236 | 1.527.657 |
| 5 | | Variable expenses | 485.617 | 495.814 | 506.227 | 516.857 |
| 6 | | Marketing expenses | 17.224 | 17.586 | 17.954 | 18.332 |
| 7 | | Operational expenses | 794.014 | 796.071 | 798.172 | 800.317 |
| 8 | | | | | | |
| 9 | | Total expenses | 1.296.855 | 1.309.471 | 1.322.353 | 1.335.506 |
| 10 | | | | | | |
| 11 | | Operational profit/loss | 138.465 | -144.009 | 73.883 | 192.151 |
| 12 | | (sum gross income minus | | | | |
| 13 | | var. and fixed expenses) | | | | |
| 14 | | | | | | |
| 15 | Gross income | Sales | 1.435.320 | 1.165.462 | 1.396.236 | 1.527.657 |
| 16 | | Rent income | 0 | 0 | 0 | 0 |
| 17 | | Investment | 0 | 0 | 0 | 0 |
| 18 | Variable expenses | Raw mat. | 478.440 | 488.487 | 498.745 | 509.219 |
| 19 | | Misc. | 0 | 0 | 0 | 0 |
| 20 | | Freight | 7.177 | 7.327 | 7.481 | 7.638 |
| 21 | Marketing expenses | Marketing | 4.784 | 4.885 | 4.987 | 5.092 |
| 22 | | Printing | 1.914 | 1.954 | 1.995 | 2.037 |
| 23 | | Mail | 6.698 | 6.839 | 6.982 | 7.129 |
| 24 | | PR | 3.828 | 3.908 | 3.990 | 4.074 |
| 25 | Fixed expenses | Salary - adm. | 415525 | 439.816 | 439.004 | 426.002 |
| 26 | | Salary - oper. | 274422 | 274422 | 274422 | 274422 |
| 27 | | Rental exp | 26.500 | 26.500 | 26.500 | 26.500 |

**Comparative analysis**

In the financial analysis, formulas do the following:
1. Calculate accumulated figures up through the current month.
2. Calculate the difference between the accumulated figures from this year, last year and this year's budget.
3. Look up current, last year's and budgeted figures for the current month.

| | A | B | C | D | E | F | G | H | I | J | K | L | M |
|---|---|---|---|---|---|---|---|---|---|---|---|---|---|
| 1 | Periode | 9 | | | | | | | | | | | 0 |
| 2 | DEVIATION FROM BUDGET | | | | | | | | | | | | 1 January |
| 3 | September | | Accumulated | | | Deviation from | | | This month | | | | 2 February |
| 4 | | To date | Budgeted | Last yr. | | Budgeted | Last yr. | | To date | Budgeted | | | 3 March |
| 5 | Gross income | 15378723 | 13050000 | 17835115 | | 2328723 | -2456393 | | 2280140 | 1450000 | | | 4 April |
| 6 | Variable expenses | 6527014 | 4567500 | 6169552 | | 1959514 | 357462 | | 964600 | 507500 | | | 5 May |
| 7 | Marketing expenses | 171091 | 162000 | 218823 | | 9091 | -47732 | | 12480 | 18000 | | | 6 June |
| 8 | Operational expenses | 7948485 | 7626600 | 9546239 | | 321885 | -1597754 | | 916248 | 847400 | | | 7 July |
| 9 | | | | | | | | | | | | | 8 August |
| 10 | Total expenses | 14646590 | 12356100 | 15934614 | | 2290490 | -1288024 | | 1893328 | 1372900 | | | 9 September |
| 11 | | | | | | | | | | | | | 10 October |
| 12 | Operational profit/loss | 732133 | 693900 | 1900501 | | 38233 | -1168368 | | 386812 | 77100 | | | 11 November |
| | | | | | | | | | | | | | 12 December |

## DEFINED NAMES

| Name | Area |
|---|---|
| ac91 | ACCOUNTS.XLS!$C$2:$N$11 |
| budget | BUDGET.XLS!$C$2:$N$11 |
| ac90 | ACCNTS90.XLS!$C$2:$N$11 |

## KEY FORMULAS

| Cell | Formula | Comments |
|---|---|---|
| B5 | =SUM(ACCOUNTS.XLS!$C4: INDEX(ac91,$L5,$B$1)) | Sums from January to the current month. Fill right for budgeted and last year's accumulated figures. |
| C5 | =SUM(BUDGET.XLS!$C4: INDEX(budget,$L5,$B$1)) | Same as above, but adjusted to calculate this year's budget. |
| D5 | =SUM(ACCNTS90.XLS!$C4: INDEX(ac90,$L5,$B$1)) | Same as above, but adjusted to calculate last year's accounts. |
| F5 | =B5-C5 | Subtracts budgeted from current figures. |
| G5 | =B5-D5 | Subtracts last year's from current figures. |
| I5 | =HLOOKUP($B$1,ac91,$L5) | Looks up figures for current month. Fill right for budgeted figures. |
| J5 | =HLOOKUP($B$1,budget,$L5) | Same as above, but adjusted to look up budgeted figures. Fill down all formulas in row 5. |
| A3 | =VLOOKUP(B1,L3:M14,2) | Looks up the name of the month. |

# Model B

## Invoice system

*This model consists of five linked spreadsheets and two macros.*

**1** a customer list

**2** an inventory list

**3** an invoice form

**4** an invoice list

**5** an employee list

**6** a macro to transfer information from the invoice form to the list, to update salesmens' records on the employee list and to prepare the invoice form for the next order

**7** a form letter to customers with overdue accounts

**8** a macro to print out form letters

## Customer list

The customer list contains standard customer information such as name, address and phone. No formulas are required.

|   | A | B | C | D | E | F |
|---|---|---|---|---|---|---|
| 1 | Cust. no. | Name | Tel. | Address | Postcode | City |
| 2 | 1111 | Genco Pura Olive Oil Ltd. | 10 00 01 | 5 Bronx St. | 5510 | Sydney |
| 3 | 1112 | Corleone & Co. | 11 00 01 | 566 Miami Ln. | 4044 | Strand |
| 4 | 1113 | Department 007 | 70 00 07 | 70 Bourke St. | 2025 | Kongsberg |
| 5 | 1114 | M & Moneypenney | 70 00 07 | 70 Bourke St. | 2025 | Kongsberg |
| 6 | 1115 | Kongsberg Weapons | 42 60 00 | 55 Moskow Way | 2025 | Kongsberg |
| 7 | 1116 | Mongstad | 28 67 55 | 999 Money St. | 0177 | Wangaratta |

## Inventory list

The inventory list contains information on amount and type of items in stock and wholesale and sales price.

Formulas then:
Produce a message if an item is low in stock and needs to be ordered.

### Inventory

|   | A | B | C | D | E | F | G | H | I |
|---|---|---|---|---|---|---|---|---|---|
| 1 | *Inventory* | | | | | | | | |
| 2 | | | | | | | | | |
| 3 | Date of last stock take | | 12.Oct.90 | | | | | | |
| 4 | | | | | | | | | |
| 5 | | | | | Deliv. | Received | | | |
| 6 | | | | | since | since | | | |
| 7 | Item no. | Description | List price | Wholesale | stock take | stock take | In stock | Stock take | |
| 8 | | | | | | | | | |
| 9 | 1111 | Yogi tea 100g bags | 18,00 | 10,80 | 3950 | 1250 | 300 | 3000 | |
| 10 | 1112 | Yogi tea250g bags | 30,00 | 18,00 | 5500 | 2500 | 0 | 3000 | Order more! |
| 11 | 1113 | Yogi tea100g loose | 12,00 | 7,20 | 750 | | 250 | 1000 | |
| 12 | 1114 | Yogi tea250g loose | 20,00 | 12,00 | 650 | | 350 | 1000 | |
| 13 | 1115 | Yogi teaper kilo | 90,00 | 54,00 | 150 | | 350 | 500 | |
| 14 | 1116 | Himalaya 100g loose | 12,00 | 7,20 | 1200 | 500 | 300 | 1000 | |

### KEY NUMBER FORMATS

| Cell | Format |
|---|---|
| I9 | General[Red] |

### KEY FORMULAS

| Cell | Formula | Comments |
|---|---|---|
| G9 | =H9-E9+F9 | This calculates amount in stock. Fill down. |
| I9 | =IF(G9<100,"Order more!","") | This produces message if stock in a particular item is low. Fill down. |

**Invoice form**

In the invoice form, customer number, salesman's initials, item numbers and amounts and freight are entered each time an order is made.

Formulas then:
1. Look up customer name, address and phone.
2. Look up item descriptions and prices.
3. Calculate totals, discount and tax and final total.

| | A | B | C | D | E | F |
|---|---|---|---|---|---|---|
| 1 | | | | Yogi Tea Import A/S | | |
| 2 | | | | 111 Collins St., Melbourne 3000 | | |
| 3 | | | | Tlf. (03) 10 44 44 | | |
| 4 | Kongsberg Weapons | | | | | |
| 5 | 55 Moskow Way | | | | | |
| 6 | Kongsberg | | | Date: | 2.Oct.90 | |
| 7 | 42 60 00 | | | Invoice no. | 242222 | |
| 8 | | | | Customer no. | 1115 | |
| 9 | | | | | | |
| 10 | | | | | | |
| 11 | Item no. | Description | Item price | No. ordered | Sum | |
| 12 | 1111 | Yogi tea 100g bags | 18,00 | 75 | 1350,00 | |
| 13 | 1113 | Yogi tea 100g loose | 12,00 | 50 | 600,00 | |
| 14 | 1115 | Yogi tea per kilo | 90,00 | 100 | 9000,00 | |
| 15 | 1118 | Himalaya per kilo | 90,00 | 40 | 3600,00 | |
| 16 | | | | | | |
| 17 | | | | | | |
| 18 | | | | Subtotal | 14550,00 | |
| 19 | Seller's initials | | -10% | Discount | -1455,00 | |
| 20 | mmm | | | Freight | 480,00 | |
| 21 | | | | Tax | 2715,00 | |
| 22 | | | | Total | 16290,00 | |

## KEY NUMBER FORMATS

| Cell | Format |
|------|--------|
| A7 | "Tlf. "00 00 00 |

## DEFINED NAMES

| Name | Area |
|------|------|
| cnr | $E$8 |
| cust | CUST.XLS!$A$3:$F$50 |
| goods | INVENTRY.XLS!$A$9:$C$30 |

## KEY FORMULAS

| Cell | Formula | Comments |
|------|---------|----------|
| A4 | =IF(VLOOKUP(cnr,cust,1)=cnr,"", "No information for to this customer number") | Even if customer no. doesn't exist, VLOOKUP will find the closest number in the table which is less than the input number. This formula tests if the number VLOOKUP finds and the number input are the same. If not, an error message is broadcast. |
| A4 | =IF(VLOOKUP(cnr,cust,1)=cnr, VLOOKUP(cnr,cust,2),"") | Looks up customer name, but remains blank if no cust. number is entered, or if an invalid cust. no. is entered. Fill down and adjust for address/phone. |
| B12 | =IF(VLOOKUP(A12,goods,1)=cnr, VLOOKUP(A12,goods,2),"") | Same as above, but looks up item name. Cell remains blank if no item number, or an invalid one, is entered. Fill right and down. |
| E12 | =IF(A12>0,C12*D12,"") | Calculates total charge per item, but remains blank if no item number is entered. Fill down for all ordered items. |
| E18 | =SUM(E12:E17) | This calculates total cost of purchase. |
| C19 | =IF(E18>5000,-10%,0%) | This gives 10% discount if sales > 5000. |
| E19 | =E18*C19 | This calculates discount. |
| E21 | =0.2*SUM(E18:E20) | This calculates tax. |
| E22 | =SUM(E18:E20)+E21 | This calculates total invoice amount. |

**Invoice list**

In the invoice list, a macro copies invoice information to the list. Payments are entered manually as they come in.

Formulas then:
1. Calculate balance.
2. Calculate overdue payments in number of days.

| | A | B | C | D | E | F | G | H | I |
|---|---|---|---|---|---|---|---|---|---|
| 1 | | | | | | Date : | 2.Oct.90 | | |
| 2 | | | | | | | | | |
| 3 | Inv.no. | Cust.no. | Name | Due | Total | Paid | Balance | Overdue | Seller |
| 5 | 242223 | 1120 | B-gang | 16.Oct.90 | 31086 | | 31086 | | ana |
| 6 | 242223 | 1112 | Corleone & Co. | 16.Oct.90 | 22500 | | 22500 | | ana |
| 7 | 242222 | 1115 | Kongsberg Weapons | 16.Oct.90 | 16506 | | 16506 | | mmm |
| 8 | 242221 | 1112 | Corleone & Co. | 15.Oct.90 | 9837 | | 9837 | | mic |
| 9 | 242220 | 1120 | B-gang | 12.Oct.90 | 1146 | 1000 | 146 | | jbo |
| 10 | 242219 | 1116 | Mongstad | 7.Oct.90 | 8424 | 8000 | 424 | | bjw |
| 11 | 242218 | 1117 | Scandia Ltd. | 3.Oct.90 | 9007 | 9000 | 7 | | fro |
| 12 | 242217 | 1119 | SPECTRU | 28.Sep.90 | 11437 | 11437 | 0 | | jej |
| 13 | 242216 | 1113 | Department 007 | 23.Sep.90 | 8035 | 6000 | 2035 | 8 days | kih |
| 14 | 242215 | 1118 | Norsk Data A/S | 19.Sep.90 | 4788 | | 4788 | 13 days | erb |
| 15 | 242214 | 1121 | Libyan Air | 14.Sep.90 | 5220 | | 5220 | 17 days | jbo |
| 16 | 242213 | 1111 | Genco Pura Olive Oil Ltd. | 10.Sep.90 | 4140 | | 4140 | 22 days | kih |
| 17 | 242212 | 1112 | Corleone & Co. | 5.Sep.90 | 9261 | 9261 | 0 | | fro |
| 18 | 242211 | 1120 | B-gang | 31.Aug.90 | 1146 | 1000 | 146 | 31 days | kih |
| 19 | 242210 | 1116 | Mongstad | 27.Aug.90 | 8424 | 8000 | 424 | 36 days | bgj |
| 20 | 242209 | 1117 | Scandia Ltd. | 22.Aug.90 | 9007 | 9000 | 7 | 40 days | hep |
| 21 | 242208 | 1119 | SPECTRU | 18.Aug.90 | 11437 | 11437 | 0 | | mic |
| 22 | 242207 | 1114 | M & Moneypenney | 13.Aug.90 | 8035 | 6000 | 2035 | 50 days | ana |
| 23 | 242206 | 1115 | Kongsberg Weapons | 8.Aug.90 | 4788 | | 4788 | 54 days | mic |
| 24 | 242205 | 1121 | Libyan Air | 4.Aug.90 | 5220 | | 5220 | 59 days | vic |

## KEY NUMBER FORMATS

| Cell | Format | Comments |
|---|---|---|
| H5:H100 | 0" days";"" | This causes cell to be blank if no. is negative. |

## DEFINED NAMES

| Name | Area |
|---|---|
| today | $G$1 |

## KEY FORMULAS

| Cell | Formula | Comments |
|---|---|---|
| G5 | =E5-F5 | This calculates balance. |
| H5 | =IF(G5>0,today-D5,"") | This calculates days overdue, but if balance is nil, the cell remains blank. |

**Department and salary tables**

These tables contain updated information on departmental and salary structures. No formulas are needed in this sheet.

|   | A | B | C | D | E | F |
|---|---|---|---|---|---|---|
| 1 | *Department table* | | | *Paytable* | | |
| 2 | Deptno. | Department | | Paycode | Annual salary | |
| 3 | 5101 | Sales | | 20 | 158574 | |
| 4 | 5102 | EDB | | 21 | 165302 | |
| 5 | 5103 | Admin. | | 22 | 172576 | |
| 6 | 5104 | Production | | 23 | 179873 | |
| 7 | 5105 | Transportation | | 24 | 187948 | |
| 8 | 5106 | Marketing | | 25 | 194525 | |
| 9 | 5107 | Finance | | 26 | 201077 | |

**Employee list**

The employee list contains name, address, department and gross salary for all employees.

Formulas look up department name and annual salary.

|    | A | B | C | D | E | F | G | H |
|----|---|---|---|---|---|---|---|---|
| 1  | *Employee table* | | | | | | | |
| 2  | | | | | | | | |
| 3  | ID no. | Name | Initials | Dept. no. | Department | Paycode | Salary | Sales |
| 4  | 3564 | Mikael Corleone | mic | 5105 | Transportation | 34 | 259018 | 45736 |
| 5  | 3565 | Anders And | ana | 5102 | EDB | 21 | 152155 | 61621 |
| 6  | 3566 | Bruce Wayne | brw | 5108 | Research | 22 | 159095 | 8424 |
| 7  | 3567 | Vito Corleone | vic | 5103 | Admin. | 42 | 358580 | 5220 |
| 8  | 3568 | Jens Jensen | jej | 5101 | Sales | 29 | 211686 | 15577 |
| 9  | 3569 | J. Bond | jbo | 5105 | Transportation | 30 | 220390 | 14790 |
| 10 | 3570 | Ernst Blofeld | erb | 5106 | Marketing | 42 | 358580 | 5934 |

**DEFINED NAMES**

| Name | Area |
|------|------|
| dptab | PERSONEL.XLS!$A$3:$B$30 |
| paytab | PERSONEL.XLS!$D$3:$E$50 |
| sales | INVOICE.XLS!$E$22 |
| seller | INVOICE.XLS!$A$20 |

**KEY FORMULAS**

| Cell | Formula | Comments |
|------|---------|----------|
| E4 | =IF(A4>0,VLOOKUP(D4,dptab,2),"") | This looks up department name. |
| G4 | =IF(A4>0,VLOOKUP(F4,paytab,2),"") | This looks up annual salary. Fill down the above formulas. |

**Macro to**
**update**
**invoice**
**list**

This macro does the following:
1. Transfers figures from the invoice form to the invoice list
2. Updates salesman's sales on the employee list
3. Prepares the invoice form for the next invoice.

Notes that this macro uses two submacros:
1. A submacro to update salesman's sales on the employee list
2. A submacro to increase a given number by 1

| STATEMENTS | EXPLANATION |
|---|---|
| =ACTIVATE("DEBITOR.XLS") | activates invoice list |
| =SELECT("R5") | selects the top row of invoice listings |
| =INSERT(2) | inserts an empty row over |
| =SELECT("R4C1:R4C9") | selects the newly received invoice listings |
| =COPY()<br>=SELECT("R5C1")<br>=PASTE.SPECIAL(3,1,FALSE,FALSE)<br>=CANCEL.COPY() | copies them to the next row, converting from<br>  to straight values |
| =SELECT("R6C1:R6C9")<br>=COPY()<br>=SELECT("R5C1")<br>=PASTE.SPECIAL(4,1,FALSE,FALSE) | selects the row below<br>  and copies the formats to the row above |
| =SELECT("R5C7:R6C8") | selects the formulas for balance and overdue |
| =FILL.UP() | and copies them to the new row |
| =SELECT("R4C1") | selects D4 |
| =SAVE() | saves the invoice list |
| =seller() | goes to the salesman submacro |
| =ACTIVATE("INVOICE.XLS") | activates invoice form |
| =SELECT("R7C5") | selects E7 |
| =SAVE.AS?() | saves as desired |
| =PRINT?() | prints as desired |
| =GOTO(cleanup)<br><br>=RETURN() | goes to submacro which prepares invoice<br>  form for new order |

# SUBMACRO TO UPDATE SALES BY SALESMAN

| STATEMENTS | EXPLANATION |
|---|---|
| seller | |
| =ACTIVATE("EMPLOYEE.XLS") | activates employee table |
| =SELECT("R1C4") | selects D1 |
| =FORMULA("=MATCH(seller,R4C3:R16C3,0)") | finds which salesman made sale |
| =SELECT("R1C5") | selects E1 |
| =FORMULA("=sales") | retrieves total sale from invoice |
| =SELECT("R1C6") | selects F1 |
| =FORMULA("=INDEX(R4C8:R16C8,R1C4)+R1C5") | retrieves salesman's sales to date and adds latest sale |
| =COPY() | copies ... |
| =SELECT(INDEX(EMPLOYEE.XLS!$H$4:$H$16, EMPLOYEE.XLS!$D$1)) | ... to salesman's sales |
| =PASTE.SPECIAL(3,1,FALSE,FALSE) | pastes in value without formula |
| =CANCEL.COPY() | |
| =SELECT("R1C4:R1C6") | clears formulas in D1 through F1 |
| =CLEAR() | |
| =SELECT("R1C1") | selects A1 |
| =SAVE() | saves |
| =RETURN() | |

# SUBMACRO TO PREPARE INVOICE SHEET FOR NEW ORDER

| STATEMENTS | EXPLANATION |
|---|---|
| cleanup | |
| =SELECT("R12C1:R18C1") | clears customer number, item numbers |
| =CLEAR(3) | and amounts ordered |
| =SELECT("R12C4:R17C4") | |
| =CLEAR(3) | |
| =SELECT("R20C5") | |
| =FORMULA("") | |
| =SELECT("R20C1") | |
| =FORMULA("") | |
| =SELECT("R8C5") | |
| =FORMULA("") | |
| =SELECT("R7C5") | |
| =increment() | increases invoice no. by 1 (subroutine) |
| =SAVE.AS?("INVOICE") | saves with name INVOICE if desired |
| =RETURN() | |

# SUBMACRO TO INCREASE VALUE BY 1

| STATEMENTS | EXPLANATION |
|---|---|
| increment<br>=FORMULA("=RC[-1]+1") | sets number 1 more than cell on left |
| =COPY()<br>=SELECT("RC[-1]") | copies to cell on left ... |
| =PASTE.SPECIAL(3,1,FALSE,FALSE)<br>=CANCEL.COPY() | ... without the formula |
| =SELECT("RC[1]")<br>=FORMULA("") | clears the formula in the cell on the right |
| =SELECT("RC[-1]")<br>=RETURN() | selects the cell on the left |

**Form letter to payment overdue customers**

In the form letter to payment overdue customers, formulas do the following:
1. Look up customer name, address and phone.
2. Calculate total amount outstanding.

| | A | B | C | D | E | F | G | H | I | J |
|---|---|---|---|---|---|---|---|---|---|---|
| 1 | | | | | | | | | | |
| 2 | | | *Warning* | | | | | | | |
| 3 | | | | | | | | cust.no. | | Balance |
| 4 | | | | | Yogi Tea Import Ltd. | | | 1111 | | >0 |
| 5 | | | | | 111 Collins St., Melbourne 3000 | | | | | |
| 6 | | | | | Tlf. (03) 10 44 44 | | | | | 1 |
| 7 | | | | | | | | | | |
| 8 | | | | | Date: | 2.Oct.90 | | | | |
| 9 | | | | | | | | Press CTRL d | | |
| 10 | Genco Pura Olive Oil Ltd. | | | | | | | for automatic printing | | |
| 11 | 5 Bronx St. | | | | | | | of letters | | |
| 12 | Sydney | | | | | | | | | |
| 13 | 10 00 01 | | | | | | | | | |
| 14 | | | | | | | | | | |
| 15 | | | | | | | | | | |
| 16 | Inv.no. | | Due | Total | Paid | Balance | | | | |
| 17 | 242214 | | 14.Sep.90 | 5220 | | 5220 | | | | |
| 18 | 242205 | | 4.Aug.90 | 5220 | | 5220 | | | | |
| 19 | 242196 | | 23.Jun.90 | 5220 | | 5220 | | | | |
| 20 | | | | Total amount due : | | 15660 | | | | |
| 21 | | | | | | | | | | |
| 22 | | | | | | | | | | |
| 23 | According to our records, the above invoices are outstanding. | | | | | | | | | |
| 24 | Kindly remit payment immediately. If you have any questions, feel free | | | | | | | | | |
| 25 | to contact our accounts office, tel. (02) 10 44 44. | | | | | | | | | |

## DEFINED NAMES

| Name | Area | Comments |
|------|------|----------|
| cnr | $H$4 | |
| cust | CUST.XLS!$A$3:$F$50 | |
| custnr | CUST.XLS!$A$3:$A$50 | |
| database | DEBITOR.XLS!$A$3:$H$50 | |
| criteria | $H$3:$K$4 | Note that this area is located out of view of the user. |

## KEY FORMULAS

| Cell | Formula | Comments |
|------|---------|----------|
| A10 | =IF(cnr>0,VLOOKUP(cnr,cust,2),"") | This looks up customer name, but remains blank if no cust. no. is entered. Fill down and adjust for address/phone. Note that customer no. is in cell H4. |
| E20 | =SUM(E17:E19) | This calculates total amount outstanding. |
| J7 | =IF(VLOOKUP(H4,cust,1)=H4,1,0) | Even if customer no. doesn't exist, VLOOKUP will find the closest number in the table which is less than the input number. This formula tests if the number VLOOKUP finds and the number input are the same. If not, this test cell is set to zero. This result is used in the macro which generates these form letters. |

**Form letter macro**

This macro does the following for each customer in the customer list:
1. Retrieves information on outstanding invoices.
2. If balance is outstanding, prints a letter in 2 copies and saves.
3. Continues automatically until all customers are processed.

Note that this macro uses the increment submacro.

| STATEMENTS | EXPLANATION |
|---|---|
| =ACTIVATE("LETTER.XLS") | activates form letter |
| =SELECT("R8C6") | selects J4 |
| =WHILE(ACTIVE.CELL()>0) | while test cell = 1 (to see if customer exists) ... |
| =SELECT("R16C1:R19C5")<br>=EXTRACT(FALSE)<br>=SELECT("R20C5") | extracts customer data from database |
| =IF(ACTIVE.CELL()>0,GOTO(D9),GOTO(D11)) | if there is an outstanding balance |
| =PRINT?(2,1,1,2,FALSE,FALSE,1)<br>=SAVE.AS?() | prints and saves as desired ... |
| =SELECT("R4C9") | ... otherwise skips to here, selects test cell I4 ... which contains customer number |
| =increment() | and goes to submacro which increases cust. no. by 1 |
| =SELECT("R7C10") | selects J7 (cell which tests if customer exists) |
| =NEXT() | returns to WHILE statement |
| =SELECT("R8C6") | selects F8 |
| =ALERT("No more customers",2) | broadcasts message: "No more customers" |
| =SELECT("R8C6") | selects J4 |
| =FORMULA("=min(custnr)")<br>=RETURN() | sets to lowest customer number |

# Model C

# Price analysis

*This model consists of three linked spreadsheets and two macros*

**1** a price list for raw materials (in this case food)

**2** a product list (in this case recipes) and the cost of raw materials (food)

**3** a macro to enter new products (recipes) in the list

**4** a price analysis for all products (recipes) and a more detailed analysis of a product (recipe)

**5** a macro to carry out a detailed analysis of a particular product (recipe)

**Raw materials**

In the list of raw materials (food), item name (food item), price, unit used in purchasing, unit used in-house and their relationship, and wastage are entered into the appropriate columns.

Formulas then:
Calculate resulting cost per in-house unit.

| | A | B | C | D | E | F | G | H |
|---|---|---|---|---|---|---|---|---|
| 1 | | *Price list* | | | | | | |
| 2 | | | | | | *recipe/store unit* | | |
| 3 | *no.* | *food* | *price* | *unit* | *recipe unit* | *ratio* | *wastage* | *cost* |
| 4 | 1 | milk | 6,40 | lt | cup | 4 | | 1,60 |
| 5 | 2 | flour | 1,30 | kg | cup | 6 | | 0,22 |
| 6 | 3 | honey | 20,00 | kg | cup | 7 | 1% | 2,89 |
| 7 | 4 | oil | 30,00 | lt | cup | 5 | | 6,00 |
| 8 | 5 | potatoes | 1,95 | kg | piece | 10 | 8% | 0,21 |
| 9 | 6 | butter | 14,90 | 500g | 1g | 500 | | 0,03 |
| 10 | 7 | garlic | 6,50 | hg | clove | 50 | 2% | 0,13 |
| 11 | 8 | ginger | 3,40 | hg | handful | 25 | 8% | 0,15 |
| 12 | 9 | bread | 11,00 | lf | slice | 20 | 3% | 0,57 |

**KEY FORMULAS**

| Cell | Formula | Comments |
|---|---|---|
| H4 | =IF(C4>0,C4/F4+(C4/F4*G4),"") | This calculates total price per in-house unit, adding wastage. |

In the product list, a macro is started which asks for amount, unit and name for each ingredient entered in a recipe.

Formulas calculate current price per ingredient used in recipe.
The macro then calculates the total price for the recipe.

|   | A | B | C | D | E | F | G | H | I |
|---|---|---|---|---|---|---|---|---|---|
| 1 | *Recipe list* | | | Press CTRL a to enter new recipe. | | | | | |
| 2 | | | | | | | | | |
| 3 | code | recipe | amount | unit | ingredient | price | total | accumulated | |
| 4 | 1 | honey toast | 0,1 | cup | honey | 0,29 | | 0,29 | |
| 5 | 1 | honey toast | 2 | slice | bread | 1,13 | | 1,42 | |
| 6 | 1 | honey toast | 25 | g | butter | 0,75 | 2,17 | 2,17 | |
| 7 | 2 | garlic bread | 5 | slice | garlic | 0,66 | | 0,66 | |
| 8 | 2 | garlic bread | 2 | slice | bread | 1,13 | | 1,80 | |
| 9 | 2 | garlic bread | 25 | g | butter | 0,75 | 2,54 | 2,54 | |

**DEFINED NAMES**

| Name | Area |
|---|---|
| food | FOOD.XLS!$B$4:$B$100 |
| foodtab | FOOD.XLS!$A$4:$H$100 |

**KEY FORMULAS**

| Cell | Formula | Comments |
|---|---|---|
| F4 | =IF(C4>0,VLOOKUP(MATCH (E4,food,0),foodtab,8)*C4,0) | Looks up the price of the ingredient in the table, then multiplies it by the amount used in the recipe. If no ingredient is entered, the result is set to 0. Fill down. |
| A5 | =IF(B5=B4,A4,A4+1) | Creates a code number for the recipe, and repeats the same number until a new recipe is started. Then the number is increased by 1. Fill down. |
| H4 | =IF(A4=A3,H3+F4,F4) | Accumulates the cost of recipe ingredients. If it is a new recipe, the ingredient price only is taken. Fill down. |
| G4 | =IF(A4=A5,"",H4) | If the next line starts a new recipe, this takes the accumulated total from column H. Otherwise, the cell remains blank. Fill down. |
| K3 | =J12 | Links to cell for easier pasting in macro. |
| L3 | =J9 | Links to cell for easier pasting in macro. |
| M3 | =J6 | Links to cell for easier pasting in macro. |

**New product macro**

The product list macro does the following:

1. Presents dialog box for user to fill in amount, unit and name of recipe ingredient.
2. When user is finished with a recipe, the macro calculates total cost.

| STATEMENTS | EXPLANATION |
|---|---|
| recipe<br>=DIALOG.BOX(B2:H15) | Selects dialog box. |
| =IF(H4=FALSE,GOTO(A4),GOTO(A20)) | If CANCEL box checked, goes to end of macro, otherwise continues. |
| =CALCULATION(3) | Turns off automatic calculation of formulas. |
| =ECHO(FALSE) | Turns off visual for updating. |
| =ACTIVATE("COST.XLM") | Activates macro sheet. |
| =SELECT("R6C8:R15C8")<br>=COPY()<br>=ACTIVATE("RECIPE.XLS")<br>=SELECT(!J3)<br>=PASTE()<br>=CANCEL.COPY() | Selects result fields from dialog box.<br>... and copies<br>... To the product spreadsheet<br>... starting at cell J3. |
| =CALCULATION(1) | Turns on automatic calculation. |
| =SELECT("RC:RC[3]") | Selects cells linked to paste-in results from dialog box. |
| =COPY() | Copies. |
| =SELECT(INDEX(!B4:!B25,MATCH<br>(MAX(!A4:!A25),!A4:!A25,0))) | Selects the first blank cell for a new entry. |
| =PASTE.SPECIAL(3,1,FALSE,FALSE)<br>=CANCEL.COPY() | Pastes in dialog box results. |
| =GOTO(A2) | Loops back to dialog box. |
| =SAVE() | Saves file. |
| =ECHO(TRUE)<br>=RETURN() | Turns on visual screen updating. |

## DIALOG DEFINITION AREA ON MACRO SHEET

|    | B    | C   | D  | E     | F      | G                     | H             | I        |
|----|------|-----|----|-------|--------|-----------------------|---------------|----------|
| 1  | item | x   | y  | width | height | text                  | init/suit     | gram     |
| 2  |      |     |    | 540   | 190    |                       |               | handful  |
| 3  | 1    | 460 | 6  | 72    | 21     | OK                    |               | kilo     |
| 4  | 13   | 385 | 30 | 147   | 21     | &Recipe finished      | TRUE          | cup      |
| 5  | 5    | 8   | 6  | 140   | 12     | &Recipe               |               | litre    |
| 6  | 6    | 8   | 30 | 140   | 18     |                       | cinnamon toa  | slice    |
| 7  | 16   | 8   | 55 | 140   | 120    | COST.XLS!R5C2:R21C2   | 6             | T-spoon  |
| 8  | 5    | 160 | 6  | 100   | 12     | &Ingredient           |               | piece    |
| 9  | 6    | 160 | 30 | 100   | 18     |                       | ginger        | t-spoon  |
| 10 | 16   | 160 | 55 | 100   | 120    | FOOD.XLS!R4C2:R18C2   | 8             |          |
| 11 | 5    | 272 | 6  | 100   | 12     | &Unit                 |               |          |
| 12 | 6    | 272 | 30 | 100   | 18     |                       | handful       |          |
| 13 | 16   | 272 | 55 | 100   | 120    | COST.XLM!R1C9:R9C9    | 2             |          |
| 14 | 5    | 385 | 60 | 60    | 12     | &Amount               |               |          |
| 15 | 8    | 385 | 80 | 60    | 18     |                       | 1             |          |
| 16 |      |     |    |       |        |                       |               |          |

## DIALOG BOX PRODUCED BY MACRO

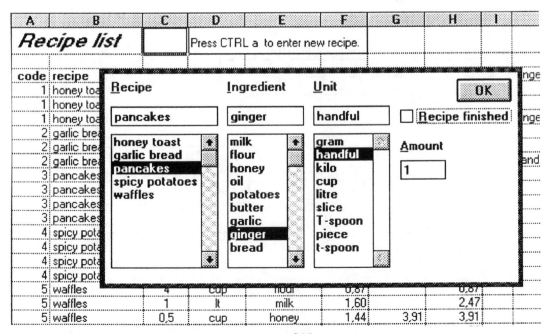

219

**Price analysis**

The price analysis has 2 parts:
1. The first part has formulas which calculate total costs for each recipe.
2. The second part retrieves more detailed information about each product (recipe), and is run by a macro.

| | A | B | C | D | E | F | G | H | I | J |
|---|---|---|---|---|---|---|---|---|---|---|
| 1 | | *Cost analysis* | | | | Press CTRL c to run cost analysis. | | | | |
| 2 | | | | | | | | | | |
| 3 | | | | | | | | | | |
| 4 | | *recipe* | *total* | | | **recipe** | **total** | | | |
| 5 | 1 | honey toast | 2,17 | | | garlic bread | **2,54** | | | |
| 6 | 2 | garlic bread | 2,54 | | | | | | | |
| 7 | 3 | pancakes | 13,23 | | | *recipe* | *amount* | *unit* | *ingredient* | *price* |
| 8 | 4 | spicy potatoes | 6,45 | | | garlic bread | 5 | slice | garlic | 0,66 |
| 9 | 5 | waffles | 3,91 | | | | 2 | slice | bread | 1,13 |
| 10 | 6 | | | | | | 25 | g | butter | 0,75 |
| 11 | 7 | | | | | | | | | |
| 12 | 8 | | | | | | | | | |
| 13 | 9 | | | | | | | | | |
| 14 | 10 | | | | | | | | | |
| 15 | 11 | | | | | | | | | |
| 16 | 12 | | | | | | | | | |
| 17 | 13 | | | | | | | | | |
| 18 | 14 | | | | | | | | | |
| 19 | 15 | | | | | | | | | |
| 20 | 16 | | | | | | | | | |
| 21 | 17 | | | | | | | | | |

**DEFINED NAMES**

| Name | Area |
|---|---|
| database | FOOD.XLS!$B$4:$H$100 |
| criteria | $F$4:$F$5 |
| rtab | RECIPE.XLS!$A$4:$G$100 |

**KEY FORMULAS**

| Cell | Formula | Comments |
|---|---|---|
| B5 | =IF(VLOOKUP($A5,rtab,3)>0, VLOOKUP($A5,rtab,2),"") | Looks up recipe name, and remains blank if none exists. Fill right for total recipe cost. |
| C5 | =IF(VLOOKUP($A5,rtab,3)>0, VLOOKUP($A5,rtab,7),"") | Same as above, but adjusted to calculate total recipe cost. Fill down both of the above formulas. |
| G5 | =SUM(J8:J21) | Calculates total recipe cost. |

**Product analysis macro**

The single product analysis macro retrieves information about a specified product (recipe).

| STATEMENTS | EXPLANATION |
|---|---|
| lookup<br>=SELECT("R7C6:R20C10") | Selects result area. |
| =EXTRACT(FALSE) | Retrieves information. |
| =SELECT("R9C6:R20C6")<br>=CLEAR(3) | Clears repetitive recipe names. |
| =SELECT("R8C6")<br>=COPY()<br>=SELECT("R5C6")<br>=PASTE()<br>=CANCEL.COPY() | Copies full recipe name to criteria area. |
| =RETURN() | |

# Model D

## Payroll system

*This model consists of five linked spreadsheets and a macro*

**1**   a department table and a salary table

**2**   an employee list

**3**   an income tax table

**4**   a payroll list

**5**   a payslip form

**6**   a macro to produce payslips for all employees

**Department and salary tables**

These tables contain updated information on departmental and salary structures. No formulas are needed in this sheet.

|  | A | B | C | D | E | F |
|---|---|---|---|---|---|---|
| **1** | **Department table** | | | **Paytable** | | |
| **2** | *Deptno.* | *Department* | | *Paycode* | *Annual salary* | |
| **3** | 5101 | Sales | | 20 | 158574 | |
| **4** | 5102 | EDB | | 21 | 165302 | |
| **5** | 5103 | Admin. | | 22 | 172576 | |
| **6** | 5104 | Production | | 23 | 179873 | |
| **7** | 5105 | Transportation | | 24 | 187948 | |
| **8** | 5106 | Marketing | | 25 | 194525 | |
| **9** | 5107 | Finance | | 26 | 201077 | |
| **10** | 5108 | Research | | 27 | 208277 | |
| **11** | 5109 | Purchasing | | 28 | 216015 | |

**Employee list**

The employee list contains name, address, department and gross salary for all employees.

Formulas look up department name and annual salary.

|  | A | B | C | D | E | F | G |
|---|---|---|---|---|---|---|---|
| **1** | **Employee table** | | | | | | |
| **2** | | | | | | | |
| **3** | *ID no.* | *Name* | *Initials* | *Dept. no.* | *Department* | *Paycode* | *Salary* |
| **4** | 3564 | Mikael Corleone | mic | 5105 | Transportation | 34 | 259018 |
| **5** | 3565 | Anders And | ana | 5102 | EDB | 21 | 152155 |
| **6** | 3566 | Bruce Wayne | brw | 5108 | Research | 22 | 159095 |
| **7** | 3567 | Vito Corleone | vic | 5103 | Admin. | 42 | 358580 |
| **8** | 3568 | Jens Jensen | jej | 5101 | Sales | 29 | 211686 |
| **9** | 3569 | J. Bond | jbo | 5105 | Transportation | 30 | 220390 |

**DEFINED NAMES**

| Name | Area |
|---|---|
| dptab | PERSONEL.XLS!$A$3:$B$30 |
| paytab | PERSONEL.XLS!$D$3:$E$50 |

**KEY FORMULAS**

| Cell | Formula | Comments |
|---|---|---|
| E4 | =IF(A3>0,VLOOKUP(D3,dptab,2),"") | This looks up department name. |
| G4 | =IF(A3>0,VLOOKUP(F3,paytab,2),"") | This looks up annual salary. Fill down the above formulas. |

223

**Tax table**

The tax table contains tax tables for state and local tax for class 1 and class 2 tax payers.

|  | A | B | C | D | E | F |
|---|---|---|---|---|---|---|
| 1 | tax class 1 | | | | class 2 | |
| 2 | annual income | local tax | state tax | | local tax | state tax |
| 3 | 150000 | 27762 | 10903 | | 24024 | 6906 |
| 4 | 151000 | 27972 | 11149 | | 24234 | 7062 |
| 5 | 152000 | 28182 | 11395 | | 24444 | 7218 |
| 6 | 153000 | 28392 | 11641 | | 24654 | 7374 |
| 7 | 154000 | 28602 | 11887 | | 24864 | 7530 |
| 8 | 155000 | 28812 | 12133 | | 25074 | 7686 |
| 9 | 156000 | 29022 | 12379 | | 25284 | 7842 |
| 10 | 157000 | 29232 | 12625 | | 25494 | 7998 |
| 11 | 158000 | 29442 | 12871 | | 25704 | 8154 |
| 12 | 159000 | 29652 | 13117 | | 25914 | 8310 |
| 13 | 160000 | 29862 | 13363 | | 26124 | 8466 |
| 14 | 161000 | 30072 | 13609 | | 26334 | 8622 |
| 15 | 162000 | 30282 | 13855 | | 26544 | 8778 |

**Payroll list**

The payroll list contains payroll information on all employees.

Formulas do the following:
1. Look up gross salary, tax classification and tax payable.
2. Calculate net salary and holiday pay.

|  | A | B | C | D | E | F | G | H | I |
|---|---|---|---|---|---|---|---|---|---|
| 1 | Month | 10 | | *October 1990* | | | | | |
| 2 | Year | 1990 | | | | | | | |
| 3 | | | | Press CTRL a to produce payslips. | | | | | |
| 4 | ID no. | Salary | Tax | Net sal. | Holid. pay | Tax class | | class 1 | class 2 |
| 5 | 3564 | 22575 | 7943 | 14632 | 225749 | 2 | | 8894 | 7943 |
| 6 | 3567 | 13775 | 4334 | 9441 | 137752 | 1 | | 4334 | 3469 |
| 7 | 3568 | 14381 | 3713 | 10669 | 143813 | 2 | | 4638 | 3713 |
| 8 | 3569 | 30913 | 12286 | 18628 | 309133 | 2 | | 13237 | 12286 |
| 9 | 3575 | 18678 | 5771 | 12906 | 186775 | 2 | | 6722 | 5771 |
| 10 | 3576 | 16210 | 4642 | 11568 | 162104 | 2 | | 5593 | 4642 |
| 11 | 3579 | 30913 | 12286 | 18628 | 309133 | 2 | | 13237 | 12286 |
| 12 | 3582 | 19390 | 7157 | 12233 | 193898 | 1 | | 7157 | 6206 |
| 13 | 3585 | 18678 | 5771 | 12906 | 186775 | 2 | | 6722 | 5771 |
| 14 | 3588 | 14989 | 3991 | 10999 | 149894 | 2 | | 4942 | 3991 |
| 15 | 3591 | 19390 | 6206 | 13184 | 193898 | 2 | | 7157 | 6206 |
| 16 | 3594 | 14381 | 3713 | 10669 | 143813 | 2 | | 4638 | 3713 |
| 17 | 3597 | 13215 | 4030 | 9185 | 132145 | 1 | | 4030 | 3225 |

## KEY NUMBER FORMATS

| Cell | Format | Comments |
|------|--------|----------|
| A5:A100 | 0;"" | This causes cell to be blank if no. is negative. |

## DEFINED NAMES

| Name | Area |
|------|------|
| month | $K$4:$L$15 |
| wtab | WORKERS.XLS!$A$3:$G$100 |
| ttab | TAX.XLS!A$3:$F$150 |

## KEY FORMULAS

| Cell | Formula | Comments |
|------|---------|----------|
| B5 | =IF(A5>0,VLOOKUP(A5,wtab,6)/12,"") | Looks up gross salary and transfers to monthly salary. It remains blank if no employee number is entered. |
| C5 | =IF(A5>0,IF(month=6,0,IF(month=12, IF(F5=1,H5*0.5,I5*0.5), IF(F5=1,H5,I5))),"") | Tests first for month (no tax for June, half for December). It tests as well for tax classification (1 or 2). Based on this, the appropriate tax is retrieved and calculated. |
| D5 | =IF(A5>0,B5-C5,"") | Calculates net salary. |
| E5 | =IF(A5>0,B5*month,"") | Calculates basis for holiday pay. |
| F5 | =IF(A5>0,VLOOKUP(A5,wtab,7),"") | Looks up tax classification (1 or 2). |
| H5 | =IF(A5>0,(VLOOKUP(B5*12,ttab,2)+ VLOOKUP(B5*12,ttab,3))/10.5,"") | Converts monthly salary back to annual salary, then looks up tax in tax table. Local and national tax is added together. Fill right and adjust for tax class 2. |
| I5 | =IF(A5>0,(VLOOKUP(B5*12,ttab,5)+ VLOOKUP(B5*12,ttab,6))/10.5,"") | Same as above, adjusted for tax class 2. fill down all above formulas. |
| E1 | =VLOOKUP(B1,K4:L15,2) | Looks up name of month. |
| E19 | =B2 | Retrieves year. |

225

The payslip form retrieves its information from the payroll list. Here, the information is placed in a payslip format.

Formulas do the following:
1. Look up employee information.
2. Look up payroll information.
3. Test if employee number given is valid, and broadcast error message if not.

A macro uses this form to produce payslips for all of the employees.

|  | A | B | C | D | E | F | G | H |
|---|---|---|---|---|---|---|---|---|
| 1 | | | | | | | | |
| 2 | **Mikael Corleone** | | | | | | | |
| 3 | | | | | | | | |
| 4 | Yogi Tea Import Ltd. | | | | ID no. | 3564 | Department | 5105 |
| 5 | | | | | Period | 1.Oct.90 - 31.Oct.90 | Date | 20.Oct.90 |
| 6 | | | | | | | | |
| 7 | | 1100 Gross salary | 22.575 | | | | | |
| 8 | | 1101 Income tax | 7.943 | | | | | |
| 9 | | 1200 Net salary | 14.632 | | | | | |
| 10 | | | | | | | | |
| 11 | | | | | | | | |
| 12 | | | | | | Holiday pay | 225.749 | |
| 13 | | | | | | | | |
| 14 | | | | | | | | |
| 15 | | | | | | | | |
| 16 | | | | | | | | |
| 17 | | | | | | | | |
| 18 | | | | | | | | |
| 19 | | | | | | | | |
| 20 | | 1 | | | | | | |
| 21 | | 1 | | | | | | |

## DEFINED NAMES

| Name | Area |
|------|------|
| enr | $E$4 |
| wtab | WORKERS.XLS!$A$3:$G$100 |
| ptab | PAYROLL.XLS!$A$5:$E$100 |
| wnr | WORKERS.XLS!$A$3:$A$100 |

## KEY FORMULAS

| Cell | Formula | Comments |
|------|---------|----------|
| A2 | =IF(B20>0,VLOOKUP(enr,wtab,2),"") | Looks up employee name. Remains blank if test cell = 0  (employee no. invalid). |
| H4 | =IF(B20>0,VLOOKUP(enr,wtab,3),"") | Similar to the above, but adjusted for department no. |
| C7 | =IF(B$20>0, VLOOKUP(enr,ptab,2),"") | Similar to the above, but looks in payroll table for gross salary. |
| C8 | =IF(B$20>0, VLOOKUP(enr,ptab,3),"") | Similar to the above, but adjusted for tax payable. |
| C9 | =IF(B$20>0, VLOOKUP(enr,ptab,4),"") | Similar to the above, but adjusted for net salary. |
| G12 | =IF(B$20>0, VLOOKUP(enr,ptab,5),"") | Similar to the above, but adjusted for holiday pay. |
| C3 | =IF(B20>0,"", "No information for this cust. no.") | Broadcasts message if test cell = 0 (employee number invalid) |
| B20 | =IF(VLOOKUP(enr,wtab,1)=wnr,1,0) | This tests if employee no. is valid by comparing it with the no. retrieved by VLOOKUP (which will find the closest number to it if it can't find an identical no.) |
| E4 | =MIN(wnr) | This sets employee no. to the employee no. with the lowest value (for use by macro). |
| B21 | =IF(E4>MAX(wnr),2,1) | This tests if employee no. is higher than the employee no. with the highest value. If so, this is a signal to the macro that all employee payslips have been processed. |

**Payslip producing macro**

This macro produces payslips in duplicate for each employee.

| STATEMENTS | EXPLANATION |
|---|---|
| =ACTIVATE("PAYSLIP.XLS") | activates payslip |
| =SELECT(!B21) | selects test cell B21 |
| =WHILE(ACTIVE.CELL()=1) | while employee no. is not too high, continues, otherwise, goes to ALERT statement |
| =SELECT(!B20) | selects test cell B20 |
| =IF(ACTIVE.CELL()>0,GOTO(A7), GOTO(A8)) <br> =PRINT?(2,1,1,2,FALSE,FALSE,1) | prints twice if employee no. is valid |
| =SELECT(!F4) | selects cell beside employee no. |
| =increment() | increases employee no. by 1 (submacro) |
| =SELECT(!B21) | selects test cell B21 |
| =NEXT() | returns to WHILE statement |
| =ALERT("No more employees",2) | Broadcasts message: "No more employees" |
| =SELECT("R4C5") | selects employee no. |
| =FORMULA("=MIN(wnr)") <br><br> =RETURN() | writes formula setting no. to employee no. with lowest value. |

### SUBMACRO TO INCREASE VALUE BY 1

| STATEMENTS | EXPLANATION |
|---|---|
| increment <br> =FORMULA("=RC[-1]+1") | sets number 1 more than cell on left |
| =COPY() <br> =SELECT("RC[-1]") | copies to cell on left ... |
| =PASTE.SPECIAL(3,1,FALSE,FALSE) <br> =CANCEL.COPY() | ... without the formula |
| =SELECT("RC[1]") <br> =FORMULA("") | clears the formula in the cell on the right |
| =SELECT("RC[-1]") <br> =RETURN() | selects the cell on the left |

# Part 4 | Solutions to Exercises

| | Date: | =NOW() |
|---|---|---|
| **Balance** | **Fee** | **Overdue** |
| 5220 | =IF(D675>100;$B$672;0) | =IF(D675>0;$G$671-B675;"") |
| 4788 | =IF(D676>100;$B$672;0) | =IF(D676>0;$G$671-B676;"") |
| 2035 | =IF(D677>100;$B$672;0) | =IF(D677>0;$G$671-B677;"") |
| 0 | =IF(D678>100;$B$672;0) | =IF(D678>0;$G$671-B678;"") |
| 9007 | =IF(D679>100;$B$672;0) | =IF(D679>0;$G$671-B679;"") |
| 0 | =IF(D680>100;$B$672;0) | =IF(D680>0;$G$671-B680;"") |
| 146 | =IF(D681>100;$B$672;0) | =IF(D681>0;$G$671-B681;"") |
| 0 | =IF(D682>100;$B$672;0) | =IF(D682>0;$G$671-B682;"") |
| | | |
| 21196 | 250 | =SUM(G678:G685) |
| 2650 | 31 | =AVERAGE(G678:G685) |
| 9007 | 50 | =MAX(G678:G685) |
| 0 | 0 | =MIN(G678:G685) |

|    | A | B | C | D | E | F | G | H |
|----|---|---|---|---|---|---|---|---|
| 1  | # Solutions to exercises |||||||
| 2  | | | | | | | | |
| 3  | *Exercise 1a - employee register* |||||||
| 4  | You have nine employees in your department. Type out a list with name, |||||||
| 5  | hours worked per week and hourly wage. Calculate weekly wage for |||||||
| 6  | each employee, based on hours worked and hourly wage. |||||||
| 7  | Save with the name "employee". |||||||
| 8  | | | | | | | | |
| 9  | | | hours | hr.wage | wk.wage | | | |
| 10 | Andersen | 40 | 120 | =B10*C10 | | | |
| 11 | Bond | 35 | 100 | =B11*C11 | | | |
| 12 | Caudillo | 40 | 130 | =B12*C12 | | | |
| 13 | Colombo | 50 | 60 | =B13*C13 | | | |
| 14 | Corleone | 25 | 80 | =B14*C14 | | | |
| 15 | Greer | 38 | 85 | =B15*C15 | | | |
| 16 | Kuiyakin | 38 | 105 | =B16*C16 | | | |
| 17 | | | | | | | | |
| 18 | | | | | | | | |
| 19 | | | | | | | | |
| 20 | | | | | | | | |

|  | A | B | C | D | E | F | G | H |
|---|---|---|---|---|---|---|---|---|
| 21 | *Exercise 1b - accounts receivable* | | | | | | | |
| 22 | You have eight customers who have ordered goods. Make a debtor | | | | | | | |
| 23 | list containing customer no., total amount purchased and amount already | | | | | | | |
| 24 | paid. Calculate balance due based on amount purchased and amount | | | | | | | |
| 25 | paid. Save with the name "accounts". | | | | | | | |
| 26 | | | | | | | | |
| 27 | | | | | | | | |
| 28 | | | | | | | | |
| 29 | | | | | | | | |
| 30 | Cust.no. | Total | Paid | Balance | | | | |
| 31 | 1112 | 9261 | 9261 | =B31-C31 | | | | |
| 32 | 1120 | 1146 | 1000 | =B32-C32 | | | | |
| 33 | 1116 | 8424 | 8424 | =B33-C33 | | | | |
| 34 | 1117 | 9007 | 0 | =B34-C34 | | | | |
| 35 | 1119 | 11437 | 11437 | =B35-C35 | | | | |
| 36 | 1113 | 8035 | 6000 | =B36-C36 | | | | |
| 37 | 1115 | 4788 | 0 | =B37-C37 | | | | |
| 38 | 1121 | 5220 | 0 | =B38-C38 | | | | |
| 39 | | | | | | | | |
| 40 | | | | | | | | |

|    | A | B | C | D | E | F | G | H |
|----|---|---|---|---|---|---|---|---|
| 41 | ***Exercise 1c - tax return*** | | | | | | | |
| 42 | Make a form for a tax return, using Excel. Type out the text for items 1 to 5. | | | | | | | |
| 43 | Then fill out name, tax classification and age, as well as items 1-5. | | | | | | | |
| 44 | You can use a tax return information pamphlet to help you fill out the form. | | | | | | | |
| 45 | Calculate the sums for items 1d to 5. Save with the name "taxcalc". | | | | | | | |
| 46 | | | | | | | | |
| 47 | | | | | | | | |
| 48 | | | | | | | | |
| 49 | | | | | | | | |
| 50 | | | | | | | | |
| 51 | | | | TAX RETURN | | | | |
| 52 | | | | | | | | |
| 53 | name | Kuliyakin | | classif. | 1 | age | 35 | |
| 54 | | | | | | | | |
| 55 | | | | | INCOME | | | |
| 56 | | | | | | | | |
| 57 | Item 1a | Salary | | | 250000 | | | |
| 58 | | Social security | | | | | | |
| 59 | | Loan advantage | | | 2000 | | | |
| 60 | | Company car | | | 15000 | | | |
| 61 | Item 1d | Other income | | | 5600 | | | |
| 62 | | Total income | | | =E57+E58+E59+E60+E61 | | | |
| 63 | | | | | | | | |
| 64 | | | | | | | | |
| 65 | Item 3b | Other benefits | | | 0 | | | |
| 66 | Item 5 | SUM (basis for min. deduction) | | | =E62+E65 | | | |
| 67 | | | | | | | | |

|    | A | B | C | D | E | F | G | H |
|----|---|---|---|---|---|---|---|---|
| 68 | ***Exercise 2a - deleting, moving, copying*** | | | | | | | |
| 69 | Two departments have been merged, with you as department leader! To the | | | | | | | |
| 70 | right of the original employees, write the names of the six new employees | | | | | | | |
| 71 | in your department, together with hours worked and hourly wage (headings, too). | | | | | | | |
| 72 | | | | | | | | |
| 73 | Use Edit - Cut to move the new information (headings included) down under the | | | | | | | |
| 74 | original list, so that the two lists are merged into one. Select the row with the | | | | | | | |
| 75 | superfluous headings and use Edit - Delete to delete the row. Weekly wages | | | | | | | |
| 76 | also have to be calculated for the new staff. Instead of writing new formulas | | | | | | | |
| 77 | for these, use Edit - Fill down to copy down the formula in the last line in the original | | | | | | | |
| 78 | list (Greer). | | | | | | | |
| 79 | | | | | | | | |
| 80 | | | | | | | | |
| 81 | | | | | | | | |
| 82 | | | | | | | | |
| 83 | | | | | | | | |
| 84 | | | hours | hr.wage | wk.wage | | | |
| 85 | Andersen | | 40 | 120 | =B85*C85 | | | |
| 86 | Bond | | 35 | 100 | =B86*C86 | | | |
| 87 | Caudillo | | 40 | 130 | =B87*C87 | | | |
| 88 | Colombo | | 50 | 60 | =B88*C88 | | | |
| 89 | Corleone | | 25 | 80 | =B89*C89 | | | |
| 90 | Greer | | 38 | 85 | =B90*C90 | | | |
| 91 | Marple | | 40 | 185 | =B91*C91 | | | |
| 92 | Jones | | 40 | 120 | =B92*C92 | | | |
| 93 | Blofeld | | 25 | 80 | =B93*C93 | | | |
| 94 | Solo | | 40 | 130 | =B94*C94 | | | |
| 95 | Syse | | 35 | 100 | =B95*C95 | | | |
| 96 | Iacocca | | 25 | 95 | =B96*C96 | | | |
| 97 | | | | | | | | |

| | A | B | C | D | E | F | G | H |
|---|---|---|---|---|---|---|---|---|
| 98 | **_Exercise 2b - editing, deleting, copying_** | | | | | | | |
| 99 | Use Edit - Clear (DEL RET) to remove the formulas for balance. | | | | | | | |
| 100 | Write the first formula again, and copy down with Edit - Fill down. | | | | | | | |
| 101 | Use Edit - Insert to insert a new column for invoice no. | | | | | | | |
| 102 | Insert the column to the left of customer no. | | | | | | | |
| 103 | | | | | | | | |
| 104 | | | | | | | | |
| 105 | | | | | | | | |
| 106 | | | | | | | | |
| 107 | | | | | | | | |
| 108 | Inv. no. | Cust.no. | Total | Paid | Balance | | | |
| 109 | | 1112 | 9261 | 9261 | =C109-D109 | | | |
| 110 | | 1120 | 1146 | 1000 | =C110-D110 | | | |
| 111 | | 1116 | 8424 | 8424 | =C111-D111 | | | |
| 112 | | 1117 | 9007 | 0 | =C112-D112 | | | |
| 113 | | 1119 | 11437 | 11437 | =C113-D113 | | | |
| 114 | | 1113 | 8035 | 6000 | =C114-D114 | | | |
| 115 | | 1115 | 4788 | 0 | =C115-D115 | | | |
| 116 | | 1121 | 5220 | 0 | =C116-D116 | | | |
| 117 | | | | | | | | |

|     | A | B | C | D | E | F | G | H |
|-----|---|---|---|---|---|---|---|---|
| 118 | *Exercise 2c - tax table* | | | | | | | |
| 119 | On a new sheet, make a table which shows federal and local tax for | | | | | | | |
| 120 | classification 1 and 2, for yearly income from 175000 to and including 375000. | | | | | | | |
| 121 | As income increases by 1000, local tax increases by 210, federal tax by 246. | | | | | | | |
| 122 | Use the figures below when writing the first line in the table. | | | | | | | |
| 123 | | | | | | | | |
| 124 | classification 1 | | | | classification 2 | | | |
| 125 | income | local tax | fed. tax | | local tax | fed. tax | | |
| 126 | 175000 | 33012 | 17053 | | 29274 | 10806 | | |
| 127 | | | | | | | | |
| 128 | In the second line of the table come the following formulas: | | | | | | | |
| 129 | | | | | | | | |
| 130 | income | local tax | fed. tax | | local tax | fed. tax | | |
| 131 | 175000 | 33012 | 17053 | | 29274 | 10806 | | |
| 132 | ( + 1000 ) | ( +210 ) | ( +246 ) | | ( +210 ) | ( +246 ) | | |
| 133 | | | | | | | | |
| 134 | Then use Edit - Fill to copy down in all columns so that the | | | | | | | |
| 135 | table continues on to where income is 375000. | | | | | | | |
| 136 | | | | | | | | |
| 137 | | | | | | | | |
| 138 | | | | | | | | |
| 139 | | | | | | | | |
| 140 | **Tax tables** | | | | | | | |
| 141 | | | | | | | | |
| 142 | classif. 1 | | | | classif. 2 | | | |
| 143 | income | local tax | fed. tax | | local tax | fed. tax | | |
| 144 | 175000 | 33012 | 17053 | | 29274 | 10806 | | |
| 145 | =A144+1000 | =B144+210 | =C144+246 | | =E144+210 | =F144+246 | | |
| 146 | =A145+1000 | =B145+210 | =C145+246 | | =E145+210 | =F145+246 | | |
| 147 | =A146+1000 | =B146+210 | =C146+246 | | =E146+210 | =F146+246 | | |
| 148 | =A147+1000 | =B147+210 | =C147+246 | | =E147+210 | =F147+246 | | |
| 149 | =A148+1000 | =B148+210 | =C148+246 | | =E148+210 | =F148+246 | | |
| 150 | =A149+1000 | =B149+210 | =C149+246 | | =E149+210 | =F149+246 | | |
| 151 | =A150+1000 | =B150+210 | =C150+246 | | =E150+210 | =F150+246 | | |
| 152 | =A151+1000 | =B151+210 | =C151+246 | | =E151+210 | =F151+246 | | |
| 153 | =A152+1000 | =B152+210 | =C152+246 | | =E152+210 | =F152+246 | | |
| 154 | =A153+1000 | =B153+210 | =C153+246 | | =E153+210 | =F153+246 | | |
| 155 | =A154+1000 | =B154+210 | =C154+246 | | =E154+210 | =F154+246 | | |
| 156 | =A155+1000 | =B155+210 | =C155+246 | | =E155+210 | =F155+246 | | |
| 157 | | | | | | | | |

| | A | B | C | D | E | F | G | H |
|---|---|---|---|---|---|---|---|---|
| 158 | ***Exercise 3a - locking, linking and mass copying*** | | | | | | | |
| 159 | Your department has shown good results. All employees will therefore get | | | | | | | |
| 160 | a bonus of 500. Add two rows on the top of the employee list. In the top row, | | | | | | | |
| 161 | type 'Bonus', and in the next cell, '500'. Add columns for weekly wage + bonus. | | | | | | | |
| 162 | | | | | | | | |
| 163 | Write a formula to calculate weekly wage + bonus for the first employee. Use | | | | | | | |
| 164 | cell references in the formula instead of numbers. Copy down with Edit - Fill down. | | | | | | | |
| 165 | But first lock the appropriate cell reference in the formula with $. | | | | | | | |
| 166 | | | | | | | | |
| 167 | | | | | | | | |
| 168 | | | | | | | | |
| 169 | | | | | | | | |
| 170 | Bonus | | 500 | | | | | |
| 171 | | | | | | | | |
| 172 | emp.no. | name | hours | hr.wage | wk.wage | + bonus | | |
| 173 | 1111 | Andersen | 40 | 120 | 4800 | =E173+$B$170 | | |
| 174 | 1119 | Blofeld | 25 | 80 | 2000 | =E174+$B$170 | | |
| 175 | 1112 | Bond | 35 | 100 | 3500 | =E175+$B$170 | | |
| 176 | 1113 | Caudillo | 40 | 130 | 5200 | =E176+$B$170 | | |
| 177 | 1114 | Colombo | 50 | 60 | 3000 | =E177+$B$170 | | |
| 178 | 1115 | Corleone | 25 | 80 | 2000 | =E178+$B$170 | | |
| 179 | 1116 | Greer | 38 | 85 | 3230 | =E179+$B$170 | | |
| 180 | 1122 | Iacocca | 25 | 95 | 2375 | =E180+$B$170 | | |
| 181 | 1118 | Jones | 40 | 120 | 4800 | =E181+$B$170 | | |
| 182 | 1117 | Marple | 40 | 185 | 7400 | =E182+$B$170 | | |
| 183 | 1120 | Solo | 40 | 130 | 5200 | =E183+$B$170 | | |
| 184 | 1121 | Syse | 35 | 100 | 3500 | =E184+$B$170 | | |
| 185 | | | | | | | | |
| 186 | | | | | | | | |
| 187 | | | | | | | | |

| | A | B | C | D | E | F | G | H |
|---|---|---|---|---|---|---|---|---|
| 188 | *Exercise 3b - naming cells, linking and mass copying* | | | | | | | |
| 189 | The boss has decided that a fee of 50 will be instituted for overdue invoices. | | | | | | | |
| 190 | Add two lines at the top of the debtor list. In the top line, type 'Fee', and in the | | | | | | | |
| 191 | next line, '50'. Add another column for balance + overdue fee. | | | | | | | |
| 192 | | | | | | | | |
| 193 | Write a formula to calculate balance + fee for the first invoice. Use cell | | | | | | | |
| 194 | references instead of numbers. Copy down with Edit - Fill down. But first | | | | | | | |
| 195 | lock the appropriate cell reference in the formula. This time, however, don't | | | | | | | |
| 196 | use $ to lock the reference, but instead give the cell (where the new fee is) | | | | | | | |
| 197 | a name (using Formula - Define name). | | | | | | | |
| 198 | | | | | | | | |
| 199 | Then delete the fee in the rows where balance is nil. | | | | | | | |
| 200 | | | | | | | | |
| 201 | | | | | | | | |
| 202 | | | | | | | | |
| 203 | | | | | | | | |
| 204 | | | | | | | | |
| 205 | Fee | 50 | | | | | | |
| 206 | | | | | | | | |
| 207 | Inv. no. | Cust.no. | Total | Paid | Balance | + fee | | |
| 208 | 24207 | 1121 | 5220 | 0 | 5220 | =E208+Fee | | |
| 209 | 24206 | 1115 | 4788 | 0 | 4788 | =E209+Fee | | |
| 210 | 24205 | 1113 | 8035 | 6000 | 2035 | =E210+Fee | | |
| 211 | 24204 | 1119 | 11437 | 11437 | 0 | =E211+Fee | | |
| 212 | 24203 | 1117 | 9007 | 0 | 9007 | =E212+Fee | | |
| 213 | 24202 | 1116 | 8424 | 8424 | 0 | =E213+Fee | | |
| 214 | 24201 | 1120 | 1146 | 1000 | 146 | =E214+Fee | | |
| 215 | 24200 | 1112 | 9261 | 9261 | 0 | =E215+Fee | | |
| 216 | | | | | | | | |

|   | A | B | C | D | E | F | G | H |
|---|---|---|---|---|---|---|---|---|
| 217 | *Exercise 3c - Naming cells* | | | | | | | |
| 218 | Tax class and age will be used in subsequent formulas in the tax return. | | | | | | | |
| 219 | Give these cells names using Formula - Define name, so that these names | | | | | | | |
| 220 | can be used later on in formulas, instead of cell references. | | | | | | | |
| 221 | | | | | | | | |
| 222 | | | | | | | | |
| 223 | | | | | | | | |
| 224 | | | | | | | | |
| 225 | | | | | TAX RETURN | | | |
| 226 | | | | | | | | |
| 227 | name | Kuliyakin | | class | 1 | age | 35 | |
| 228 | | | | | | | | |
| 229 | | | | | INCOME | | | |
| 230 | | | | | | | | |
| 231 | Item 1a | Salary | | | 250000 | | | |
| 232 | | Social security | | | | | | |
| 233 | | Loan advantage | | | 2000 | | | |
| 234 | | Company car | | | 15000 | | | |
| 235 | Item 1d | Other income | | | 5600 | | | |
| 236 | | Total income | | | =E231+E232+E233+E234+E235 | | | |
| 237 | | | | | | | | |
| 238 | | | | | | | | |
| 239 | Item 3b | Other benefits | | | 1000 | | | |
| 240 | Item 5 | SUM (basis for min. deduction) | | | =E236+E239 | | | |
| 241 | | | | | | | | |

|     | A | B | C | D | E | F | G | H |
|-----|---|---|---|---|---|---|---|---|
| 242 | ***Exercise 4a - number series and sorting*** | | | | | | | |
| 243 | Use Edit - Insert to insert a new column for employee no. to the left | | | | | | | |
| 244 | of employee name. Use Data - Series to generate employee numbers. | | | | | | | |
| 245 | The first number is 1111, which you simply type in, and then the numbers | | | | | | | |
| 246 | increase by 1. | | | | | | | |
| 247 | | | | | | | | |
| 248 | Use Data - Sort to sort alphabetically by name. | | | | | | | |
| 249 | | | | | | | | |
| 250 | | | | | | | | |
| 251 | | | | | | | | |
| 252 | | | | | | | | |
| 253 | | | | | | | | |
| 254 | emp.no. | name | hours | hr.wage | wk.wage | | | |
| 255 | 1111 | Andersen | 40 | 120 | 4800 | | | |
| 256 | 1119 | Blofeld | 25 | 80 | 2000 | | | |
| 257 | 1112 | Bond | 35 | 100 | 3500 | | | |
| 258 | 1113 | Caudillo | 40 | 130 | 5200 | | | |
| 259 | 1114 | Colombo | 50 | 60 | 3000 | | | |
| 260 | 1115 | Corleone | 25 | 80 | 2000 | | | |
| 261 | 1116 | Greer | 38 | 85 | 3230 | | | |
| 262 | 1122 | Iacocca | 25 | 95 | 2375 | | | |
| 263 | 1118 | Jones | 40 | 120 | 4800 | | | |
| 264 | 1117 | Marple | 40 | 185 | 7400 | | | |
| 265 | 1120 | Solo | 40 | 130 | 5200 | | | |
| 266 | 1121 | Syse | 35 | 100 | 3500 | | | |
| 267 | | | | | | | | |
| 268 | | | | | | | | |
| 269 | | | | | | | | |

| | A | B | C | D | E | F | G | H |
|---|---|---|---|---|---|---|---|---|
| 270 | **_Exercise 4b - number series and sorting_** | | | | | | | |
| 271 | Use Data - Series to generate invoice numbers. Type in the first number: | | | | | | | |
| 272 | 24200. Afterwards, this increases by 1. | | | | | | | |
| 273 | | | | | | | | |
| 274 | Use Data - Sort to sort the debtor list by invoice number in descending | | | | | | | |
| 275 | order. | | | | | | | |
| 276 | | | | | | | | |
| 277 | | | | | | | | |
| 278 | | | | | | | | |
| 279 | | | | | | | | |
| 280 | | | | | | | | |
| 281 | Inv. no. | Cust.no. | Total | Paid | Balance | | | |
| 282 | 24207 | 1121 | 5220 | 0 | 5220 | | | |
| 283 | 24201 | 1120 | 1146 | 1000 | 146 | | | |
| 284 | 24204 | 1119 | 11437 | 11437 | 0 | | | |
| 285 | 24203 | 1117 | 9007 | 0 | 9007 | | | |
| 286 | 24202 | 1116 | 8424 | 8424 | 0 | | | |
| 287 | 24206 | 1115 | 4788 | 0 | 4788 | | | |
| 288 | 24205 | 1113 | 8035 | 6000 | 2035 | | | |
| 289 | 24200 | 1112 | 9261 | 9261 | 0 | | | |
| 290 | | | | | | | | |
| 291 | | | | | | | | |

| | A | B | C | D | E | F | G | H |
|---|---|---|---|---|---|---|---|---|
| 292 | *Exercise 5a - linking spreadsheets* | | | | | | | |
| 293 | On another sheet, make a form for information about a single employee. | | | | | | | |
| 294 | The form should include name, employee number, hourly wage, hours worked, | | | | | | | |
| 295 | weekly wage, bonus and total wage paid out. | | | | | | | |
| 296 | | | | | | | | |
| 297 | Retrieve information from the employee register, using linking | | | | | | | |
| 298 | (formulas with  =, not copying information) | | | | | | | |
| 299 | | | | | | | | |
| 300 | | | | | | | | |
| 301 | | | | | | | | |
| 302 | | | | | | | | |
| 303 | | | | | *Uke  42* | | | |
| 304 | | | | | | | | |
| 305 | **Andersen, Jaques** | | | *Employee no.* | =A173 | | | |
| 306 | | | | | | | | |
| 307 | *Rate* | =D173 | | *Salary* | =E173 | | | |
| 308 | *Hours* | =C173 | | *Bonus* | =B170 | | | |
| 309 | | | | | | | | |
| 310 | | | | *Total* | =F173 | | | |
| 311 | | | | | | | | |
| 312 | | | | | | | | |
| 313 | | | | | | | | |

| | A | B | C | D | E | F | G | H |
|---|---|---|---|---|---|---|---|---|
| 314 | *Exercise 6a - formatting* | | | | | | | |
| 315 | Format the employee list so that headings appear in italic type. | | | | | | | |
| 316 | One of the employees, Caudillo, has mentioned to you that actually his name is | | | | | | | |
| 317 | "El Caudillo". Change this. As a result, the column will have to be widened. | | | | | | | |
| 318 | | | | | | | | |
| 319 | Centre and put a box around the cell at the top of the sheet containing bonus | | | | | | | |
| 320 | of 500. Right-justify the headings, except for name which can stay as it is, and | | | | | | | |
| 321 | employee number. Centre the latter along with the rest of its column. | | | | | | | |
| 322 | | | | | | | | |
| 323 | Add two lines at the top of the sheet and write the name of the department in | | | | | | | |
| 324 | bold type, with 18-pt. size, and in grey (shadow). Remove gridlines from the | | | | | | | |
| 325 | screen. | | | | | | | |
| 326 | | | | | | | | |
| 327 | Give a name to the cell containing bonus amount. Insert the name in all formulas | | | | | | | |
| 328 | which contain references to bonus. | | | | | | | |
| 329 | | | | | | | | |
| 330 | | | | | | | | |
| 331 | | | | | | | | |
| 332 | | | | | | | | |
| 333 | EDB Service | | | | | | | |
| 334 | | | | | | | | |
| 335 | Bonus | | 500 | | | | | |
| 336 | | | | | | | | |
| 337 | *emp.no.* | *name* | | *hours* | *hr.wage* | *wk.wage* | *+ bonus* | |
| 338 | 1111 | Andersen | | 40 | 120 | 4800 | 4800 | |
| 339 | 1119 | Blofeld | | 25 | 80 | 2000 | 2000 | |
| 340 | 1112 | Bond | | 35 | 100 | 3500 | 3500 | |
| 341 | 1113 | El Caudillo | | 40 | 130 | 5200 | 5200 | |
| 342 | 1114 | Colombo | | 50 | 60 | 3000 | 3000 | |
| 343 | 1115 | Corleone | | 25 | 80 | 2000 | 2000 | |
| 344 | 1116 | Greer | | 38 | 85 | 3230 | 3230 | |
| 345 | 1122 | Iacocca | | 25 | 95 | 2375 | 2375 | |
| 346 | 1118 | Jones | | 40 | 120 | 4800 | 4800 | |
| 347 | 1117 | Marple | | 40 | 185 | 7400 | 7400 | |
| 348 | 1120 | Solo | | 40 | 130 | 5200 | 5200 | |
| 349 | 1121 | Syse | | 35 | 100 | 3500 | 3500 | |
| 350 | | | | | | | | |
| 351 | | | | | | | | |
| 352 | | | | | | | | |

| | A | B | C | D | E | F | G | H |
|---|---|---|---|---|---|---|---|---|
| 353 | *Exercise 6b - formatting* | | | | | | | |
| 354 | Format the debtor list so that headings appear in italic type. | | | | | | | |
| 355 | Format the amounts so that they appear with no decimals, and "$" before. | | | | | | | |
| 356 | You will have to widen some of the columns. | | | | | | | |
| 357 | | | | | | | | |
| 358 | Centre and put a box around the cell at the top of the sheet containing the fee | | | | | | | |
| 359 | of 50. Right-justify the headings, except for invoice and customer number, | | | | | | | |
| 360 | which should be centred along with the rest of their columns. | | | | | | | |
| 361 | | | | | | | | |
| 362 | Insert a new column to the right of 'Total', and give it the heading 'Due'. | | | | | | | |
| 363 | Write in due dates similar to the example below. | | | | | | | |
| 364 | | | | | | | | |
| 365 | Add two lines at the top of the sheet and write "Invoice List" in bold type, | | | | | | | |
| 366 | with 18-pt. size, and in grey (shadow). Write today's date in the top righthand | | | | | | | |
| 367 | corner of the sheet. Remove gridlines from the screen. | | | | | | | |
| 368 | | | | | | | | |
| 369 | | | | | | | | |
| 370 | | | | | | | | |
| 371 | | | | | | | | |
| 372 | Invoice List | | | | | | | |
| 373 | | | | | | Date: | 8.Oct.90 | |
| 374 | Fee : | | 50 | | | | | |
| 375 | | | | | | | | |
| 376 | *Inv. no.* | *Cust.no.* | *Total* | *Due* | *Paid* | *Balance* | *+ fee* | |
| 377 | 24207 | 1121 | $5220 | 7.Oct | $0 | $5220 | $5270 | |
| 378 | 24206 | 1115 | $4788 | 5.Oct | $0 | $4788 | $4838 | |
| 379 | 24205 | 1113 | $8035 | 3.Oct | $6000 | $2035 | $2085 | |
| 380 | 24204 | 1119 | $11437 | 1.Oct | $11437 | $0 | $50 | |
| 381 | 24203 | 1117 | $9007 | 30.Sep | $0 | $9007 | $9057 | |
| 382 | 24202 | 1116 | $8424 | 28.Sep | $8424 | $0 | $50 | |
| 383 | 24201 | 1120 | $1146 | 26.Sep | $1000 | $146 | $196 | |
| 384 | 24200 | 1112 | $9261 | 25.Sep | $9261 | $0 | $50 | |
| 385 | | | | | | | | |
| 386 | | | | | | | | |

|     | A | B | C | D | E | F | G | H |
|-----|---|---|---|---|---|---|---|---|
| 387 | *Exercise 6c - formatting* | | | | | | | |
| 388 | Format your tax form with boxes, grey fields (shadow), justifying and | | | | | | | |
| 389 | fonts as shown in the example below. Remove gridlines. | | | | | | | |
| 390 | | | | | | | | |
| 391 | | | | | | | | |
| 392 | | | | | | | | |
| 393 | | | | | | | | |
| 394 | | | | | | | | |
| 395 | | | | | | | | |
| 396 | | | | TAX RETURN | | | | |
| 397 | | | | | | | | |
| 398 | name | Kuliyakin | | class | 1 | age | 35 | |
| 399 | | | | | | | | |
| 400 | | | | INCOME | | | | |
| 401 | | | | | | | | |
| 402 | Item 1a | Salary | | | 250000 | | | |
| 403 | | Social security | | | | | | |
| 404 | | Loan advantage | | | 2000 | | | |
| 405 | | Company car | | | 15000 | | | |
| 406 | Item 1d | Other income | | | 5600 | | | |
| 407 | | Total income | | | 272600 | | | |
| 408 | | | | | | | | |
| 409 | | | | | | | | |
| 410 | Item 3b | Other benefits | | | 1000 | | | |
| 411 | Item 5 | SUM (basis for min. deduction) | | | 273600 | | | |
| 412 | | | | | | | | |
| 413 | | | | | | | | |

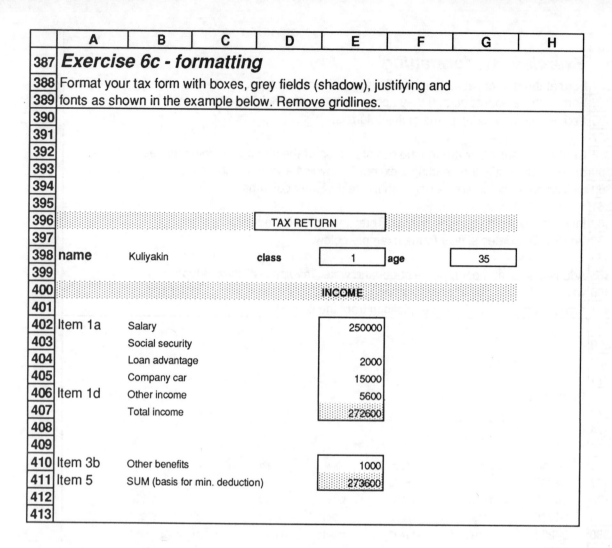

| | A | B | C | D | E | F | G | H |
|---|---|---|---|---|---|---|---|---|
| 414 | *Exercise 7a - printout* | | | | | | | |
| 415 | Use File - Printer setup to select printer. | | | | | | | |
| 416 | | | | | | | | |
| 417 | Use File - Page setup to remove gridlines and row/column headings | | | | | | | |
| 418 | (A, B, C ... and 1, 2, 3 ...) from the printout. | | | | | | | |
| 419 | | | | | | | | |
| 420 | Use File - Page setup to remove page headings, | | | | | | | |
| 421 | and to change the footer to "p." instead of "Page". | | | | | | | |
| 422 | Cause the footer to be written in italic font. | | | | | | | |
| 423 | | | | | | | | |
| 424 | Print out, but first look at Preview. | | | | | | | |
| 425 | | | | | | | | |
| 426 | | | | | | | | |
| 427 | | | | | | | | |
| 428 | | | | | | | | |
| 429 | | | | | | | | |
| 430 | EDB Service | | | | | | | |
| 431 | | | | | | | | |
| 432 | Bonus | 500 | | | | | | |
| 433 | | | | | | | | |
| 434 | *emp.no.* | *name* | *hours* | *hr.wage* | *wk.wage* | *+ bonus* | | |
| 435 | 1111 | Andersen | 40 | 120 | 4800 | 4800 | | |
| 436 | 1119 | Blofeld | 25 | 80 | 2000 | 2000 | | |
| 437 | 1112 | Bond | 35 | 100 | 3500 | 3500 | | |
| 438 | 1113 | El Caudillo | 40 | 130 | 5200 | 5200 | | |
| 439 | 1114 | Colombo | 50 | 60 | 3000 | 3000 | | |
| 440 | 1115 | Corleone | 25 | 80 | 2000 | 2000 | | |
| 441 | 1116 | Greer | 38 | 85 | 3230 | 3230 | | |
| 442 | 1122 | Iacocca | 25 | 95 | 2375 | 2375 | | |
| 443 | 1118 | Jones | 40 | 120 | 4800 | 4800 | | |
| 444 | 1117 | Marple | 40 | 185 | 7400 | 7400 | | |
| 445 | 1120 | Solo | 40 | 130 | 5200 | 5200 | | |
| 446 | 1121 | Syse | 35 | 100 | 3500 | 3500 | | |
| 447 | | | | | | | | |
| 448 | | | | | | | | |
| 449 | | | | | | | | |

| | A | B | C | D | E | F | G | H |
|---|---|---|---|---|---|---|---|---|
| 450 | *Exercise 7b - printout* | | | | | | | |
| 451 | Use File - Printer setup and then Setup to get a horizontal printout. | | | | | | | |
| 452 | | | | | | | | |
| 453 | Use File - Page setup to remove gridlines and row/column headers | | | | | | | |
| 454 | (A, B, C ... and 1, 2, 3 ...) from the printout. | | | | | | | |
| 455 | | | | | | | | |
| 456 | Use File - Page setup to remove page headings, | | | | | | | |
| 457 | and to change the footer to "p." instead of "Page". | | | | | | | |
| 458 | Cause the footer to be written in italic font. | | | | | | | |
| 459 | | | | | | | | |
| 460 | Print out, but first look at Preview. | | | | | | | |
| 461 | | | | | | | | |
| 462 | | | | | | | | |
| 463 | | | | | | | | |
| 464 | | | | | | | | |
| 465 | | | | | | | | |
| 466 | Invoice List | | | | | | | |
| 467 | | | | | | Date: | 8.Oct.90 | |
| 468 | Fee : | 50 | | | | | | |
| 469 | | | | | | | | |
| 470 | Inv. no. | Cust.no. | Total | Due | Paid | Balance | + fee | |
| 471 | 24207 | 1121 | $5220 | 7.Oct | $0 | $5220 | $5220 | |
| 472 | 24206 | 1115 | $4788 | 5.Oct | $0 | $4788 | $4788 | |
| 473 | 24205 | 1113 | $8035 | 3.Oct | $6000 | $2035 | $2035 | |
| 474 | 24204 | 1119 | $11437 | 1.Oct | $11437 | $0 | $0 | |
| 475 | 24203 | 1117 | $9007 | 30.Sep | $0 | $9007 | $9007 | |
| 476 | 24202 | 1116 | $8424 | 28.Sep | $8424 | $0 | $0 | |
| 477 | 24201 | 1120 | $1146 | 26.Sep | $1000 | =C477-E477 | =F477+$B$55 | |
| 478 | 24200 | 1112 | $9261 | 25.Sep | $9261 | =C478-E478 | =F478+$B$55 | |
| 479 | | | | | | | | |
| 480 | | | | | | | | |

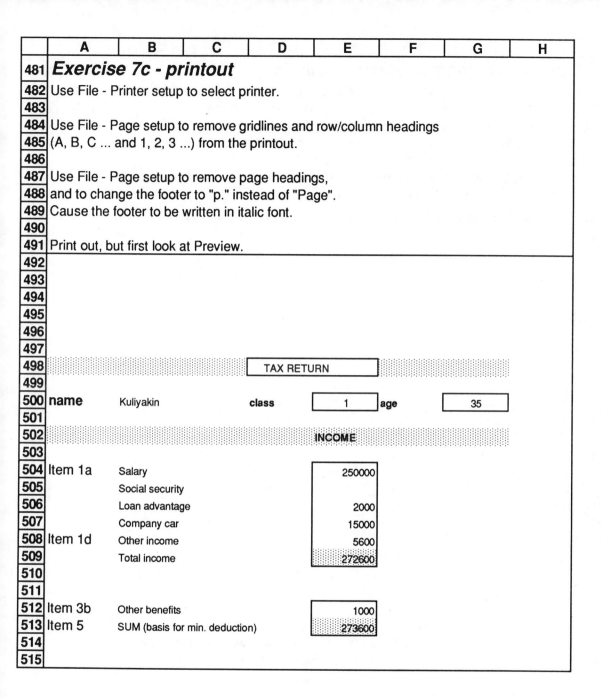

|     | A | B | C | D | E | F | G | H |
|-----|---|---|---|---|---|---|---|---|
| 481 | *Exercise 7c - printout* | | | | | | | |
| 482 | Use File - Printer setup to select printer. | | | | | | | |
| 483 | | | | | | | | |
| 484 | Use File - Page setup to remove gridlines and row/column headings | | | | | | | |
| 485 | (A, B, C ... and 1, 2, 3 ...) from the printout. | | | | | | | |
| 486 | | | | | | | | |
| 487 | Use File - Page setup to remove page headings, | | | | | | | |
| 488 | and to change the footer to "p." instead of "Page". | | | | | | | |
| 489 | Cause the footer to be written in italic font. | | | | | | | |
| 490 | | | | | | | | |
| 491 | Print out, but first look at Preview. | | | | | | | |
| 492 | | | | | | | | |
| 493 | | | | | | | | |
| 494 | | | | | | | | |
| 495 | | | | | | | | |
| 496 | | | | | | | | |
| 497 | | | | | | | | |
| 498 | | | | TAX RETURN | | | | |
| 499 | | | | | | | | |
| 500 | **name** | Kuliyakin | | **class** | 1 | age | 35 | |
| 501 | | | | | | | | |
| 502 | | | | INCOME | | | | |
| 503 | | | | | | | | |
| 504 | Item 1a | Salary | | | 250000 | | | |
| 505 | | Social security | | | | | | |
| 506 | | Loan advantage | | | 2000 | | | |
| 507 | | Company car | | | 15000 | | | |
| 508 | Item 1d | Other income | | | 5600 | | | |
| 509 | | Total income | | | 272600 | | | |
| 510 | | | | | | | | |
| 511 | | | | | | | | |
| 512 | Item 3b | Other benefits | | | 1000 | | | |
| 513 | Item 5 | SUM (basis for min. deduction) | | | 273600 | | | |
| 514 | | | | | | | | |
| 515 | | | | | | | | |

|     | A | B | C | D | E | F | G | H |
|-----|---|---|---|---|---|---|---|---|
| 516 | *Exercise 8a - mathematical functions* | | | | | | | |
| 517 | Use the SUM-function to add the figures in each column. | | | | | | | |
| 518 | Use the AVERAGE-function to average the figures in each column. | | | | | | | |
| 519 | Use the MAX-function to get the highest number in each column. | | | | | | | |
| 520 | Use the MIN-function to get the lowest number in each column. | | | | | | | |
| 521 | Use Edit - Fill right to copy the formulas to the right. | | | | | | | |
| 522 | Use the COUNT-function to count the number of employees. | | | | | | | |
| 523 | Use the NOW-function to get the day's date. | | | | | | | |
| 524 | (Format - Number to get date format) | | | | | | | |
| 525 | | | | | | | | |
| 526 | | | | | | | | |
| 527 | | | | | | | | |
| 528 | | | | | | | | |
| 529 | | | | | | | | |
| 530 | EDB Service | | | | | | =NOW() | |
| 531 | | | | | | | | |
| 532 | Bonus | 500 | | | | | | |
| 533 | | | | | | | | |
| 534 | *emp.no.* | *name* | *hours* | *hr.wage* | *wk.wage* | *+ bonus* | | |
| 535 | 1111 | Andersen | 40 | 120 | 4800 | 4840 | | |
| 536 | 1119 | Blofeld | 25 | 80 | 2000 | 2040 | | |
| 537 | 1112 | Bond | 35 | 100 | 3500 | 3540 | | |
| 538 | 1113 | El Caudillo | 40 | 130 | 5200 | 5240 | | |
| 539 | 1114 | Colombo | 50 | 60 | 3000 | 3040 | | |
| 540 | 1115 | Corleone | 25 | 80 | 2000 | 2040 | | |
| 541 | 1116 | Greer | 38 | 85 | 3230 | 3270 | | |
| 542 | 1122 | Iacocca | 25 | 95 | 2375 | 2415 | | |
| 543 | 1118 | Jones | 40 | 120 | 4800 | 4840 | | |
| 544 | 1117 | Marple | 40 | 185 | 7400 | 7440 | | |
| 545 | 1120 | Solo | 40 | 130 | 5200 | 5240 | | |
| 546 | 1121 | Syse | 35 | 100 | 3500 | 3540 | | |
| 547 | | | | | | | | |
| 548 | | *Sum* | =SUM(C535: | =SUM(D535: | =SUM(E535: | =SUM(F535:F546) | | |
| 549 | | *Average* | =AVERAGE( | =AVERAGE( | =AVERAGE( | =AVERAGE(F535:F546) | | |
| 550 | | *Highest* | =MAX(C535: | =MAX(D535: | =MAX(E535: | =MAX(F535:F546) | | |
| 551 | | *Lowest* | =MIN(C535:C | =MIN(D535:C | =MIN(E535:E | =MIN(F535:F546) | | |
| 552 | | *Count* | =COUNT(C535:C546) | | | | | |
| 553 | | | | | | | | |
| 554 | | | | | | | | |

| | A | B | C | D | E | F | G | H |
|---|---|---|---|---|---|---|---|---|
| **555** | ***Exercise 8b - mathematical functions*** | | | | | | | |
| **556** | Use the SUM-function to add the figures in each column. | | | | | | | |
| **557** | Use the AVERAGE-function to average the figures in each column. | | | | | | | |
| **558** | Use the MAX-function to get the highest number in each column. | | | | | | | |
| **559** | Use the MIN-function to get the lowest number in each column. | | | | | | | |
| **560** | Use Edit - Fill right to copy the formulas to the right. | | | | | | | |
| **561** | Press DEL and RET to clear away sum, average, etc. for due date. | | | | | | | |
| **562** | Use the COUNT-function to count the number of invoices. | | | | | | | |
| **563** | Use the NOW-function to get the day's date. | | | | | | | |
| **564** | (Format - Number to get date format) | | | | | | | |
| **565** | | | | | | | | |
| **566** | | | | | | | | |
| **567** | | | | | | | | |
| **568** | | | | | | | | |
| **569** | | | | | | | | |
| **570** | Invoice List | | | | | | | |
| **571** | | | | | | Date: =NOW() | | |
| **572** | Fee : | 50 | | | | | | |
| **573** | | | | | | | | |
| **574** | *Inv. no.* | *Cust.no.* | *Total* | *Due* | *Paid* | *Balance* | *+ fee* | |
| **575** | 24207 | 1121 | $5220 | 7.Oct | $0 | $5220 | $5220 | |
| **576** | 24206 | 1115 | $4788 | 5.Oct | $0 | $4788 | $4788 | |
| **577** | 24205 | 1113 | $8035 | 3.Oct | $6000 | $2035 | $2035 | |
| **578** | 24204 | 1119 | $11437 | 1.Oct | $11437 | $0 | $0 | |
| **579** | 24203 | 1117 | $9007 | 30.Sep | $0 | $9007 | $9007 | |
| **580** | 24202 | 1116 | $8424 | 28.Sep | $8424 | $0 | $0 | |
| **581** | 24201 | 1120 | $1146 | 26.Sep | $1000 | $146 | $146 | |
| **582** | 24200 | 1112 | $9261 | 25.Sep | $9261 | $0 | $0 | |
| **583** | | | | | | | | |
| **584** | | *Sum* | =SUM(C575: | =SUM(D575: | =SUM(E575: | =SUM(F575:F582) | | |
| **585** | | *Average* | =AVERAGE( | =AVERAGE( | =AVERAGE( | =AVERAGE(F575:F582) | | |
| **586** | | *Highest* | =MAX(C575: | =MAX(D575: | =MAX(E575: | =MAX(F575:F582) | | |
| **587** | | *Lowest* | =MIN(C575:( | =MIN(D575:[ | =MIN(E575:E | =MIN(F575:F582) | | |
| **588** | | *Count* | =COUNT(C575:C582) | | | | | |

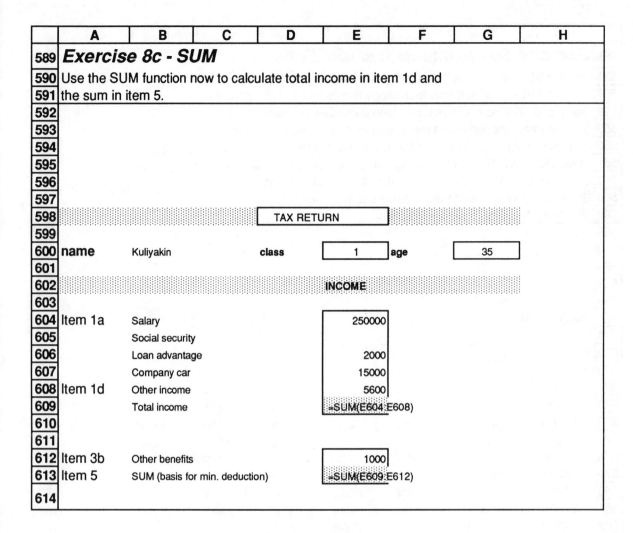

| | A | B | C | D | E | F | G | H |
|---|---|---|---|---|---|---|---|---|
| 589 | **Exercise 8c - SUM** | | | | | | | |
| 590 | Use the SUM function now to calculate total income in item 1d and | | | | | | | |
| 591 | the sum in item 5. | | | | | | | |
| 592 | | | | | | | | |
| 593 | | | | | | | | |
| 594 | | | | | | | | |
| 595 | | | | | | | | |
| 596 | | | | | | | | |
| 597 | | | | | | | | |
| 598 | | | | | TAX RETURN | | | |
| 599 | | | | | | | | |
| 600 | **name** | Kuliyakin | | **class** | 1 | age | 35 | |
| 601 | | | | | | | | |
| 602 | | | | | INCOME | | | |
| 603 | | | | | | | | |
| 604 | Item 1a | Salary | | | 250000 | | | |
| 605 | | Social security | | | | | | |
| 606 | | Loan advantage | | | 2000 | | | |
| 607 | | Company car | | | 15000 | | | |
| 608 | Item 1d | Other income | | | 5600 | | | |
| 609 | | Total income | | | =SUM(E604:E608) | | | |
| 610 | | | | | | | | |
| 611 | | | | | | | | |
| 612 | Item 3b | Other benefits | | | 1000 | | | |
| 613 | Item 5 | SUM (basis for min. deduction) | | | =SUM(E609:E612) | | | |
| 614 | | | | | | | | |

| | A | B | C | D | E | F | G | H |
|---|---|---|---|---|---|---|---|---|
| 615 | *Exercise 9a - IF* | | | | | | | |
| 616 | Insert a column to the left of '+ bonus'. Give it the heading 'bonus'. | | | | | | | |
| 617 | Use the IF-function to test if hours worked is more than 20. | | | | | | | |
| 618 | If it is, than the employee gets a bonus, and if not, forget it (0). | | | | | | | |
| 619 | Use Edit - Fill down to copy the formulas down, and Edit - Fill right | | | | | | | |
| 620 | to copy the formulas on the bottom line, to the right. | | | | | | | |
| 621 | | | | | | | | |
| 622 | | | | | | | | |
| 623 | | | | | | | | |
| 624 | | | | | | | | |
| 625 | | | | | | | | |
| 626 | EDB Service | | | | | | | |
| 627 | | | | | | | | |
| 628 | Bonus | 500 | | | | | | |
| 629 | | | | | | | | |
| 630 | emp.no. | name | hours | hr.wage | wk.wage | bonus | | + bonus |
| 631 | 1111 | Andersen | 40 | 120 | 4800 | =IF(C631>20;$B$628;0) | | 5300 |
| 632 | 1119 | Blofeld | 25 | 80 | 2000 | =IF(C632>20;$B$628;0) | | 2500 |
| 633 | 1112 | Bond | 40 | 100 | 4000 | =IF(C633>20;$B$628;0) | | 4500 |
| 634 | 1113 | El Caudillo | 40 | 130 | 5200 | =IF(C634>20;$B$628;0) | | 5700 |
| 635 | 1114 | Colombo | 40 | 60 | 2400 | =IF(C635>20;$B$628;0) | | 2900 |
| 636 | 1115 | Corleone | 25 | 80 | 2000 | =IF(C636>20;$B$628;0) | | 2500 |
| 637 | 1116 | Greer | 10 | 85 | 850 | =IF(C637>20;$B$628;0) | | 850 |
| 638 | 1122 | Iacocca | 25 | 95 | 2375 | =IF(C638>20;$B$628;0) | | 2875 |
| 639 | 1118 | Jones | 40 | 120 | 4800 | =IF(C639>20;$B$628;0) | | 5300 |
| 640 | 1117 | Marple | 40 | 185 | 7400 | =IF(C640>20;$B$628;0) | | 7900 |
| 641 | 1120 | Solo | 10 | 130 | 1300 | =IF(C641>20;$B$628;0) | | 1300 |
| 642 | 1121 | Syse | 25 | 100 | 2500 | =IF(C642>20;$B$628;0) | | 3000 |
| 643 | | | | | | | | |
| 644 | | Sum | 360 | 1285 | 39625 | =SUM(F631:F642) | | 44625 |
| 645 | | Average | 30 | 107 | 3302 | =AVERAGE(F631:F642) | | 3719 |
| 646 | | Highest | 40 | 185 | 7400 | =MAX(F631:F642) | | 7900 |
| 647 | | Lowest | 10 | 60 | 850 | =MIN(F631:F642) | | 850 |
| 648 | | Count | 12 | | | | | |
| 649 | | | | | | | | |
| 650 | | | | | | | | |

|     | A | B | C | D | E | F | G | H |
|-----|---|---|---|---|---|---|---|---|
| 651 | ***Exercise 9b - IF*** | | | | | | | |
| 652 | Insert a column to the left of '+ fee'. Give it the heading 'Fee'. | | | | | | | |
| 653 | Use the IF-function to test if balance is higher than 100. | | | | | | | |
| 654 | If it is, the customer is charged a fee, and otherwise, the cell remains empty. | | | | | | | |
| 655 | Use already-defined cell names, and adjust the formulas for '+ fee'. | | | | | | | |
| 656 | | | | | | | | |
| 657 | Insert a column after '+ fee'. Give it the heading 'overdue'. | | | | | | | |
| 658 | Write a formula to find number of days overdue. Use IF first to test | | | | | | | |
| 659 | if balance is nil, and if so, the cell can remain empty (""). Otherwise, | | | | | | | |
| 660 | a formula calculates days overdue (today's date minus due date). | | | | | | | |
| 661 | Write this formula as the third parameter inside of the IF-function. | | | | | | | |
| 662 | | | | | | | | |
| 663 | Use Edit - Fill down to copy the formulas down, and | | | | | | | |
| 664 | Edit - Fill right to copy the formulas on the bottom line, to the right. | | | | | | | |
| 665 | | | | | | | | |
| 666 | | | | | | | | |
| 667 | | | | | | | | |
| 668 | | | | | | | | |
| 669 | | | | | | | | |
| 670 | Invoice List | | | | | | | |
| 671 | | | | | | Date: | 8.Oct.90 | |
| 672 | Fee : | 50 | | | | | | |
| 673 | | | | | | | | |
| 674 | | *Total* | *Due* | *Paid* | *Balance* | *Fee* | *+ fee* | *Overdue* |
| 675 | 5220 | 7.Oct | 0 | 5220 | =IF(D675>100;$B$672;0) | =IF(D675>0;$G$671-B675;"") | |
| 676 | 4788 | 5.Oct | 0 | 4788 | =IF(D676>100;$B$672;0) | =IF(D676>0;$G$671-B676;"") | |
| 677 | 8035,2 | 3.Oct | 6000 | 2035 | =IF(D677>100;$B$672;0) | =IF(D677>0;$G$671-B677;"") | |
| 678 | 11437,2 | 1.Oct | 11437,2 | 0 | =IF(D678>100;$B$672;0) | =IF(D678>0;$G$671-B678;"") | |
| 679 | 9007,2 | 30.Sep | 0 | 9007 | =IF(D679>100;$B$672;0) | =IF(D679>0;$G$671-B679;"") | |
| 680 | 8424 | 28.Sep | 8424 | 0 | =IF(D680>100;$B$672;0) | =IF(D680>0;$G$671-B680;"") | |
| 681 | 1146 | 26.Sep | 1000 | 146 | =IF(D681>100;$B$672;0) | =IF(D681>0;$G$671-B681;"") | |
| 682 | 9261 | 25.Sep | 9261 | 0 | =IF(D682>100;$B$672;0) | =IF(D682>0;$G$671-B682;"") | |
| 683 | | | | | | | | |
| 684 | | Sum | 36122 | 21196 | 250 | 21446 | 27 | |
| 685 | | Average | 4515 | 2650 | 31 | 2681 | 5 | |
| 686 | | Highest | 11437 | 9007 | 50 | 9057 | 11 | |
| 687 | | Lowest | 0 | 0 | 0 | 0 | 1 | |
| 688 | | | | | | | | |
| 689 | | | | | | | | |

| | A | B | C | D | E | F | G | H |
|---|---|---|---|---|---|---|---|---|
| 690 | *Exercise 9c - cell naming and IF* | | | | | | | |
| 691 | Type in the following variables on the top of the sheet, and define with | | | | | | | |
| 692 | Formula - Define name: | | | | | | | |
| 693 | 1. Tax free limit for shares (class 1 and 2) | | | | | | | |
| 694 | 2. Standard deduction (minimum and maximum limits) | | | | | | | |
| 695 | 3. Travel amount that cannot be deducted | | | | | | | |
| 696 | | | | | | | | |
| 697 | Tax free amount in item 11 is 3000 in class 1, 6000 in class 2. | | | | | | | |
| 698 | Use IF to test for tax class. | | | | | | | |
| 699 | Sum of federal tax is the sum of item 10a, 10b and stock dividend, minus tax-free amount. | | | | | | | |
| 700 | Sum of local tax is the sum of item 10a and 10b minus tax-free amount. | | | | | | | |
| 701 | However, you don't want any negative numbers in these cells, and that is exactly | | | | | | | |
| 702 | what you would get if the tax-free amount is higher than the sum of the other items. | | | | | | | |
| 703 | So you will need to include an IF to test if this is the case, and if so, make the result 0. | | | | | | | |
| 704 | | | | | | | | |
| 705 | As for standard deduction, it is = the low limit (mindeduct) if income * 13% is lower | | | | | | | |
| 706 | than the low limit. If income * 13% is higher than the high limit (maxdeduct), then | | | | | | | |
| 707 | the result would be the high limit. For example: | | | | | | | |
| 708 | If income = 200000, 200000*13% =26000, so standard deduction would be 7000. | | | | | | | |
| 709 | If income is 18000, 18000*13% =2340, so standard deduction would be 3000. | | | | | | | |
| 710 | | | | | | | | |
| 711 | Sum of deductibles can't be a negative number either, so here an IF needs to | | | | | | | |
| 712 | be included, in the same way as with sum of federal and local tax. | | | | | | | |
| 713 | | | | | | | | |
| 714 | | | | | | | | |
| 715 | | | | | | | | |
| 716 | | | | | | | | |
| 717 | | | | | | | | |
| 718 | | | | | | | | |

| | A | B | C | D | E | F | G | H |
|---|---|---|---|---|---|---|---|---|
| 719 | freediv1 | 3000 | item 11 | | | | | |
| 720 | freediv2 | 6000 | | | | | | |
| 721 | mindeduct | 3000 | item 21a | | | | | |
| 722 | maxdeduct | 7000 | | | | | | |
| 723 | mintravel | 5000 | item 24b | | | | | |
| 724 | | | | | | | | |
| 725 | | | | | | | | |
| 726 | | | | TAX RETURN | | | | |
| 727 | | | | | | | | |
| 728 | **name** | Kuliyakin | | **class** | 1 | age | 35 | |
| 729 | | | | | | | | |
| 730 | | | | INCOME | | | | |
| 731 | | | | | | | | |
| 732 | Item 1a | Salary | | | 250000 | | | |
| 733 | | Social security | | | | | | |
| 734 | | Loan advantage | | | 2000 | | | |
| 735 | | Company car | | | 15000 | | | |
| 736 | Item 1d | Other income | | | 5600 | | | |
| 737 | | Total income | | | 272600 | | | |
| 738 | | | | | | | | |
| 739 | | | | | | | | |
| 740 | Item 3b | Other benefits | | | 1000 | | | |
| 741 | Item 5 | SUM (basis for min. deduction) | | | 273600 | | | |
| 742 | | | | | | | | |
| 743 | Item 10a | Interest | | | 5000 | | | |
| 744 | Item 10b | Insurance, savings div. | | | 3000 | | | |
| 745 | Item 11 | Stock dividend | | | 4000 | | | |
| 746 | | Tax-free allowance (for p. 10/11) | | | =-IF(E728 =1;freediv1;freediv2) | | | |
| 747 | | Sum federal tax | | | =IF(SUM(E743:E746)>0;SUM(E743:E746);0) | | | |
| 748 | | Sum local tax | | | =IF(E743+E744+E746>0;E743+E744+E746;0) | | | |
| 749 | Item 12-19 | Other income | | | 2500 | | | |
| 750 | | | | | | | | |
| 751 | | | | | | | | |
| 752 | Item 20 | SUM gross income | | | =E741+E747+E749 | | | |
| 753 | | | | | | | | |
| 754 | | | | | | | | |
| 755 | | | | | | | | |
| 756 | | | | | | | | |
| 757 | | | | | | | | |

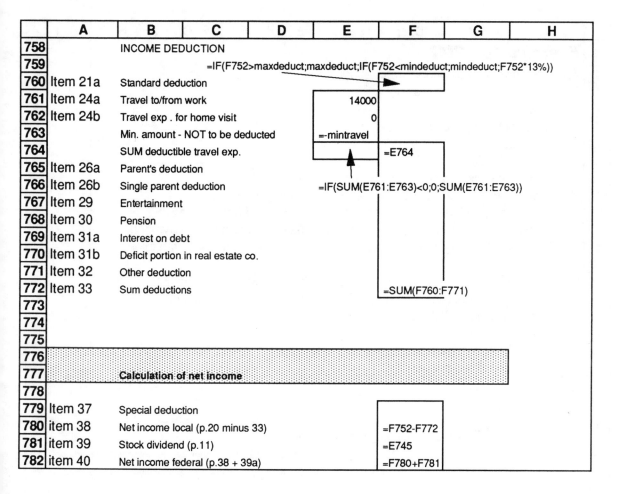

|     | A | B | C | D | E | F | G | H |
|-----|---|---|---|---|---|---|---|---|
| 758 |   | INCOME DEDUCTION | | | | | | |
| 759 |   | =IF(F752>maxdeduct;maxdeduct;IF(F752<mindeduct;mindeduct;F752*13%)) | | | | | | |
| 760 | Item 21a | Standard deduction | | | | | | |
| 761 | Item 24a | Travel to/from work | | | 14000 | | | |
| 762 | Item 24b | Travel exp . for home visit | | | 0 | | | |
| 763 |   | Min. amount - NOT to be deducted | | | =-mintravel | | | |
| 764 |   | SUM deductible travel exp. | | | | =E764 | | |
| 765 | Item 26a | Parent's deduction | | | | | | |
| 766 | Item 26b | Single parent deduction | | | =IF(SUM(E761:E763)<0;0;SUM(E761:E763)) | | | |
| 767 | Item 29 | Entertainment | | | | | | |
| 768 | Item 30 | Pension | | | | | | |
| 769 | Item 31a | Interest on debt | | | | | | |
| 770 | Item 31b | Deficit portion in real estate co. | | | | | | |
| 771 | Item 32 | Other deduction | | | | | | |
| 772 | Item 33 | Sum deductions | | | | =SUM(F760:F771) | | |
| 773 |   | | | | | | | |
| 774 |   | | | | | | | |
| 775 |   | | | | | | | |
| 776 |   | | | | | | | |
| 777 |   | **Calculation of net income** | | | | | | |
| 778 |   | | | | | | | |
| 779 | Item 37 | Special deduction | | | | | | |
| 780 | item 38 | Net income local (p.20 minus 33) | | | | =F752-F772 | | |
| 781 | item 39 | Stock dividend (p.11) | | | | =E745 | | |
| 782 | item 40 | Net income federal (p.38 + 39a) | | | | =F780+F781 | | |

|   | A | B | C | D | E | F | G | H | I |
|---|---|---|---|---|---|---|---|---|---|
| 1 | *Exercise 10 - PMT* | | | | | | | | |
| 2 | You are considering buying a car for 80000. | | | | | | | | |
| 3 | The finance plan is as follows: | | | | | | | | |
| 4 | - 35% down payment | | | | | | | | |
| 5 | - monthly loan repayments for 3 years | | | | | | | | |
| 6 | - at 15,9% interest | | | | | | | | |
| 7 | | | | | | | | | |
| 8 | Use the PMT-function to calculate the amount of each repayment. | | | | | | | | |
| 9 | Make some variables at the top of the sheet for annuity, interest, | | | | | | | | |
| 10 | number of years, periods per year, amount of loan, price of car, % financing | | | | | | | | |
| 11 | and down payment. Use simple formulas to calculate price and down payment. | | | | | | | | |
| 12 | Use Formula - Create Names to define names for the cells containing variables. | | | | | | | | |
| 13 | | | | | | | | | |
| 14 | Make a table on the same sheet which shows a breakdown of repayments | | | | | | | | |
| 15 | into payments on principal, interest repayments and resulting balance for | | | | | | | | |
| 16 | each period. Use the PPMT and IPMT functions. | | | | | | | | |
| 17 | | | | | | | | | |
| 18 | Use Formula - Apply Names to replace cell references in the formulas | | | | | | | | |
| 19 | with the newly-defined names. | | | | | | | | |
| 20 | | | | | | | | | |
| 21 | | | | | | | | | |
| 22 | | | | | period | interest | | principal | balance |
| 23 | | Annuity | =-PMT(Interest;Number_of_yrs.*Periods;Loan_amount) | | | | | | |
| 24 | | Interest | 15,9% | | 2 | =-IPMT(Interest;$D24;Number_of_yrs.*Periods;Loan_amount) | | | |
| 25 | | Number of yrs. | 3 | | 3 | =-IPMT(Inter | =-PPMT(Interest;$D25;Number_of_yrs.*Periods; | | |
| 26 | | Periods | 12 | | 4 | =-IPMT(Inter | =-PPMT( | =G25-F26 | Loan_amount) |
| 27 | | Loan amount | 52000 | | 5 | =-IPMT(Inter | =-PPMT( | =G26-F27 | |
| 28 | | Price | =Loan_amount/Financing | | | =-IPMT(Inter | =-PPMT( | =G27-F28 | |
| 29 | | Financing | 65% | | 7 | =-IPMT(Inter | =-PPMT( | =G28-F29 | |
| 30 | | Down payment | =Price*(1-Financing) | | 8 | =-IPMT(Inter | =-PPMT( | =G29-F30 | |
| 31 | | | | | 9 | =-IPMT(Inter | =-PPMT( | =G30-F31 | |
| 32 | | | | | 10 | =-IPMT(Inter | =-PPMT( | =G31-F32 | |
| 33 | | | | | 11 | =-IPMT(Inter | =-PPMT( | =G32-F33 | |
| 34 | | | | | 12 | =-IPMT(Inter | =-PPMT( | =G33-F34 | |
| 35 | | | | | 13 | =-IPMT(Inter | =-PPMT( | =G34-F35 | |
| 36 | | | | | 14 | =-IPMT(Inter | =-PPMT( | =G35-F36 | |
| 37 | | | | | 15 | =-IPMT(Inter | =-PPMT( | =G36-F37 | |
| 38 | | | | | 16 | =-IPMT(Inter | =-PPMT( | =G37-F38 | |
| 39 | | | | | 17 | =-IPMT(Inter | =-PPMT( | =G38-F39 | |
| 40 | | | | | 18 | =-IPMT(Inter | =-PPMT( | =G39-F40 | |
| 41 | | | | | | | | | |
| 42 | | | | | | | | | |

# Exercise 11 - PV

You have decided to buy a house, but need to find out which price range
you can afford. What you know is that you can afford repayments of 5000 per
month, and have 100000 in savings which can be used as down payment.

The finance plan is as follows:
- 15% down payment
- monthly loan repayments for 30 years
- at 12,4% interest

Use the PV-function to calculate the loan amount you could handle.
Make some variables at the top of the sheet for annuity, interest,
number of years, periods per year, amount of loan, price of car, % financing
and down payment. Use simple formulas to calculate price and down payment.
Use Formula - Create Names to define names for the cells containing variables.

Make a table on the same sheet which shows a breakdown of repayments
into payments on principal, interest repayments and resulting balance for
each period. Use the PPMT and IPMT functions.

Use Formula - Apply Names to replace cell references in the formulas
with the newly-defined names.

| A | B | | period | interest | principal | balance |
|---|---|---|---|---|---|---|
| | | | | | | |
| Annuity | 5000 | | 1 | 4876 | 124 | 471795 |
| Interest | 12,4% | | 2 | 4875 | 125 | 471671 |
| Number of yrs. | 30 | | 3 | 4874 | 126 | 471545 |
| Periods | 12 | | 4 | 4873 | 127 | 471417 |
| Loan amount | =PV(Interest;Number_of_yrs.*Periods;-Annuity) | | | | 129 | 471288 |
| Price | =Loan_amount/Financing | | | 4870 | 130 | 471158 |
| Financing | 85% | | 7 | 4869 | 131 | 471027 |
| Down payment | =Price-Loan_amount | | | 4867 | 133 | 470894 |
| | | | 9 | 4866 | 134 | 470760 |
| | | | 10 | 4865 | 135 | 470625 |
| | | | 11 | 4863 | 137 | 470488 |
| | | | 12 | 4862 | 138 | 470350 |
| | | | 13 | 4860 | 140 | 470210 |
| | | | 14 | 4859 | 141 | 470069 |
| | | | 15 | 4857 | 143 | 469926 |

|   | A | B | C | D | E | F | G | H | I |
|---|---|---|---|---|---|---|---|---|---|
| 86 | *Exercise 12 - RATE* | | | | | | | | |
| 87 | You are considering several savings plans. | | | | | | | | |
| 88 | Use the RATE function to compare interest rates of the different plans. | | | | | | | | |
| 89 | | | | | | | | | |
| 90 | Plan 1: you receive 800000 after 20 years if you deposit 5000 twice a year. | | | | | | | | |
| 91 | Plan 2: you receive 500000 after 20 years if you deposit 7000 once a year. | | | | | | | | |
| 92 | Plan 3: you receive 50450 after 20 years if you make a one-time deposit of 5000. | | | | | | | | |
| 93 | | | | | | | | | |
| 94 | | | | | | | | | |
| 95 | | | | | | | | | |
| 96 | | | | | | | | | |
| 97 | | | | | | | | | |
| 98 | | | | | | | | | |
| 99 | Interest | =RATE(B103*B104;-B102;-B101;B100;1)*B104 | | | | | Interest | 12,3% | |
| 100 | Future amount | 800000 | | Future amount | 500000 | | Future amount | 50450 | |
| 101 | 1-time deposit | | | 1-time deposit | | | 1-time deposit | 5000 | |
| 102 | Annuity | 5000 | | Annuity | 7000 | | Annuity | | |
| 103 | Number of yrs. | 20 | | Number of yrs. | 20 | | Number of yrs. | 20 | |
| 104 | No. of periods | 2 | | No. of periods | 1 | | No. of periods | 1 | |
| 105 | | | | | | | | | |
| 106 | | | | | | | | | |

258

|  | A | B | C | D | E | F | G | H | I |
|---|---|---|---|---|---|---|---|---|---|
| 107 | *Exercise 13 - FV* | | | | | | | | |
| 108 | You are thinking of saving 750 each quarter for 10 years. | | | | | | | | |
| 109 | Interest is 11,4%. Use the FV-function to calculate how much you will | | | | | | | | |
| 110 | have saved up after 10 years. | | | | | | | | |
| 111 | | | | | | | | | |
| 112 | Make some variables at the top of the sheet for annuity, interest, | | | | | | | | |
| 113 | number of years, periods per year and total amount saved. | | | | | | | | |
| 114 | Use Formula - Create Names to define names for the cells containing variables. | | | | | | | | |
| 115 | | | | | | | | | |
| 116 | Make a table on the same sheet which shows interest and balance. | | | | | | | | |
| 117 | for each period. | | | | | | | | |
| 118 | | | | | | | | | |
| 119 | Use Formula - Apply Names to replace cell references in the formulas | | | | | | | | |
| 120 | with the newly-defined names. | | | | | | | | |
| 121 | | | | | | | | | |
| 122 | | | | | | | | | |
| 123 | | | | | | Interest | Balance | | |
| 124 | | Annuity | 750 | | 1 | =Annuity*Interest/Periods | | | |
| 125 | | Interest | 11,4% | | 2 | =(Annuity+F124)*Interest/Periods | | | |
| 126 | | Number of yrs. | 10 | | 3 | =(Annuity+F125)*Interest/Periods | | | |
| 127 | | Periods | 4 | | 4 | 89 | =Annuity+F126+E127 | | |
| 128 | | Savings | =FV(Interest;Number_of_yrs.*Periods;-Annuity;0;1) | | | | | | |
| 129 | | | | | 6 | 138 | =Annuity+F128+E129 | | |
| 130 | | | | | 7 | 163 | 5884 | | |
| 131 | | | | | 8 | 189 | 6823 | | |
| 132 | | | | | 9 | 216 | 7789 | | |
| 133 | | | | | 10 | 243 | 8782 | | |
| 134 | | | | | 11 | 272 | 9804 | | |
| 135 | | | | | 12 | 301 | 10855 | | |
| 136 | | | | | 13 | 331 | 11935 | | |
| 137 | | | | | 14 | 362 | 13047 | | |
| 138 | | | | | 15 | 393 | 14190 | | |
| 139 | | | | | 16 | 426 | 15366 | | |
| 140 | | | | | 17 | 459 | 16575 | | |
| 141 | | | | | 18 | 494 | 17819 | | |
| 142 | | | | | 19 | 529 | 19098 | | |
| 143 | | | | | 20 | 566 | 20414 | | |
| 144 | | | | | 21 | 603 | 21767 | | |
| 145 | | | | | 22 | 642 | 23159 | | |
| 146 | | | | | | | | | |
| 147 | | | | | | | | | |

| | A | B | C | D | E | F | G | H | I |
|---|---|---|---|---|---|---|---|---|---|
| 148 | **Exercise 14 - IRR** | | | | | | | | |
| 149 | You are considering an investment which involves providing 50000 in capital. | | | | | | | | |
| 150 | You have estimated your investment return each year for 10 years. Use the | | | | | | | | |
| 151 | IRR function to calculate the actual interest return on your investment. | | | | | | | | |
| 152 | | | | | | | | | |
| 153 | | | | | | | | | |
| 154 | | | | | | | | | |
| 155 | | | | | | | | | |
| 156 | | | | | | | | | |
| 157 | | | | | Investment: | =-B158 | | | |
| 158 | Investment | 50000 | | Return: Year 1 | | -1000 | | | |
| 159 | Interest return | =IRR(F157:F167) | | Year 2 | | 1000 | | | |
| 160 | Number of yrs. | 10 | | Year 3 | | 2500 | | | |
| 161 | | | | Year 4 | | 6500 | | | |
| 162 | | | | Year 5 | | 8000 | | | |
| 163 | | | | Year 6 | | 10000 | | | |
| 164 | | | | Year 7 | | 12000 | | | |
| 165 | | | | Year 8 | | 14000 | | | |
| 166 | | | | Year 9 | | 16000 | | | |
| 167 | | | | Year 10 | | 18000 | | | |

|   | A | B | C | D | E | F | G |
|---|---|---|---|---|---|---|---|
| 1 | *Exercise 15 - charts* | | | | | | |
| 2 | Type in the sales information shown in the example below. | | | | | | |
| 3 | Present this information in the form of a readable, self-explanatory chart. | | | | | | |
| 4 | | | | | | | |
| 5 | | | | | | | |
| 6 | | | | | | | |
| 7 | | | | | | | |
| 8 | **Sales in Northern Norway** | | | | | | |
| 9 | *District* | *Sales 86* | *Sales 87* | *Sales 88* | *Sales 89* | *Sales 90* | |
| 10 | Troms | 69320 | 90116 | 117151 | 152296 | 185263 | |
| 11 | Nordland | 13900 | 18070 | 23491 | 32154 | 41800 | |
| 12 | Finnmark | 8630 | 11219 | 9588 | 9642 | 10254 | |
| 13 | | | | | | | |
| 14 | | | | | | | |
| 15 | | | | | | | |

**Sales in Northern Norway**

Bar chart with y-axis from 0 to 160000, x-axis categories: Sales 86, Sales 87, Sales 88, Sales 89, Sales 90. Legend: Troms, Nordland, Finnmark.

| | A | B | C | D | E | F | G |
|---|---|---|---|---|---|---|---|
| 35 | *Exercise 16a - VLOOKUP* | | | | | | |
| 36 | Use the employee form you made in exercise 5a. | | | | | | |
| 37 | Use VLOOKUP-formulas to look up name, hourly rate, hours worked, | | | | | | |
| 38 | weekly wage, bonus and total wages corresponding to the employee | | | | | | |
| 39 | number which is input. | | | | | | |
| 40 | | | | | | | |
| 41 | | | | | | | |
| 42 | | | | | | | |
| 43 | | | | | | | |
| 44 | | | | *Week 42* | | | |
| 45 | | | | | | | |
| 46 | **Andersen, Jaques** | | *Emp. no.* | 1111 | | | |
| 47 | | | | | | | |
| 48 | *Rate* | =VLOOKUP($ | *Wage* | =VLOOKUP($D$46;table;5) | | | |
| 49 | *Hours* | =VLOOKUP($ | *Bonus* | =VLOOKUP($D$46;table;6) | | | |
| 50 | | | | | | | |
| 51 | | | *Total* | =D48+D49 | | | |
| 52 | | | | | | | |
| 53 | | | | | | | |
| 54 | | | | | | | |

|    | A | B | C | D | E | F | G |
|----|---|---|---|---|---|---|---|
| 55 | *Exercise 16b - VLOOKUP* | | | | | | |
| 56 | On a new sheet, make a form for information about a single invoice. | | | | | | |
| 57 | Use VLOOKUP-formulas to find customer no., invoice no., due date, | | | | | | |
| 58 | amount paid, balance, penalty fee and total payable. These should | | | | | | |
| 59 | correspond to the invoice number which is input. | | | | | | |
| 60 | | | | | | | |
| 61 | | | | | | | |
| 62 | | | | | | | |
| 63 | | | | | | | |
| 64 | | | | | | | |
| 65 | | | | | | | |
| 66 | | | | | | | |
| 67 | | | | | | | |
| 68 | *Inv. no.* | 24205 | | *Cust.no.* | =VLOOKUP($B$68;table;2) | | |
| 69 | | | | | | | |
| 70 | *Inv. total* | =VLOOKUP($B$68;table;3) | | *Balance* | =B70-B72 | | |
| 71 | *Due date* | =VLOOKUP($B$68;table;4) | | *Penalty fee* | =VLOOKUP($B$68;table;7) | | |
| 72 | *Paid* | =VLOOKUP($B$68;table;5) | | Total payable | =E70+E71 | | |
| 73 | | | | | | | |
| 74 | | | | | | | |
| 75 | | | | | | | |
| 76 | | | | | | | |

| | A | B | C | D | E | F | G |
|---|---|---|---|---|---|---|---|
| 77 | *Exercise 16c - VLOOKUP* | | | | | | |
| 78 | Add some variables to the list at the top of the sheet, using Formula - Define name: | | | | | | |
| 79 | 1. Welfare | | | | | | |
| 80 | 2. Taxfree amount for special state tax (class 1 and 2) | | | | | | |
| 81 | 3. Special tax  % | | | | | | |
| 82 | | | | | | | |
| 83 | Welfare is 7,9% of gross income (p. 1d) | | | | | | |
| 84 | The taxfree amount for special state tax is 195000 for class 1 and 235000 for class 2. | | | | | | |
| 85 | Special tax is 8,5% of above amount. | | | | | | |
| 86 | | | | | | | |
| 87 | **Special state tax** | | | | | | |
| 88 | Sum salary and pension is taken from the sum in item 1d. | | | | | | |
| 89 | Stock dividend is taken from item 39. | | | | | | |
| 90 | For taxfree amount, use IF to test for tax class (1 or 2). | | | | | | |
| 91 | The basis for calculating special tax is the sum of 'sum salary and pension' | | | | | | |
| 92 | and 'stock dividend' minus 'taxfree amount'. An IF-function will be needed | | | | | | |
| 93 | here to avoid negative numbers in the results. | | | | | | |
| 94 | Special tax is special tax % (8,5%) of 'amount for special tax'. | | | | | | |
| 95 | | | | | | | |
| 96 | **Income tax to state, city and district** | | | | | | |
| 97 | Net income local is taken from item 38. | | | | | | |
| 98 | For 'local and district tax", use the VLOOKUP-function. The lookup key is | | | | | | |
| 99 | net income local. The tax table you made in exercise 2c is the lookup table. | | | | | | |
| 100 | Column number depends on whether tax class is 1 or 2. | | | | | | |
| 101 | So in the last parameter of the VLOOKUP-formula, you'll need IF. | | | | | | |
| 102 | Net income state is taken from item 40. | | | | | | |
| 103 | For state tax, use the VLOOKUP-function. The lookup key is net income | | | | | | |
| 104 | local. The tax table here is also the lookup table, and the column number | | | | | | |
| 105 | also depends on whether tax class is 1 or 2 (IF). | | | | | | |
| 106 | | | | | | | |
| 107 | *(example on following page)* | | | | | | |

| | A | B | C | D | E | F | G |
|---|---|---|---|---|---|---|---|
| 108 | freediv1 | 3000 | item 11 | | | | |
| 109 | freediv2 | 6000 | | | | | |
| 110 | mindeduct | 3000 | item 21a | | | | |
| 111 | maxdeduct | 7000 | | | | | |
| 112 | mintravel | 5000 | item 24b | | | | |
| 113 | welfare | 7,9% | | | | | |
| 114 | freespec1 | 195000 | | | | | |
| 115 | freespec2 | 235000 | | | | | |
| 116 | spectax | 8,5% | | | | | |
| 117 | | | | | | | |
| 118 | | | | | | | |
| 119 | | | | TAX RETURN | | | |
| 120 | | | | | | | |
| 121 | **name** | Kuliyakin | | **class** | 1 | age | 35 |
| 122 | | | | | | | |
| 123 | | | | INCOME | | | |
| 124 | | | | | | | |
| 125 | Item 1a | Salary | | | 250000 | | |
| 126 | | Social security | | | | | |
| 127 | | Loan advantage | | | 2000 | | |
| 128 | | Company car | | | 15000 | | |
| 129 | Item 1d | Other income | | | 5600 | | |
| 130 | | Total income | | | 272600 | | |
| 131 | | | | | | | |
| 132 | | | | | | | |
| 133 | Item 3b | Other benefits | | | 1000 | | |
| 134 | Item 5 | SUM (basis for min. deduction) | | | 273600 | | |
| 135 | | | | | | | |
| 136 | Item 10a | Interest | | | 5000 | | |
| 137 | Item 10b | Insurance, savings div. | | | 3000 | | |
| 138 | Item 11 | Stock dividend | | | 4000 | | |
| 139 | | Taxfree allowance (for p. 10/11) | | | 3000 | | |
| 140 | | Sum state tax | | | 15000 | | |
| 141 | | Sum local tax | | | 5000 | | |
| 142 | Item 12-19 | Other income | | | 2500 | | |
| 143 | | | | | | | |
| 144 | | | | | | | |
| 145 | Item 20 | SUM gross income | | | | 291100 | |
| 146 | | | | | | | |

|     | A | B | C | D | E | F | G |
|-----|---|---|---|---|---|---|---|
| 147 |   | INCOME DEDUCTION | | | | | |
| 148 |   | | | | | | |
| 149 | Item 21a | Standard deduction | | | | 7000 | |
| 150 | Item 24a | Travel to/from work | | | 14000 | | |
| 151 | Item 24b | Travel exp . for home visit | | | 0 | | |
| 152 |   | Min. amount - NOT to be deducted | | | 5000 | | |
| 153 |   | SUM deductible travel exp. | | | 19000 | 19000 | |
| 154 | Item 26a | Parent's deduction | | | | | |
| 155 | Item 26b | Single parent deduction | | | | | |
| 156 | Item 29 | Entertainment | | | | | |
| 157 | Item 30 | Pension | | | | | |
| 158 | Item 31a | Interest on debt | | | | | |
| 159 | Item 31b | Deficit portion in real estate co. | | | | | |
| 160 | Item 32 | Other deduction | | | | | |
| 161 | Item 33 | Sum deductions | | | | 26000 | |
| 162 |   | | | | | | |
| 163 |   | | | | | | |
| 164 |   | | | | | | |
| 165 |   | | | | | | |
| 166 |   | Calculation of net income | | | | | |
| 167 |   | | | | | | |
| 168 | Item 37 | Special deduction | | | | | |
| 169 | item 38 | Net income local (p.20 minus 33) | | | | 265100 | |
| 170 | item 39 | Stock dividend (p.10b) | | | | 4000 | |
| 171 | item 40 | Net income fed. (p.38 + 39a) | | | | 269100 | |
| 172 |   | | | | | | |
| 173 |   | | | | | | |
| 174 |   | | | | | | |
| 175 |   | Life insurance | | | | | |
| 176 |   | | | | | | |
| 177 | Item 41a | Group life insurance | | | | 0 | |
| 178 | Item 41b | Individual life insurance | | | | 1000 | |
| 179 |   | | | | | | |
| 180 |   | | | | | | |

| | A | B | C | D | E | F | G |
|---|---|---|---|---|---|---|---|
| 181 | Basis for calculating tax | | | | | | |
| 182 | | | | | | | |
| 183 | **Welfare** | | | | | | |
| 184 | 7,9% of gross income (P.1) | | | | | =7,9%*E130 | |
| 185 | | | | | | | |
| 186 | | | | | | | |
| 187 | **Special federal tax** | | | | | | |
| 188 | Sum salary and pension (P.1) | | | | =E130 | | |
| 189 | Stock dividend (P.39) | | | | =F170 | | |
| 190 | Tax-free amount | | | | =-IF(E121 =1;freespec1;freespec2) | | |
| 191 | Basis for calculation of special tax | | | | =SUM(E188:E190) | | |
| 192 | Special tax, 8,5% of above | | | | =8,5%*E191 | | |
| 193 | | | | | | | |
| 194 | | | | | | | |
| 195 | **Income tax to fed., city, district** | | | | | | |
| 196 | Net income local (P.38) | | | | =F169 | | |
| 197 | Local and district tax | | | | =VLOOKUP(E196;localtax;IF(E121 =1;1;2 | | |
| 198 | Net income fed. (P.40) | | | | =F171 | | |
| 199 | Federal tax | | | | =VLOOKUP(E198;fedtax;IF(E121 =1;1;2)) | | |
| 200 | | | | | | | |
| 201 | | | | | | | |

|     | A | B | C | D | E | F | G |
|-----|---|---|---|---|---|---|---|
| 202 | *Exercise 17a - database* | | | | | | |
| 203 | On a new sheet, make a criteria and result area, and use Data - Extract to | | | | | | |
| 204 | generate a list with name, hours worked and salary + bonus for all | | | | | | |
| 205 | employees that worked 40 hours. | | | | | | |
| 206 | | | | | | | |
| 207 | | | | | | | |
| 208 | | | | | | | |
| 209 | | | | | | | |
| 210 | | | | | | | |
| 211 | EDB Service | | | | | | |
| 212 | | | | | Date: | 8.Oct.90 | |
| 213 | CRITERIA | | | | | | |
| 214 | *emp.no.* | *name* | *hours* | *hr.wage* | *wk.wage* | *bonus* | *+ bonus* |
| 215 | | | 40 | | | | |
| 216 | | | | | | | |
| 217 | RESULT | | | | | | |
| 218 | | *name* | *hours* | *hr.wage* | | | |
| 219 | | Andersen | 40 | 5300 | | | |
| 220 | | Bond | 40 | 4500 | | | |
| 221 | | El Caudillo | 40 | 5700 | | | |
| 222 | | Colombo | 40 | 2900 | | | |
| 223 | | Jones | 40 | 5300 | | | |
| 224 | | Marple | 40 | 7900 | | | |
| 225 | | | | | | | |
| 226 | | | | | | | |

|    | A | B | C | D | E | F | G |
|----|---|---|---|---|---|---|---|
| 227 | **_Exercise 17B - database_** | | | | | | |
| 228 | On a new sheet, make a criteria and result area, and use Data - Extract to | | | | | | |
| 229 | generate a list with invoice number, customer number, balance and overdue | | | | | | |
| 230 | for all outstanding invoices (overdue and with remaining balance). | | | | | | |
| 231 | | | | | | | |
| 232 | | | | | | | |
| 233 | | | | | | | |
| 234 | | | | | | | |
| 235 | | | | | | | |
| 236 | Invoice List | | | | | | |
| 237 | | | | | | Date: | 8.Oct.90 |
| 238 | CRITERIA | | | | | | |
| 239 | _Inv. no._ | _Cust.no._ | _Balance_ | _Overdue_ | | | |
| 240 | | | >0 | >0 | | | |
| 241 | | | | | | | |
| 242 | RESULT | | | | | | |
| 243 | _Inv. no._ | _Cust.no._ | _Total_ | _Due_ | _Paid_ | _Balance_ | _Overdue_ |
| 244 | 24207 | 1121 | 5220 | 7.Oct | 0 | 5220 | 1 day |
| 245 | 24206 | 1115 | 4788 | 5.Oct | 0 | 4788 | 3 day |
| 246 | 24205 | 1113 | 8035 | 3.Oct | 6000 | 2035 | 4 day |
| 247 | 24203 | 1117 | 9007 | 30.Sep | 0 | 9007 | 8 day |
| 248 | 24201 | 1120 | 1146 | 26.Sep | 1000 | 146 | 11 day |
| 249 | | | | | | | |
| 250 | | | | | | | |

| | A | B | C | D | E | F | G |
|---|---|---|---|---|---|---|---|
| 251 | *Exercise 18a - database functions* | | | | | | |
| 252 | On a new sheet, make two criteria areas, one for those who work over 35 hours, | | | | | | |
| 253 | and one for those who work 35 hours or less. | | | | | | |
| 254 | | | | | | | |
| 255 | Use DSUM to calculate total weekly wages and DAVERAGE to find average | | | | | | |
| 256 | weekly wages and hourly rate. | | | | | | |
| 257 | | | | | | | |
| 258 | | | | | | | |
| 259 | | | | | | | |
| 260 | | | | | | | |
| 261 | | | | | | | |
| 262 | EDB Service | | | | | | |
| 263 | | | | | Date: | 8.Oct.90 | |
| 264 | | | | | | | |
| 265 | | | *hours* | *rate* | | | |
| 266 | | | >35 | <36 | | | |
| 267 | | | | | | | |
| 268 | Total wk. wages | | =DSUM(dbase;5;C$265:C$266) | | | | |
| 269 | Avg. wk. wages | | =DAVERAGE(c | =DAVERAGE(dbase;5;D$265:D$266) | | | |
| 270 | Avg. rate | | =DAVERAGE(c | =DAVERAGE(dbase;4;D$265:D$266) | | | |
| 271 | | | | | | | |
| 272 | | | | | | | |

| | A | B | C | D | E | F | G |
|---|---|---|---|---|---|---|---|
| 273 | *Exercise 18b - database functions* | | | | | | |
| 274 | On a new sheet, make three criteria areas, one for all overdue invoices, | | | | | | |
| 275 | one for all invoices more than 7 days overdue, and one for more than 10 days | | | | | | |
| 276 | overdue. | | | | | | |
| 277 | | | | | | | |
| 278 | Use DSUM to calculate total balance and DAVERAGE to find average | | | | | | |
| 279 | balance. | | | | | | |
| 280 | | | | | | | |
| 281 | | | | | | | |
| 282 | | | | | | | |
| 283 | | | | | | | |
| 284 | | | | | | | |
| 285 | | | | | | | |
| 286 | Invoice List | | | | | | |
| 287 | | | | | | Date: | 8.Oct.90 |
| 288 | | | | | | | |
| 289 | | | *Overdue* | *Overdue* | *Overdue* | | |
| 290 | | | >0 | >7 | >10 | | |
| 291 | | | | | | | |
| 292 | | Total balance | =DSUM(dbase;6;C$289:C$290) | | =DSUM(dbase;6;E$289:E$290) | | |
| 293 | | Avg. balance | | =DAVERAGE(dbase;6;D$289:D$290) | | | |
| 294 | | | | | | | |
| 295 | | | | | | | |

| | A | B | C | D | E | F | G |
|---|---|---|---|---|---|---|---|
| 296 | *Exercise 19a - macros* | | | | | | |
| 297 | On the same sheet you made criteria and result areas (exercise 16), | | | | | | |
| 298 | create a macro to: | | | | | | |
| 299 | | | | | | | |
| 300 | 1. Select the result area. | | | | | | |
| 301 | 2. Choose Data - Extract and OK. | | | | | | |
| 302 | 3. Move the curser back to the criteria area. | | | | | | |
| 303 | | | | | | | |
| 304 | Write some instructions to future users of the macro. | | | | | | |
| 305 | | | | | | | |
| 306 | | | | | | | |
| 307 | | | | | | | |
| 308 | | | | | | | |
| 309 | | | | | | | |
| 310 | EDB Service | | | | | | |
| 311 | | | | | Date: | 8.Oct.90 | |
| 312 | | | | | | | |
| 313 | Type in criteria and press CTRL A to get your information. | | | | | | |
| 314 | | | | | | | |
| 315 | CRITERIA | | | | | | |
| 316 | *emp.no.* | *name* | | *hours* | *hr.wage* | *wk.wage* | *bonus* | *+ bonus* |
| 317 | | | | 40 | | | | |
| 318 | | | | | | | |
| 319 | RESULT | | | | | | |
| 320 | | *name* | | *hours* | *hr.wage* | | |
| 321 | | Andersen | | 40 | 5300 | | |
| 322 | | Bond | | 40 | 4500 | | |
| 323 | | El Caudillo | | 40 | 5700 | | |
| 324 | | Colombo | | 40 | 2900 | | |
| 325 | | Jones | | 40 | 5300 | | |
| 326 | | Marple | | 40 | 7900 | | |
| 327 | | | | | | | |
| 328 | | | | | | | |

| | A | B | C | D | E | F | G |
|---|---|---|---|---|---|---|---|
| 329 | *Exercise 19b - macros* | | | | | | |
| 330 | On the same sheet you made criteria and result areas (exercise 16), | | | | | | |
| 331 | create a macro to: | | | | | | |
| 332 | | | | | | | |
| 333 | 1. Select the result area. | | | | | | |
| 334 | 2. Choose Data - Extract and OK. | | | | | | |
| 335 | 3. Move the curser back to the criteria area. | | | | | | |
| 336 | | | | | | | |
| 337 | Write some instructions to future users of the macro. | | | | | | |
| 338 | | | | | | | |
| 339 | | | | | | | |
| 340 | | | | | | | |
| 341 | | | | | | | |
| 342 | | | | | | | |
| 343 | **Invoice List** | | | | | | |
| 344 | | | | | | Date: | 8.Oct.90 |
| 345 | | | | | | | |
| 346 | Type in criteria and press CTRL D to get your information. | | | | | | |
| 347 | | | | | | | |
| 348 | CRITERIA | | | | | | |
| 349 | *Inv. no.* | *Cust.no.* | *Balance* | *Overdue* | | | |
| 350 | | | >0 | >0 | | | |
| 351 | | | | | | | |
| 352 | RESULT | | | | | | |
| 353 | *Inv. no.* | *Cust.no.* | *Total* | *Due* | *Paid* | *Balance* | *Overdue* |
| 354 | 24207 | 1121 | 5220 | 7.Oct | 0 | 5220 | 1 day |
| 355 | 24206 | 1115 | 4788 | 5.Oct | 0 | 4788 | 3 day |
| 356 | 24205 | 1113 | 8035 | 3.Oct | 6000 | 2035 | 4 day |
| 357 | 24203 | 1117 | 9007 | 30.Sep | 0 | 9007 | 8 day |
| 358 | 24201 | 1120 | 1146 | 26.Sep | 1000 | 146 | 11 day |

# Part 5

# Quick Reference

# Menu commands

## Handling files

| | |
|---|---|
| File - New | Open empty file (normal, macro or chart) |
| File - Open | Open file - you choose or type in file name |
| File - Links | Open all files linked to active spreadsheet |
| File - Save | Save current file |
| File - Save as | Save current sheet under new name |
| File - Save Workspace | Create workspace consisting of all files now open |
| File - Close | Close current file |
| File - Delete | Delete current file |
| File - Exit | Leave EXCEL program |

## Editing data

| | |
|---|---|
| Edit - Undo Entry | Cancel last action |
| Edit - Clear | Clear contents of selected cells (alternative - press DEL) |
| Edit - Copy | Copy selected cell(s) |
| Edit - Cut | Move selected cell(s) |
| Edit - Paste | Paste in, starting from selected cell (alt. press RET) |
| Edit - Insert Paste (3.0) | Paste in, adjusting rows automatically |
| Edit - Paste Special | Paste in values or formats only |
| Edit - Paste Special, Transpose (3.0) | Convert table to horizontal/vertical |
| Edit - Paste Link | Link cells to the copied cells |
| Edit - Insert | Insert selected cells - move other cells down/right |
| Edit - Delete | Delete selected cells and move other cells up/left |
| Edit - Fill Down/Right | Copy top/lefthand cell to all other selected cells |
| (shift) Edit - Fill Up/Left | Copy bottom/righthand cell to other selected cells |
| Formula - Define Name | Give a name to a cell |
| Formula - Create Names | Name several cells (mark cells AND names first) |
| Formula - Apply Names | Insert defined cell names into formulas |
| Formula - Find | Find value |
| Formula - Replace | Replace value |
| Formula - Goto | Find cell |
| Formula - Note | Attach notes to specific cell |
| Formula - Paste Function | Paste in function name and descriptions of arguments |

## Editing data (cont.-)

| | |
|---|---|
| Formula - Goal Seek (3.0) | Get desired value by adjusting value in another cell |
| Formula - Solver (3.0) | Get optimum values by adjusting values in other cells |
| Formula - Outline (3.0) | Produce automatic outline with levels of priority |
| Data - Parse | Split contents of one column to several columns |
| Data - Series | Produce series of consecutively increasing numbers |
| Data - Sort | Sort selected data by column/row you designate |
| Data - Consolidate (3.0) | Consolidate data from several spreadsheets |

## Help

| | |
|---|---|
| Help - Index | Fetch help index on commands |
| Help - Keyboard (3.0) | Fetch help index on keys |
| Help - Lotus 1-2-3 (3.0) | Fetch Lotus 1-2-3 help |
| Help - Tutorial | Online tutorial to introduce features of Excel |

## Formatting data

| | |
|---|---|
| Format - Number | Change number format, eg number of decimals, date |
| Format - Number, [red/blue/green] (2x) | Change colour of data |
| Format - Alignment | Justify contents (left, right, centre) |
| Format - Alignment, Wrap text (3.0) | Automatic word wrap of text |
| Format - Font | Change font (normal, bold, italic, bold italic) |
| Format - Font, | |
| Fonts (2x) | Edit size/style of font |
| Size/Type (3.0) | Edit size/style of font |
| Colour (3.0) | Edit colour of data |
| Format - Border | Edit outline - box, line on top/bottom/left/right, shade |
| Format - Patterns (3.0) | Edit frame, colour (foreground), pattern of graphic object |
| Format - Column Width | Edit column width |
| Format - Row Height | Edit row height |
| Format - Style (3.0) | Define format style (combination of font/border formats) |

## Handling the Screen Picture

| | |
|---|---|
| Window - <file-name> | Activate selected window and bring it to the screen |
| Window - Arrange All | Divide screen so that all open files are visible |
| Window - Hide/Unhide (3.0) | Hide/unhide active window |
| Window - New | Create additional window for the active file |
| Options - Display | Show/hide formulas, grids, headings, zero values |
| Options - Display | choose colours for worksheet |
| Options - Full/Short Menus | Show short/full form of menu |
| Options - Workspace | Show/hide menu bar, formula bar, status bar, arrow bar |
| Options - Calculation | Switch on/off automatic calculation of formulas |
| Options - Calculation | Adjust calculation conditions (e.g. iteration) |
| Options - Calculate Now | Calculate formulas (used with manual calc.) |
| Format - Cell Protection | Protect/hide cells for protected document |
| Options - Protect/Unprotect Document | Protect/unprotect document, execute cell protection as defined with Format - Cell Protection command |

## Printing out

| | |
|---|---|
| File - Print | Print file |
| File - Print, Preview | See preview of printout |
| File - Page Setup | Show/hide gridlines and column/row headings |
| File - Page Setup | Edit header and footer |
|   left-justify &L | italic &I    file name &F |
|   right-justify &R | page no. &P    today's date &D |
| File - Page Setup (3.0) | Choose vertical (portrait) or horizontal (landscape) format |
| File - Printer Setup | Choose printer |
| File - Printer Setup (2x) | Choose vertical (portrait) or horizontal (landscape) format |
| Options - Set/Remove Pg Brk | Add/remove manual page break |
| Options - Set Print Area | Define selected area as area to be printed out |

## Charts

| | |
|---|---|
| Gallery | Choose type of chart |
| Chart - Add Legend | Add legend to chart |
| Format - Legend | Move legend to another part of chart |
| Format - Patterns | Format graphic objects |
| Format - Font | Format tekst |
| Format - 3D View (3.0) | Rotate 3-dimensional object |
| (shift) Edit - Copy Picture | Copy chart (to another program) |

## Databaser

| | |
|---|---|
| Data - Set Database | Define area (on same file) as database (include headings) |
| Data - Set Criteria | Define area as criteria area (include headings) |
| Data - Set Extract (3.0) | Define area as result area (include headings) |
| Data - Extract | Extract data from database |
| Data - Find | Find value in database |
| Data - Form | Produce dialogue box interface for database |
| Data - Activate Q+E (3.0) | Activate Q+E database interface program |
| Data - SQL Query (3.0) | Edit/write SQL query |
| Data - Paste Fieldnames (3.0) | Paste fieldnames from external database |

## Macros

| | |
|---|---|
| Macro - Record | Start macro recorder |
| Macro - Run | Run macro |
| Macro - Set Recorder | Set macro recorder |
| Macro - Start Recorder | Continue macro recorder |
| Macro - Stop Recorder | Stop macro recorder |

# Functions

## Calculating

| | |
|---|---|
| =NOW() | today's date<br>=NOW() |
| =SUM(A4:A24) | adds values<br>=SUM(cell range) |
| =PRODUCT(A4:A24) | multiplies values<br>=PRODUCT(cell range) |
| =AVG(A4:A24) | averages values<br>=AVERAGE(cell range) |
| =MIN(A4:A24) | fetches the lowest value<br>=MIN(cell range) |
| =MAX(A4:A24) | fetches the highest value<br>=MAX(cell range) |
| =COUNT(A4:A24) | counts cells containing numeric values<br>=COUNT(cell range) |
| =COUNTA(A4:A24)   (3.0) | counts non-blanc cells<br>=COUNTA(cell range) |
| =ROUND(A15,0) | rounds value to nearest designated decimal<br>(eg. 2 to be rounded to 2 decimals,<br>and -3 to be rounded to thousands<br>=ROUND(value,number of decimals to be rounded to) |
| =TRUNC(A15) | truncates value to nearest whole number<br>=TRUNC(value) |
| =VALUE(A5) | converts text to numeric value<br>=VALUE(text) |
| =MID(A5,3,2) | extracts characters from text<br>=MID(text,start number, number of characters to extract) |

## Logical choice

=IF(A5>0,10%,"no discount")    based on test, gives value if true,
value if false
=IF(test,value if true,value if false)

=IF(AND(A5>0,G5>500),    true if both true, otherwise false
10%,0%)    =AND(value,value)

=IF(OR(A5>0,G5>500),10%," ")    true if either true, otherwise false
=OR(value,value)

=IF(NOT(A5>0),"Contact","")    true if not true, otherwise false
=NOT(value,value)


## Financial

=FV(12%/2,2*10,-1000)    future value based on regular payments made
=FV(interest per period,total no. of payments,
payment amount)

=PMT(12%/2,2*10,50000)    payment amount on a loan (shown as negative no.)
=PMT(interest per period,total no.of payments,loan amount)

=PV(16%/12,12*4,-1000)    loan attainable based on regular payments made
=PV(interest per period,total no. of payments,
payment amount)

=RATE(2*10,-1000,0,50000)    interest rate returned on investment
=RATE(total no. of payments,payment amount,
initial deposit,future value)

=SLN(50000,20000,5)    annual depreciation amount of an asset
=SLN(purchase price,eventual appraised value,
after how many years)

## Information tables

| | |
|---|---|
| =VLOOKUP(B5,table,2) | finds value from table<br>=VLOOKUP(index value,index table,row no. in table) |
| =HLOOKUP(B5,table,2) | finds value from table<br>=HLOOKUP(index value,index table,column no. in table) |
| =VLOOKUP(MATCH<br>(B5,B2:B100,0),table,2) | finds relative position of value<br>=MATCH(index value,row/column in table,0 for exact match) |
| =SUM(Jan89:INDEX<br>(Jan89:Dec89,month90)) | finds cell reference in range, based on row/column number.<br>=INDEX(range,column no.,row no.) |
| =DSUM(database,2,criteria) | adds values within database<br>=DSUM(database table,row no. in table,criteria area) |
| =DPRODUCT<br>(database,2,criteria) | multiplies values within database<br>=DPRODUCT(database table,row no. in table,criteria area) |
| =DAVERAGE<br>(database,2,criteria) | averages values within database<br>=DAVERAGE(database table,row no.in table,criteria area) |
| =DCOUNT<br>(database,2,criteria) | counts rows in database<br>=DCOUNT(database table,row no.in table,criteria area) |
| =DMIN(database,2,criteria) | fetches lowest value within database<br>=DMIN(database table,row no.in table,criteria area) |
| =DMAX(database,2,criteria) | fetches highest value within database<br>=DMAX(database table,row no.in table,criteria area) |
| =DGET(database,2,criteria) | fetches value (number or text) from database<br>=DGET(database table,row no.in table,criteria area) |

## Statistical

| | |
|---|---|
| =STDEV(B2:B52) | estimates standard deviation based on sample<br>=STDEV(cell range in row/column) |
| =VAR(B2:B52) | estimates standard variance based on sample<br>=VAR(cell range in row/column) |
| =TREND(A2:C2,{1,2,3},{4,5,6}) | gives values on linear trend<br>=TREND(known values,no. sequence of<br>known values,no. seq. of unknown values) |

# Macro statements

Macro statements corresponding directly to menu commands such
as PRINT() or SORT(), or to worksheet functions such as VLOOKUP()
have been omitted from this list.

## Command statements

=ACTIVATE("CUST.XLS")    activates sheet
                                     =ACTIVATE("sheet-name")

=FORMULA("=VLOOKUP    enters text/number/formula into active cell
(RC[-1],tab,2)")          =FORMULA("text")

=RETURN()    ends the macro
                                     =RETURN()

=SELECT(!A4:A24)    selects cell or range of cells
                                     =SELECT(cell/cell range)

=SELECT(INDEX(!B4:M4,!B1)) selects the cell returned by index function
                                     =SELECT(INDEX(range,column no./row no.))

## Interactive statements

=ALERT    displays dialogue box with message
("All rows are now updated",2)  =ALERT("message",box-type)
                                      Type 1offers choice, 2 gives message,3 gives warning

=MESSAGE(TRUE,    displays message on status (bottom) line of screen
"Data is being transferred ...")  =MESSAGE(TRUE,"message")

=MESSAGE(FALSE)    removes message and returns status line to normal

=FORMULA(INPUT    prompts user to type something
("Type in invoice number",1))  =FORMULA(INPUT("prompt",input-type))
                                      Type 0 - formula, 1 - number, 2 - text

=PRINT?()    optional menu command -
                                      user decides if it will be executed
                                      =<command>?()

## Program statements

| | |
|---|---|
| =WHILE(ACTIVE.CELL()>0) | refers to active cell<br>    ACTIVE.CELL() |
| =ECHO(FALSE) | turns off screen updating |
| =ECHO(TRUE) | turns on screen updating |
| =GOTO(A13) | moves control to another line in macro<br>  =GOTO(cell reference) |
| =STEP() | stops the macro - gives user option<br>to stop, continue or step through the macro |
| =IF(ACTIVE.CELL()="",<br>GOTO(A3),GOTO(A8)) | if condition is met, does one thing,<br>otherwise, does another thing<br>  =IF(condition,if yes,if no) |
| =SET.NAME<br>("total",ACTIVE.CELL()) | remembers cell by giving it name<br>  =SET.NAME("name",cell reference) |
| =cleanup() | calls another macro, and returns control<br>to original macro when called macro<br>is finished<br>  =name of called macro() |
| =WAIT("11:00 PM")<br>=WAIT(NOW()+.00001) | causes macro to wait until given time -<br>.00001 = 1 second<br>  =WAIT("time") |
| =WHILE(!K2=1)<br>- - - - -<br>=NEXT() | at WHILE, executes statements up til NEXT if condition is<br>met, otherwise skips until after NEXT -<br>at NEXT, returns to WHILE<br>  =WHILE(condition) |
| =FOR("counter",1,50)<br>- - - - -<br>=NEXT() | repeats statements after FOR and up til NEXT for specified<br>number of times<br>  =FOR("counter name",start number,stop number) |

# Customizing

=ADD.COMMAND(1,5,A8:B8)   adds command to pull-down menu
                        =ADD.COMMAND(menu type,
                        menu position,menu definition area)
                        Type 1 - worksheet menu, 2 - chart menu

=ADD.MENU(1,A7:B8)       adds item to menu
                        =ADD.MENU(menu type,menu definition area)
                        Type 1 - worksheet menu, 2 - chart menu
                        in table,criteria area)

=DELETE.COMMAND      deletes command from pull-down menu
(1,5,"Query")                   =DELETE.COMMAND
                        (menu type,menu position,command)
                        Type 1 - worksheet menu, 2 - chart menu

=DELETE.MENU          deletes item from menu
(1,"Database")                =DELETE.MENU(menu type,menu definition area)
                        Type 1 - worksheet menu, 2 - chart menu

=DIALOGUE.BOX(B6:H22)   brings dialogue box onto the screen
                        =DIALOGUE.BOX(dialogue box definition area)

=RENAME.COMMAND     renames command in pull-down menu
(1,5,2,"Report")               =DELETE.COMMAND(menu type,
                        menu position,command position,new name)
                        Type 1 - worksheet menu, 2 - chart menu

Following is a short reference to the icons in the icon bar at the top of the screen in Excel 3.0. The icons are explained in the same order as they appear on the screen.

| Normal |

Here you can read and edit already-defined format combinations.

 Click here to fetch an already-defined format combination.

 Click here to reduce priority in an outline.
Click here to remove an outline from the spreadsheet.

 Click here to increase priority in an outline.

 Click here to remove plus and minus symbols from an outline.

 Click here to select just the visible rows in an outline.

 Click here to get an automatic SUM formula.

 Click here for bold font.

 Click here for italic font.

Click here to left-justify.

Click here to centre-justify.

Click here to right-justify.

Click here to select several graphic objects at a time.

Click at these icons to draw graphic shapes.

Click here to create a chart on your spreadsheet.
Also click here to edit a chart on the spreadsheet.

Click here to draw a text box.

Click here to draw a macro button.

Click here to take a picture of a part of the spreadsheet, including graphic objects.

# Index